99

THE DIETER'S GOURMET COOKBOOK

**No Sugar No Salt
Low Fat Low Cholesterol**

THE DIETER'S GOURMET COOKBOOK

No Sugar No Salt
Low Fat Low Cholesterol

by Francine Prince

W. FOULSHAM & CO. LTD
LONDON · NEW YORK · TORONTO ·
CAPE TOWN · SYDNEY

W. FOULSHAM & COMPANY LIMITED
Yeovil Road, SLOUGH, Berkshire SL1 4JH ENGLAND

ISBN 0-572-01142-3

Photoset in Great Britain by
Rowland Phototypesetting Ltd
Bury St Edmunds, Suffolk
and printed by St Edmundsbury Press
Bury St Edmunds, Suffolk.

CONTENTS

How to Use This Book

My new cuisine is for food lovers no matter what kind of diet they're on: weight-losing, maintenance, low-fat, low-saturated fat, low-sodium, low-carbohydrate or low-cholesterol. And it's a gastronomic extravaganza for nondieters who are turning from the egg-butter-cream-sugar-and-salt-laden meals of the past to repasts that are as light as they are nutritious.

Every recipe has been tested in my own kitchen, which is very much like yours, and in the kitchens of my students and friends. If you're not an expert cook, all you have to do is follow my instructions, which I've made so explicit and so detailed that you're bound to come up with a perfect dish the first time. If you're an experienced cook, you can appreciate the painstaking care that went into every recipe—the careful calculation of the right quantities of ingredients and the exact techniques for blending them. You'll never have to repeat that age-old recipe follower's lament, "But will it turn out as good the next time?" Every recipe will produce the same mouth-watering results every time.

Good cooking! And good health!

Following each recipe, you'll find this line:

CAL	F	P:S	SOD	CAR	CHO

CAL stands for food energy in calories; F for fat in grams; P:S for the ratio of polyunsaturated fats to saturated fats; SOD for sodium in milligrams; CAR for carbohydrates in grams; and CHO for cholesterol in milligrams. Figures under each heading represent quantities per serving. Figures have been rounded out but, and where a quantity is less than 1, it is regarded as nil.

Here is the maximum daily intake recommended by most doctors for restricted and maintenance diets in each of the six categories:

CAL	F	P:S	SOD	CAR	CHO
Restricted Diets					
1200	47	>1:1	500	120	160-185
Maintenance Diets					
>1200*	60-70	1:1	2000	>120**	300

> *means greater than.*

*To calculate your maintenance calories, multiply your weight in pounds by 12 and 15 (or your weight in kilograms by 26.5 and 33). Example: You weigh 130 pounds, so 130 × 12 = 1,560 and 130 × 15 = 1,950. To maintain your weight, take only between 1,560 and 1,950 calories per day.

**Divide your maintenance calories above by 10 to obtain maximum carbohydrate intake.

To stay under all, or any, of the limits of these diets, just select a daily menu in which the sum of the relevant figures per serving never exceeds the corresponding figures in the foregoing chart.

The Ingredients of My New Cuisine

Here's a list of the basic ingredients I use for my recipes. Use them as a guide when you create new recipes of your own.

Vegetable oils. Corn oil. Other high polyunsaturated vegetables oils can be used as well, but I prefer corn oil because it's the best tasting.

Mayonnaise. My low-calorie, no-cholesterol, no-sugar-or-salt mayonnaise, which has a high polyunsaturated:saturated fat ratio (Page 103).

Milk. Low-fat dry milk, buttermilk made from skimmed milk, and low-fat yogurt.

Eggs. Egg whites, which contain no cholesterol or fats of any kind. (I use a half egg yolk in a handful of recipes for flavour and to hold ingredients together. It adds just a few milligrams of cholesterol per portion.)

Cheeses. Low-fat cheeses, cottage cheese. Other part skim-milk cheeses which I use sparingly include: Jarlsberg, Esrom, Tilsit Havarti, St. Paulin, Samsoe, Danbo, Cantal, Cheddar, Valembert, Fin de Pres, and Elbo.

Sweeteners. Rather than cook with white or brown sugars, which are high in sucrose, I prefer to use the following sweet-tasting foods: fresh and cooked fruits, dried fruits (no sugar added), fresh fruit juices and canned or bottled fruit juices no sugar added, sweet vegetables such as carrots, tomatoes and onions, and a small amount of honey. I also use sweet spices and herbs including allspice, anise, basil, cinnamon, cardamom, coriander, ginger, nutmeg and mace, as well as flavouring essences such as vanilla and almond.

Salt. For a salty taste, I use tangy spices, and fresh and dried herbs and vegetables, as well as aromatic seeds. These include: bay leaf, caraway seed, celery (but not celery salt or celery flakes), chives, cloves, cumin, curry powder (no salt or pepper added), dill, fennel, garlic and garlic powder (but not garlic salt), marjoram, mint, mustard (but not prepared mustard), onions and onion powder, oregano, mild paprika, parsley, poppy seed, rosemary, sage, sesame seed, taragon and thyme. On rare occasions, I make use of a small amount of a powdered vegetable concentrate (no salt added).

Pepper. Cayenne pepper which, some herbologists believe, has a salutory effect on the circulatory system.

Sauces. I rely on blendings of herbs and spices to create new and pungent flavours. I also use small amounts of a sodium-free soya sauce.

Baking Powders. I use low-sodium baking powder, if available, which substitutes potassium for sodium.

Flour. For my breads I insist on unbleached wheat flour, and I use wholewheat, rye, gluten and buckwheat as well. Stone grinding preserves the taste, texture and the nutritional value of the grains. For my other baked goods, I also use rolled oats, unprocessed bran, cracked wheat and wheat germ.

Pasta. Whole wheat spaghetti and macaroni made without eggs and salt.

Rice. A short-grained brown rice flecked with green, which can be found in health food stores. When brown rice is not compatible with the other ingredients of a recipe, I use white rice, cooking it in such a way that each kernel is plump and fluffy and quite separate from every other kernel.

Nuts. Walnuts and almonds which have very high polyunsaturated:saturated fat ratios.

Meats. I use mainly lean cheaper cuts of meat. They're tougher than prime meats, but you can tenderize them by marinating, braising or, when applicable, by pounding, as for a veal escalope. Prime meats, though, can be lean. Use your eye to judge whether a cut is sufficiently fat-free to earn a place on your table.

Fish. Fresh fish, with the following leaner fish (listed in order of ascending fatness) preferred: cod, sea bass, sole, flounder, halibut, whiting and tuna.

Poultry. Chicken and turkey, which are among the least fatty and lowest in cholesterol of all fowl. Younger chickens are less fatty; and young turkeys are leaner than mature ones.

Canned and bottled foods. I use those packed in water or in their own juices, such as tomatoes, tomato paste, tomato purée, red pimentos and waterchestnuts (which I use to add crunchiness to some of my dishes), as well as pineapples, apple juice, tuna fish, sardines and salmon.

Gelatine. Unflavoured gelatine or agar-agar. Agar-agar makes a spreadable, custardy mixture; gelatine, a stiffer one.

Thickening agents. Arrowroot. It's as effective a thickening agent as cornflour and has more nutritional value, cooks more quickly, and never alters the taste of the ingredients with which it is combined.

Coffee and chocolate. I use a coffee substitute made from a blend of cereals, which contains no caffeine or other harmful ingredients. Carob, which is ground from the pod of the carob tree, has a pleasant chocolate flavour, is low in saturated fat, easily digested, and rich in natural sweeteners.

Where to Shop for the Ingredients You Need

I've found that, by and large, fruiterers, greengrocers, fishmongers and butchers' shops offer a wide variety of fresher, tastier and higher quality foods than supermarkets. The food, moreover, is generally unpackaged, and you can eye-test it before purchase. (How often have you been unpleasantly surprised when you opened a supermarket package?) Prices tend to be a bit higher than supermarkets', but not always, and the careful shopper can come away with some amazing bargains. And you don't have to fret in a checkout queue.

Health food stores are usually more expensive than other food shops. Nowadays, supermarkets stock many of the items that were once health food store exclusives, and often at better prices. On the other hand, some items can actually be purchased cheaper in health food stores. For example, 100 g/4 oz packets of yeast provide great savings over the supermarkets' pre-measured smaller packets. (Don't worry about the remaining yeast keeping, once you've opened the pack. Just follow label instructions for sealing, and the yeast will keep up to a month.)

Some of my ingredients are obtainable only in health food or continental foodstores. Here's a list of those ingredients: Cold-pressed corn oil. Low-fat dry milk. Vegetable concentrate, no salt added. Sodium-free soya sauce. Low-sodium baking powder. Gluten and buckwheat flours. Pasta made without eggs or salt. Unprocessed bran. Short-grained brown rice (organic). Tomato paste and tomato purée, no salt added. Coffee substitute. Carob powder, no sugar added. Agar-agar.

Some of the recipes call for sweet potatoes, sometimes called yams, and blueberries. These are often available at specialist greengrocers' or continental food shops.

STOCKS

Stocks are the foundation of great gourmet cooking. They are clear, concentrated broths made by gently simmering meats and bones—or fish parts—with water, vegetables, herbs and spices. They are used to impart flavour to sauces, soups, vegetables, stews, braised meats and poached chicken or fish. They can instantly convert a plain side dish such as boiled rice into a gastronomic treat. And they are made with ease, simmering along with the minimum of attention.

I recommend the use of five stocks.

Chicken stock is the easiest to make. It's really a rich chicken soup, its flavour augmented by many chicken bones and longer cooking time. Its uses seem endless. It's a base for a variety of soups and sauces, a flavouring for rice, barley and kasha (buckwheat), and it does wonders when you're poaching either fish or poultry.

Beef stock is used for meat sauces, braised meats and vegetables, and to add a hearty flavour to soups.

Brown beef stock imparts a dark brown colour as rich as its flavour to sauces and braised meats.

Fish stock is employed for fish sauces and fish soups. Used in poaching, it adds appeal to the simplest fish and enriches the most flavoursome.

Veal stock provides a fine delicate flavour for sauces, soups, and braised veal. It is sometimes substituted for chicken stock.

Stocks keep well in the freezer, so be sure to have

them on hand always. (For 'instant frozen stocks,' see Page 147).

Note: If you run out of stock, or if you haven't enough stock, use a commercial vegetable concentrate.

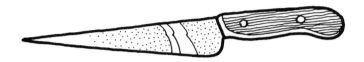

CHICKEN STOCK

	Metric	Imperial	American
Chicken giblets, backs and wings, or boiling chicken, cut, plus its giblets	1.75 kg	4 lb	4 lb
Large carrot, peeled and cut into 4 pieces	1	1	1
Large cloves garlic, finely chopped	4	4	4
Large onion, cut into quarters	1	1	1
Large shallots, finely chopped	2	2	2
Leek, white part only, washed, trimmed and coarsely chopped	1	1	1
Small parsnip, peeled and cut in half	1	1	1
Small turnip, peeled and diced	1	1	1
Large fresh mushrooms, washed, trimmed and coarsely chopped	4	4	4
Large stick celery, cut into 4 pieces	1	1	1
Water, enough to cover	2-2.5 l	3½-4 pt	2-2½ qt
Dry Vermouth or white wine	180 ml	6 fl oz	¾ cup
Cayenne pepper	6 pinches	6 pinches	6 pinches
Large bouquet garni which includes dill sprigs as well as parsley	1	1	1

Remove all skin from chicken and necks. Trim off fat and discard. Wash well.

Place all ingredients in large saucepan. Bring to simmering point and simmer, uncovered, for 10 minutes, removing scum that rises to top. Cover partially, and continue simmering for 2½-3 hours, removing scum occasionally. Uncover partially and let cool in pan.

Transfer to a sieve, placing bowl underneath, and press ingredients to remove all stock. Reserve chicken pieces for light lunch or hors d'oeuvre. Transfer stock to freezeproof containers. Cover loosely with foil and cool at room temperature. Cover tightly, and refrigerate overnight. Then cut away and discard hardened fat from top of stock. Refrigerate some of the stock for use within a few days, covering tightly, and freeze the remainder.

Yield: About 2 litres /3½ pt /2 qt

CAL	F	P:S	SOD	CAR	CHO
Per 240 ml /8 fl oz /1 cup					
41	0	0	17	3	0

FISH STOCK

	Metric	Imperial	American
Bones and heads of any white-fleshed fish, chopped into 7.5-cm /3-inch pieces	1.25-1.5 kg	2½-3 lb	2½-3 lb
Corn oil	3 tbsp	3 tbsp	3 tbsp
Large onion, coarsely chopped	1	1	1
Large stick celery, cut into 4 pieces	1	1	1
Large shallots, finely chopped	2	2	2
Carrot, peeled and diced	1	1	1
Large fresh mushrooms, washed, trimmed and coarsely chopped	5	5	5
Large cloves garlic, finely chopped	2	2	2
Dry Vermouth or white wine	80 ml	3 fl oz	⅓ cup
Water, enough to cover	1.5 l	2½ pt	5½-6 cups
Vegetable concentrate	½ tsp	½ tsp	½ tsp
Whole cloves	3	3	3
Bouquet garni	1	1	1
Dried marjoram leaves, crushed	¼ tsp	¼ tsp	¼ tsp
Dried tarragon leaves, crushed	½ tsp	½ tsp	½ tsp

Wash bones and heads under cold running water. Pat dry with paper towels. Heat oil until hot in heavy saucepan. (Diameter of pan should not exceed 23 cm /9 inches.) Sauté bones, heads, vegetables and garlic for 3 minutes. Add wine and cook for 5 minutes. Add remainder of ingredients except herbs and bring to simmering point. Cook, uncovered for 5 minutes, removing scum that rises to top. Add herbs, partially cover and continue to simmer for another 25 minutes, periodically removing scum that rises to top. Uncover and let stock cool in pan.

Pour into a sieve, placing bowl underneath, and press to remove all stock. Transfer to freezerproof containers. Let cool, uncovered, at room temperature. Cover tightly, and refrigerate overnight. Cut away and discard thin film of hardened fat which may rise to top. Refrigerate some of the stock for immediate use and freeze the remainder.

Yield: About 900 ml /1½ pt /1 qt

CAL	F	P:S	SOD	CAR	CHO
Per 240 ml /8 fl oz /1 cup					
20	0	0	28	3	0

VEAL STOCK

	Metric	Imperial	American
Corn oil	2 tbsp	2 tbsp	2 tbsp
Veal bones, cracked	680 g	1½ lb	1½ lb
Veal knuckle, cracked	680 g	1½ lb	1½ lb
Large onion, finely chopped	1	1	1
Large cloves garlic, finely chopped	3	3	3
Small stick celery, diced	1	1	1
Large shallot, finely chopped	1	1	1
Water, enough to cover	2.25 l	4 pt	2½ qt
Carrots, peeled and diced	2	2	2
Large fresh mushrooms, washed, trimmed and thickly sliced	4	4	4
Swede, peeled and diced	50 g	2 oz	¼ cup
Tomato paste, no salt added	1 tbsp	1 tbsp	1 tbsp
Dried tarragon leaves, crushed	½ tsp	½ tsp	½ tsp
Dry Vermouth or white wine	120 ml	4 fl oz	½ cup
Bouquet garni	1	1	1

Heat oil in a large heavy saucepan until hot. Add bones, onion, garlic, celery and shallot. Sauté over medium high heat until lightly browned. Add water and bring to simmering point. Simmer, uncovered, for 10 minutes, removing scum that rises to top. Add remaining ingredients. Partially cover and simmer for about 2½ hours. Let cool in pan.

Remove bones with slotted spoon. Pour stock and other ingredients into a sieve, placing bowl underneath, and press to remove all stock. Transfer stock to freezerproof containers. Cover loosely with foil and cool at room temperature. Cover tightly, and refrigerate overnight. Cut away and discard hardened fat from top of stock. Cover tightly and refrigerate some of the stock for use within a few days and freeze the remainder.

10

Yield: About 2 litres/3½ pt/2 qt

CAL	F	P:S	SOD	CAR	CHO
Per 240 ml/8 fl oz/1 cup					
40	0	0	65	3	0

BEEF STOCK

	Metric	Imperial	American
Beef shin, each shin cut in half	1.75 kg	4 lb	4 lb
Beef bones, cracked	1.5 kg	3 lb	3 lb
Water, enough to cover	2-2.25 l	3½-4 pt	2-2½ qt
Carrots, peeled and thickly sliced	2	2	2
Large onion, cut into quarters	1	1	1
Cloves garlic, finely chopped	3	3	3
Large shallot, finely chopped	1	1	1
Whole cloves	6	6	6
Large fresh mushrooms, washed, trimmed and coarsely chopped	6	6	6
Swede, peeled and diced	75 g	3 oz	½ cup
Sticks celery, cut into 4 pieces	2	2	2
Sodium-free soya sauce	½ tsp	½ tsp	½ tsp
Bouquet garni	1	1	1

Trim away fat from meat and bones. Wash under cold running water. Place in large saucepan no wider than 23 cm/9 inches in diameter. Add water to cover. Bring to boil, then reduce heat. Cover partially and simmer for 5 minutes. Drain contents of pan in colander.

Rinse pan. Rinse meat and bones briefly under cold running water and return to pan. Add fresh water to cover. Add remainder of ingredients. Bring to simmering point. Cover partially and simmer for 3 hours, occasionally removing scum that rises to top.

Remove meat and bones from pan with slotted spoon. Discard bones and reserve meat for leftovers. Pour stock and other ingredients into a sieve, placing bowl underneath, andd press to remove all stock. Transfer stock to freezerproof containers. Cover loosely with foil and cool at room temperature. Cover tightly, and refrigerate overnight. Then cut away and discard hardened fat from top of stock. Refrigerate some of the stock for use within a few days, covering tightly, and freeze the remainder.

Yield: About 2 litres/3½ pt/2 qt

CAL	F	P:S	SOD	CAR	CHO
Per 240 ml/8 fl oz/1 cup					
45	0	0	49	3	0

BROWN BEEF STOCK

	Metric	Imperial	American
Veal bones, cracked	450 g	1 lb	1 lb
Veal knuckle, cracked	700–900 g	1½–2 lb	1½–2 lb
Lean beef such as topside, shin or shoulder, cut into large chunks	900 g	2 lb	2 lb
Celery, sliced into large pieces	2	2	2
Leeks, white part only, well washed and coarsely chopped	2	2	2
Large carrot, peeled and thickly sliced	1	1	1
Large onions, cut into quarters	2	2	2
Fresh mushrooms, washed, trimmed and thickly sliced	6	6	6
Swede, peeled and diced	100 g	4 oz	¾ cup
Large cloves garlic, coarsely chopped	4	4	4
Robust red wine	80 ml	3 fl oz	⅓ cup
Water, enough to cover	2.75 l	4½ pt	3 qt
Coriander seeds, toasted and crushed (see method)	2 tbsp	2 tbsp	2 tbsp
Whole cloves	8	8	8
Cayenne pepper	5 pinches	5 pinches	5 pinches
Large bouquet garni	1	1	1

Trim and discard fat from bones and meat. Wash under cold running water. Pat dry. Arrange bones, meat knuckle, vegetables and garlic in roasting tin large enough to hold all ingredients in one layer. Roast, uncovered, in preheated 230°C/450°F/Gas mark 8 oven for 45 minutes, turning frequently so that all ingredients are well browned. Remove from oven and pour off fat.

Transfer all ingredients to a large saucepan not wider than 23 cm/9 inches in diameter. Place roasting tin on top of stove over high heat. Add wine and cook for 2 minutes, scraping pan to loosen browned particles. Pour into pan with browned ingredients. Add water. Bring to simmering point. Cook, uncovered, for 20 minutes, removing scum that rises to top.

To toast coriander seeds, heat small frying pan until hot. Add seeds, shaking around in pan for 2 minutes. Crush seeds finely in pestle and mortar. Add spices and bouquet garni to pan. Cover partially and continue simmering for 5 hours.

Remove meat and bones with slotted spoon. Save meat for leftovers. Pour stock into a sieve, placing bowl underneath, and drain, pressing to remove all stock. Then pour through muslin.

Pour into freezerproof containers and cool at room temperature. Cover tightly and refrigerate overnight. When cold, cut away hardened fat. Then cover tightly and store in freezer, reserving some for refrigerator if planning to use within a few days.

Yield: About 2 litres/3½ pt/2 qt

CAL	F	P:S	SOD	CAR	CHO
Per 240 ml/8 fl oz/1 cup					
63	0	0	98	3	0

VEGETABLES, GRAINS AND PASTA

DUXELLES

The French know the value of duxelles. They use it in the preparation of sauces, omelettes, stuffings and vegetables for added flavour and texture. It's an excellent filling for crêpes, and spread on thinly sliced bread, it makes a delicious canapé. Keep some in the freezer. Duxelles is pronounced 'dew-zelles.'

	Metric	Imperial	American
Corn oil	3 tbsp	3 tbsp	3 tbsp
Large clove garlic, finely chopped	1	1	1
Large shallots, finely chopped	2	2	2
Fresh mushrooms, washed and trimmed	225 g	8 oz	½ lb
Dried tarragon leaves, crushed	½ tsp	½ tsp	½ tsp
Cayenne pepper	3 pinches	3 pinches	3 pinches
Freshly chopped parsley	1 tsp	1 tsp	1 tsp

Heat oil in large heavy frying pan until hot. Add garlic and shallots and cook, turning constantly, for 1 minute. Add mushrooms, spreading smoothly over pan. Cook for 2 minutes. Turn over with large spoon, and smooth out in pan. Continue turning over and smoothing out in pan until all liquid is evaporated (about 8-10 minutes). Sprinkle with tarragon, cayenne and chopped parsley. Stir to blend.

Yield: 175 g/6 oz/1 cup

CAL	F	P:S	SOD	CAR	CHO
Per tablespoon					
26	3	4.5:1	2	1	0

BRAISED CHICORY

When it's time for a change why not serve chicory? This luxury vegetable will add sophistication to any main course.

	Metric	Imperial	American
Heads chicory	4	4	4
Corn oil	1 tbsp	1 tbsp	1 tbsp
Fresh lemon juice	1 tbsp	1 tbsp	1 tbsp
Sodium-free soya sauce	2 dashes	2 dashes	2 dashes
Cayenne pepper	4 pinches	4 pinches	4 pinches
Chicken or veal stock (Pages 8 and 10)	80 ml	3 fl oz	⅓ cup
Honey	1 tsp	1 tsp	1 tsp
Freshly chopped chives or finely chopped spring onions	1 tbsp	1 tbsp	1 tbsp

Choose fresh chicory. They should be white with pale green outer leaves. Wash and pat dry. Cut lengthwise. Heat oil in non-stick frying pan until very warm. Sauté chicory briefly on both sides, cut side down first—about 2 minutes. Sprinkle with lemon juice, sodium-free soya sauce and cayenne. Add stock and honey. Bring to simmering point. Reduce heat, partially cover, and simmer gently for 30-35 minutes, basting frequently, until tender. Serve piping hot sprinkled with chopped chives or spring onion.

Yield: Serves 4

Variations:
1. Sprinkle with low-fat cheese and place under grill for 3 minutes.
2. Instead of chives or spring onion, sprinkle lightly with nutmeg before serving.

CAL	F	P:S	SOD	CAR	CHO
59	4	4.5:1	18	5	0
Sprinkled with cheese					
60	4+	4.4:1	19	5+	0

ASPARAGUS WITH TOASTED CORIANDER

Cooked to perfection, then adorned with lemon juice, shallots and toasted coriander, this luxury vegetable makes one of the most elegant side dishes. Use it to add glamour to any of your main courses.

	Metric	Imperial	American
Fresh asparagus, washed	500 g	1¼ lb	1¼ lb
Chicken stock (Page 8)	240 ml	8 fl oz	1 cup
Toasted coriander seeds, finely crushed (see method)	1 tbsp	1 tbsp	1 tbsp
Corn oil	2 tbsp	2 tbsp	2 tbsp
Shallots, finely chopped	2	2	2
Fresh lemon juice	½ tsp	½ tsp	½ tsp
Dried thyme leaves, crushed	¼ tsp	¼ tsp	¼ tsp
Honey	1 tsp	1 tsp	1 tsp
Sodium-free soya sauce	2 dashes	2 dashes	2 dashes
Cayenne pepper	2 pinches	2 pinches	2 pinches

Remove tough ends of asparagus (about 5 cm/ 2 inches from the bottom). From cut end, peel back tough layer of skin, revealing soft flesh underneath. Cut each asparagus into 3 pieces.

Bring stock to boil in saucepan wide enough to hold asparagus laying down. Add asparagus. Reduce heat and simmer, partially covered, for 8 minutes. The time will vary with the thickness of the asparagus. Transfer to colander. Rinse under running water. Drain well.

To toast coriander seeds, heat small frying pan until hot. Add seeds, shaking around in pan for 2 minutes. Crush seeds finely in pestle and mortar.

Heat oil in non-stick frying pan until hot. Add shallots and sauté for 2 minutes. Add aparagus and toss gently to coat. Sprinkle with lemon juice and thyme. Dribble honey into frying pan. Add sodium-free soya sauce and cayenne. Cook for 1 minute.

Transfer to heated serving plate, sprinkle with coriander and serve.

Yield: Serves 4

CAL	F	P:S	SOD	CAR	CHO
115	7	4.5:1	10	14	0

FRENCH GREEN BEANS

This superbly refreshing green vegetable is cooked simply in chicken stock, then brought to the peak of perfection by tossing with lemon juice, herbs and spices.

	Metric	Imperial	American
Fresh green beans, washed	450 g	1 lb	1 lb
Chicken stock (Page 8)	240 ml	8 fl oz	1 cup
Enough water to barely cover beans			
Corn oil	2 tbsp	2 tbsp	2 tbsp
Large onion, thinly sliced	1	1	1
Large clove garlic, finely chopped	1	1	1
Large shallot, finely chopped	1	1	1
Dried tarragon leaves, crushed	¼ tsp	¼ tsp	¼ tsp
Ground nutmeg	¼ tsp	¼ tsp	¼ tsp
Fresh lemon juice	1 tbsp	1 tbsp	1 tbsp
Freshly chopped parsley	1 tbsp	1 tbsp	1 tbsp

Cut off ends of beans. Slice lengthwise. Bring stock to boil in heavy-bottomed saucepan. Add green beans and enough water to barely cover. Bring to boil. Lower heat to simmering point. Partially cover and cook for 15-20 minutes. Green beans should be firm yet tender. Drain in colander, reserving stock for another dish.

Heat oil in large non-stick frying pan until hot. Add onion, garlic and shallot and sauté until softened. Add green beans and toss. Sprinkle with tarragon and nutmeg. Cook for 3 minutes, or until beans are heated through. Sprinkle with lemon juice and parsley. Toss well, and serve.

Yield: Serves 4

Note: If you prefer your green beans *au naturel*, as many people do, serve them directly from the colander, sprinkled with fresh chopped parsley.

CAL	F	P:S	SOD	CAR	CHO
121	7	4.5:1	16	11	0
Au naturel					
32	0	—	7	7	0

GREEN BEAN PURÉE

Best prepared in food processor, this smoothly textured accompaniment to almost any dish can also be used in small amounts to thicken a gravy without adding many calories.

	Metric	Imperial	American
Chicken stock (Page 8)	360 ml	12½ fl oz	1½ cups
Green beans, cut into 1.5-cm/½-inch slices	700 g	1½ lb	1½ lb
Large fresh mushrooms, washed, trimmed and coarsely chopped	4	4	4
Dried tarragon leaves, crushed	½ tsp	½ tsp	½ tsp
Dried dill weed, crushed	¼ tsp	¼ tsp	¼ tsp
Cayenne pepper	3 pinches	3 pinches	3 pinches
Enough water to barely cover beans			

Bring stock to boil in heavy-bottomed saucepan. Add green beans, mushrooms, herbs and cayenne, and enough water to barely cover. Bring to boil. Reduce heat, partially cover and simmer for 25 minutes. Uncover, and let cool in liquid for 15 minutes. Drain in colander, and reserve liquid for another dish. (This stock will be particularly delicious to add to soups and sauces.)

Transfer to food processor and purée until smooth. Reheat over very low flame, and serve.

Yield: Serves 4

Variation: If you like the consistency of this purée, you may want to try carrots or fresh peas made the same way. Just substitute either vegetable, and follow recipe.

Note: If you don't have a food processor, you can use a food mill with a fine blade, and purée twice.

CAL	F	P:S	SOD	CAR	CHO
69	0	—	22	12	0
Carrots					
79	0	—	77	15	0
Peas					
73	0	—	13	13	0

STIR-FRIED COURGETTES

Here's a familiar vegetable undercooked in the classic Chinese manner. Stir-frying is quick cooking, which means the vegetable retains its crunchy texture and its garden-fresh savour. This is one of the best ways to prepare courgettes.

	Metric	Imperial	American
Corn oil	2 tbsp	2 tbsp	2 tbsp
Large cloves garlic, finely chopped	2	2	2
Medium-sized courgettes, washed, trimmed, cut in half then cut into 1.5-cm/½-inch strips	4	4	4

	Metric	Imperial	American
Fresh lemon juice	1 tsp	1 tsp	1 tsp
Cayenne pepper	4 pinches	4 pinches	4 pinches
Dried tarragon leaves, crushed	½ tsp	½ tsp	½ tsp
Dried thyme leaves, crushed	¼ tsp	¼ tsp	¼ tsp
Sodium-free soya sauce	1 tsp	1 tsp	1 tsp

Heat oil in large heavy frying pan until hot. Add garlic and sauté for 1 minute. Add courgettes and sauté for 3 minutes, turning with spatula. Sprinkle with lemon juice, turning well to coat. Sprinkle with cayenne and herbs, and continue to sauté, turning frequently for 3-4 minutes. Add sodium-free soya sauce and cook for 1 minute. Serve immediately.

Yield: Serves 4

Notes:
1. Any dried herb of your choice may be successfully substituted for tarragon.
2. If your frying pan is not large enough to accommodate all of the courgettes at once, cook in two batches, dividing ingredients in half. When cooked, combine in one frying pan and turn with spatula to blend seasonings.

CAL	F	P:S	SOD	CAR	CHO
139	7	4.5:1	13	12	0

COURGETTE-TOMATO CASSEROLE

A dish for the summer months when both vegetables are plentiful and inexpensive. Prepare it in the morning, then just pop it into the oven at the end of a long day.

	Metric	Imperial	American
Corn oil	2 tbsp	2 tbsp	2 tbsp
Small onion, finely chopped	1	1	1
Large cloves garlic, finely chopped	2	2	2
Shallots, finely chopped	2	2	2
Green pepper, parboiled 1 minute, then sliced into strips	½	½	½
Unbleached flour	1 tsp	1 tsp	1 tsp
Courgettes, washed and cubed	450 g	1 lb	1 lb
Fresh tomatoes, cored, skinned, seeded and drained	450 g	1 lb	1 lb
Tomato paste, no salt added	1 tsp	1 tsp	1 tsp
Dried basil leaves, crushed	½ tsp	½ tsp	½ tsp
Dried oregano leaves, crushed	½ tsp	½ tsp	½ tsp
Chicken stock (Page 8)	80 ml	3 fl oz	⅓ cup
Bay leaf	1	1	1
Cayenne pepper	4 pinches	4 pinches	4 pinches
Oil for oiling casserole	½ tsp	½ tsp	½ tsp
Sharp low-fat cheese, grated (Page 6)	75 g	3 oz	½ cup
Freshly chopped parsley	1 tsp	1 tsp	1 tsp

Heat oil in large heavy frying pan until hot. Sauté onion, garlic and shallots until softened. Add green pepper and sauté for 1 minute. Sprinkle with flour and cook for 1 minute, stirring well. Add remainder of ingredients, with exception of cheese and parsley, and bring to simmering point.

Pour into lightly oiled ovenproof casserole dish, cover loosely with foil and bake in preheated 180°C/350°F/Gas mark 4 oven for 20 minutes. Remove from oven and sprinkle with grated cheese. Place under grill for 2-3 minutes, or until cheese is lightly browned. Sprinkle with parsley and serve.

Yield: Serves 4

CAL	F	P:S	SOD	CAR	CHO
175	9	4.5:1	17	17	0

HONEYED WHITE ONIONS

Small white onions are a delicious accompaniment to poultry or meat. Gilded with honey, they have an enticing sheen.

	Metric	Imperial	American
Water	240 ml	8 fl oz	1 cup
Chicken or veal stock (Pages 8 and 10)	240 ml	8 fl oz	1 cup
Small white onions, peeled	700 g	1½ lb	1½ lb
Corn oil	2 tbsp	2 tbsp	2 tbsp
Shallot, finely chopped	1	1	1
Clove garlic, finely chopped	1	1	1
Fresh lemon juice	1 tsp	1 tsp	1 tsp
Cayenne pepper	2 pinches	2 pinches	2 pinches
Ground ginger	⅛ tsp	⅛ tsp	⅛ tsp
Combined dried marjoram and tarragon leaves, crushed	¼ tsp	¼ tsp	¼ tsp
Honey	1 tbsp	1 tbsp	1 tbsp

Bring water and stock to boil in heavy-bottomed saucepan. Add onions and cook, partially covered, for 15 minutes, or until almost tender when tested through their centre with a sharp knife. Drain, reserving liquid for another dish.

In non-stick frying pan, heat oil until hot. Add shallot and garlic, and cook for 3 minutes or until softened but not brown.

Arrange onions in lightly oiled shallow baking dish. Sprinkle with lemon juice, cayenne, ginger, dried herbs and sautéed ingredients. Spoon honey over onions, and bake in preheated 180°C/350°F/Gas mark 4 oven, uncovered, for 20 minutes, turning twice. Serve immediately.

Yield: Serves 4

CAL	F	P:S	SOD	CAR	CHO
150	7	4.5:1	22	8	0

HONEYED CARROTS

For a touch of colour, serve this orange-hued slightly sweet-and-sour vegetable with sliced chicken or turkey.

	Metric	Imperial	American
Large carrots, peeled and trimmed	6	6	6
Chicken stock (Page 8)	240 ml	8 fl oz	1 cup
Enough water to barely cover carrots			
Corn oil	1 tbsp	1 tbsp	1 tbsp
Large shallot, finely chopped	1	1	1
Cider vinegar	1 tbsp	1 tbsp	1 tbsp
Dried tarragon leaves, crushed	¼ tsp	¼ tsp	¼ tsp
Cayenne pepper	2 pinches	2 pinches	2 pinches
Ground ginger	¼ tsp	¼ tsp	¼ tsp
Honey	1 tbsp	1 tbsp	1 tbsp
Freshly chopped parsley	1 tbsp	1 tbsp	1 tbsp

Cut each carrot in half. Lay cut side on board. Then slice lengthwise into 1.5-cm/½-inch strips. Place carrots in medium-sized heavy-bottomed saucepan. Add stock and enough water to barely cover. Bring to boil. Turn heat down and simmer, partially covered, for 12-15 minutes. Carrots should be tender but still firm. Drain, reserving stock for another dish.

Rinse and dry saucepan. Add oil and heat until hot. Add shallot and cook for 1 minute. Add vinegar and cook for 1 minute. Add carrots. Turn to coat. Sprinkle with tarragon, cayenne and ginger. Shake the pan. Add honey and cook over very low flame until heated through. Turn into serving dish and sprinkle with freshly chopped parsley.

Yield: Serves 4

CAL	F	P:S	SOD	CAR	CHO
89	4	4.5:1	73	11	0

BROCCOLI MAGIC

Broccoli is such an adaptable vegetable. It can be eaten cold as an hors d'oeuvre, tossed in oil and herbs as a hot side dish, or embellished with cheese for your main course. It can also be puréed with other vegetables to produce an entirely different flavour and texture (see following recipe).

	Metric	Imperial	American
Fresh broccoli, washed and trimmed	680 g	1½ lb	1½ lb
Corn oil	2 tbsp	2 tbsp	2 tbsp
Large cloves garlic, finely chopped	2	2	2
Large shallots, finely chopped	2	2	2
Dried tarragon leaves, crushed	½ tsp	½ tsp	½ tsp
Dried oregano leaves, crushed	½ tsp	½ tsp	½ tsp
Freshly chopped parsley	2 tsp	2 tsp	2 tsp
Cayenne pepper	4 pinches	4 pinches	4 pinches

Both the stalks and florets are used in this recipe. To promote tenderness and reduce bitterness that sometimes accompanies broccoli, the skin must first be removed.

Cut apart each section of broccoli about 2.5 cm/1 inch down from florets, and again 2.5 cm/1 inch up from bottom of the stalk. Standing the stalks upright, cut away the thick skin all around, making a smooth cylinder. Then cut into small cubes and set aside.

Grasping the ends of the florets, gently peel off the thick skin upwards so that the meaty soft mass underneath is exposed. Place peeled florets in colander and wash under cold running water.

Fill a large saucepan with water and bring to boil. Drop cubed stalks into water and boil, partially covered, for 4 minutes. Drop the florets into the same boiling water, and when it returns to boil, cook for 5 minutes. Colour should remain bright green. Do not overcook!

Drain in colander and rinse immediately under cold water to stop the cooking action. Broccoli can now be set aside and the final preparation resumed hours later, if liked.

Heat oil in large non-stick frying pan until hot. Add garlic and shallots and sauté until softened. Add broccoli, herbs and cayenne, shaking pan gently, taking care not to break florets. Serve immediately.

Yield: Serves 4

Variation: Place cooked broccoli in lightly oiled casserole. Top with 25 g/1 oz/¼ cup bread crumbs that have been mixed with 50 g/2 oz/¼ cup tangy low-fat cheese, and place under grill until cheese is melted and lightly brown. (Pages 00 and 00). Serve as a luncheon main course.

CAL	F	P:S	SOD	CAR	CHO
79	7	4.5:1	10	5	0
Luncheon main course					
133	8	4.5:1	10	18	0

BROCCOLI-VEGETABLE PURÉES

Smooth purées are a delightful contrast to meats and poultry. They can be made from most leftover vegetables, but are particularly interesting when made with broccoli.

	Metric	Imperial	American
Large carrot, peeled and diced	1	1	1
Large potato, peeled and diced	1	1	1
Cooked broccoli	450 g	1 lb	2 cups
Freshly chopped parsley	1 tbsp	1 tbsp	1 tbsp

Cook carrot and potato together in boiling water until tender (about 15 minutes). Drain. Combine with broccoli and put through food mill or food processor while still warm. Add chopped parsley and blend. Serve hot as a side dish.

17

Variations:

1. Add 1 tablespoon non-fat plain yogurt before puréeing. Reheat, taking care not to boil.

2. Combine 225 g/8 oz/1 cup cooked broccoli, 225 g/8 oz/1 cup cooked swede (opposite), and 2 large carrots, peeled, diced and cooked in boiling water for 15 minutes. Place in food mill or food processor and proceed as before.

Yield: Serves 4

CAL	F	P:S	SOD	CAR	CHO
104	7	4.5:1	24	12	0
With yogurt					
107	8	4.1:1	25	12	0
With vegetables					
100	7	4.5:1	30	9	0

HERBED CAULIFLOWER

Start with fresh cauliflower, cook to crunchy consistency, accent with spices and herbs, and this bland vegetable is transformed into a delicacy.

	Metric	Imperial	American
Small white head cauliflower	1	1	1
Corn oil	2 tbsp	2 tbsp	2 tbsp
Large clove garlic, finely chopped	1	1	1
Large shallots, finely chopped	2	2	2
Wine vinegar	1 tbsp	1 tbsp	1 tbsp
Cayenne pepper	2 pinches	2 pinches	2 pinches
Dried tarragon leaves, crushed	½ tsp	½ tsp	½ tsp
Ground ginger	⅛ tsp	⅛ tsp	⅛ tsp
Freshly chopped dill	2 tsp	2 tsp	2 tsp

Remove outer green leaves of cauliflower. Soak cauliflower, head down, in water to cover for 15 minutes. Separate into florets. Peel back skin from stems, see Broccoli Magic (Page 17).

Bring large pan of water to boil. Drop florets into water and cook, partially covered, for 12-15 minutes, or until tender but firm. Drain in colander.

In a large non-stick frying pan, heat oil until hot. Add garlic and shallots, and sauté until softened. Add vinegar and cook for 1 minute. Add cauliflower. Stir gently with wooden spoon. Sprinkle with cayenne, tarragon and ginger and stir, being careful not to break florets. Heat through, and serve immediately, sprinkled with freshly chopped dill.

Yield: Serves 4, one leftover

Variations:

1. *Gratinéed cauliflower.* Prepare according to recipe. Transfer drained cauliflower to ovenproof baking dish. Sprinkle with 50 g/2 oz/½ cup grated low-fat cheese. Place under grill for 3-5 minutes, or until cheese is lightly browned. Serve as a luncheon main course.

2. *Cauliflower with dill sauce.* Prepare according to recipe. Transfer to heated serving dish. Pour dill sauce (Page 49) over cauliflower, and serve.

CAL	F	P:S	SOD	CAR	CHO
94	7	4.5:1	9	5	0
Gratinéed					
99	8	4.0:1	9	6	1
With dill sauce					
152	13	4.5:1	27	7	0

SAUTÉED SWEDE

Swedes—a much neglected vegetable—are very nutritious, and their natural tangy flavour and potato-like texture make them tasty, too.

	Metric	Imperial	American
Swede, peeled and cut into 2.5-cm/1-inch cubes	680 g	1½ lb	1½ lb
Corn oil	2 tbsp	2 tbsp	2 tbsp
Large cloves garlic, finely chopped	2	2	2
Shallots, finely chopped	2	2	2
Dried thyme leaves, crushed	¼ tsp	¼ tsp	¼ tsp
Dried oregano leaves, crushed	¼ tsp	¼ tsp	¼ tsp
Dried basil leaves, crushed	¼ tsp	¼ tsp	¼ tsp
Cayenne pepper	4 pinches	4 pinches	4 pinches
Combined freshly chopped parsley and dill	2 tbsp	2 tbsp	2 tbsp

Fill a large heavy-bottomed saucepan with water. Bring to boil. Add the swede. Bring to boil again. Turn heat down, partially cover and simmer for about 45 minutes. Swede should be tender yet firm. Drain well.

Wipe out pan. Add oil and heat until hot. Add garlic and shallot, and sauté until softened (3-4 minutes). Return cooked swede to saucepan turning to coat. Sprinkle with dried herbs and cayenne and toss by shaking pan. Sprinkle with freshly chopped dill, and serve.

Yield: Serves 4

Variation: *Puréed swede.* Herbed swede may be put through food mill or food processor with 1 tablespoon plain low-fat yogurt. Reheat, taking care not to boil.

CAL	F	P:S	SOD	CAR	CHO
111	7	4.5:1	26	11	0
Puréed swede					
119	9	3.7:1	36	12	7

CREAMED SPINACH

Here's how to transform this simple vegetable into a succulent dish with an intriguing edge of sweetness.

	Metric	Imperial	American
Fresh spinach	900 g	2 lb	2 lb
Corn oil	1 tsp	1 tsp	1 tsp
Small onion, finely chopped	1	1	1
Shallot, finely chopped	1	1	1
Chicken stock (Page 8)	60 ml	2 fl oz	¼ cup
Cayenne pepper	4 pinches	4 pinches	4 pinches
Honey	1 tsp	1 tsp	1 tsp
Ground nutmeg	⅛ tsp	⅛ tsp	⅛ tsp
Unbleached flour	2½ tsp	2½ tsp	2½ tsp
Low-fat milk, warmed	60 ml	2 fl oz	¼ cup

Break off and discard tough stems of spinach. Wash very well in cold water. Pat dry with paper towels. Chop coarsely.

In a heavy-bottomed saucepan, heat oil until hot. Add onion and shallot and sauté until softened (2 minutes). Add stock, spinach, cayenne, honey and nutmeg. Cover and cook over medium heat for 5-7 minutes. Sprinkle with flour, stirring well. Add warmed milk and blend until smooth and thickened. Serve immediately.

Yield: Serves 4

CAL	F	P:S	SOD	CAR	CHO
108	4	4.5:1	47	13	0

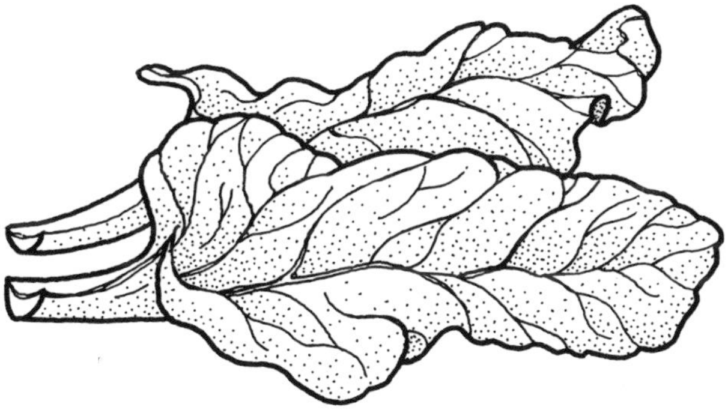

SPICED RED CABBAGE

This fragrant middle-European dish has a delicate tanginess and smooth texture that makes it vastly superior to any commercially prepared red cabbage. Try it with sweet-and-sauerbraten (Page 75).

	Metric	Imperial	American
Corn oil	2 tbsp	2 tbsp	2 tbsp
Large cloves garlic, finely chopped	2	2	2
Shallot, finely chopped	1	1	1
Small onion, finely chopped	1	1	1
Red cabbage, cut into thin strips	900 g	2 lb	2 lb
Crisp apple, cored, peeled and cubed	1	1	1
Whole cloves	8	8	8
Ground allspice	¼ tsp	¼ tsp	¼ tsp
Caraway seeds	1 tsp	1 tsp	1 tsp
Cider vinegar	2 tbsp.	2 tbsp	2 tbsp
Wine vinegar	1 tsp	1 tsp	1 tsp
Honey	1 tbsp	1 tbsp	1 tbsp
Unsweetened apple juice	120 ml	4 fl oz	½ cup
Water	120 ml	4 fl oz	½ cup
Juice of 1 lemon and grated rind of ½ lemon			
Cayenne pepper	4 pinches	4 pinches	4 pinches

Heat oil in small flameproof casserole or saucepan until hot. Add garlic, shallot and onion, and sauté until softened (about 3 minutes). Add cabbage. Turn and stir to coat well with sautéed ingredients. Add rest of ingredients and bring to boil. Reduce heat, cover and simmer for 45 minutes, stirring frequently. Turn heat off and leave cabbage in pot, covered, for 1 hour. When ready to serve, reheat over low flame, and serve in individual dishes.

Yield: Serves 4; one portion left over

Variation: Restaurants usually thicken red cabbage slightly. If you want to try it that way, dissolve 2 teaspoons arrowroot in equal amount of water, and add a little at a time to the finished cabbage, stirring well. Add enough of the mixture to give just a hint of thickening.

Note: This dish improves with age. Store in glass jar overnight, and serve reheated.

CAL	F	P:S	SOD	CAR	CHO
120	5	4.5:1	10	17	0
Thickened					
124	5	4.5:1	10	20	0

PARSLEYED POTATOES

Dressed up with generous sprinkling of herbs of your choice, the potato is a perfect accompaniment to almost any dish.

	Metric	Imperial	American
Medium-sized potatoes, peeled and each cut into 6 pieces	4	4	4
Corn oil	1 tbsp	1 tbsp	1 tbsp
Large clove garlic, finely chopped	1	1	1
Shallot, finely chopped	1	1	1
Cayenne pepper	4 pinches	4 pinches	4 pinches
Dried thyme leaves, crushed	¼ tsp	¼ tsp	¼ tsp
Dried tarragon leaves, crushed	¼ tsp	¼ tsp	¼ tsp
Freshly chopped parsley	1 tbsp	1 tbsp	1 tbsp

Place potatoes in large saucepan. Fill with water to cover. Bring to boil. Reduce heat to simmering point. Partially cover and cook for 15 minutes or until tender. Pour into colander and drain. Rinse under cold water until cooled.

Heat oil until hot in a non-stick frying pan. Add garlic and shallot and sauté for 1 minute. Add potatoes. Sprinkle with cayenne and dried herbs. Toss gently until heated through. Serve immediately, sprinkled with freshly chopped parsley.

Yield: Serves 4

Notes:
1. You can interchange herbs to match your main course.
2. Small new potatoes can be used in this recipe. Boil whole in jackets for 15-20 minutes, or until tender. Pour into colander and cool under cold running water. Peel, if liked, and follow recipe.

CAL	F	P:S	SOD	CAR	CHO
161	4	4.5:1	8	25	0

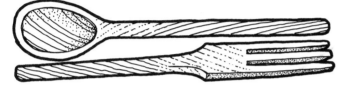

SPICED POTATOES

Serve this to your guests and challenge them to guess what it is.

	Metric	Imperial	American
Large potatoes, peeled (about 700 g/1½ lb)	4	4	4
Corn oil	1 tbsp	1 tbsp	1 tbsp
Cloves garlic, finely chopped	2	2	2
Large shallot, finely chopped	1	1	1
Cider vinegar	½ tsp	½ tsp	½ tsp
Dried rosemary leaves, crushed	¼ tsp	¼ tsp	¼ tsp
Dried thyme leaves, crushed	¼ tsp	¼ tsp	¼ tsp
Mild paprika	4 pinches	4 pinches	4 pinches
Cayenne pepper	pinch	pinch	pinch
Duxelles (Page 12)	1 tbsp	1 tbsp	1 tbsp
Sodium-free soya sauce	4 dashes	4 dashes	4 dashes
Dry mustard, dissolved in 1 tsp water	¼ tsp	¼ tsp	¼ tsp
Freshly chopped parsley and dill	2 tbsp	2 tbsp	2 tbsp
Low-fat milk	3 tbsp	3 tbsp	3 tbsp
Plain low-fat yogurt	2 tbsp	2 tbsp	2 tbsp

Cut potatoes into 2.5-cm/1-inch cubes. Place in heavy-bottomed saucepan and fill with water to cover. Bring to boil. Reduce heat to simmering point and continue to cook, partially covered, for 12-15 minutes or until tender. Pour into colander and drain for 3 minutes.

Dry saucepan and add oil. Heat until very warm. Sauté garlic and shallot until softened. Add vinegar and cook for 1 minute. Remove from heat, add dried herbs and stir well.

Mash potatoes with fork. Add spices, duxelles, sodium-free soya sauce, mustard, and parsley and dill. Blend with fork. Add sautéed mixture and blend again. Add milk, a tablespoon at a time, blending with fork. Fold in yogurt until all is absorbed.

Lightly oil 4 ovenproof individual soufflé dishes. Spoon in equal amounts of mixture. Place on baking sheet, and bake in preheated 220°C/425°F/Gas mark 7 oven for 20 minutes until puffed up. Serve immediately.

Yield: Serves 4

CAL	F	P:S	SOD	CAR	CHO
181	8	3.4:1	59	29	0

STUFFED POTATOES

You'll want to serve this dish often with braised meats, roasts or grills.

	Metric	Imperial	American
Large potatoes	2	2	2
Corn oil	1 tbsp	1 tbsp	1 tbsp
Small onion, finely chopped	½	½	½
Clove garlic, finely chopped	1	1	1
Large shallot, finely chopped	1	1	1
Wine vinegar	½ tsp	½ tsp	½ tsp
Dried tarragon, oregano or basil leaves, crushed	½ tsp	½ tsp	½ tsp

Freshly chopped parsley and dill	2 tsp	2 tsp	2 tsp
Cayenne pepper	3 pinches	3 pinches	3 pinches
Low-fat milk	3 tbsp	3 tbsp	3 tbsp
Finely grated low-fat cheese (Page 6)	25 g	1 oz	¼ cup
Mild paprika	2-3 pinches	2-3 pinches	2-3 pinches

Scrub potatoes. Dry well. Bake for 1 hour in preheated 200°C/400°F/Gas mark 6 oven, or until baked through.

In a small frying pan, heat oil until very hot. Add onion, garlic and shallot and sauté until lightly browned. Add vinegar and cook for 1 minute. Stir and set aside.

Cut each potato in half lengthwise. Scoop out potato, being careful not to break shell. Set shells aside. Transfer potatoes to bowl and mash. Add herbs and cayenne. Blend well. Add sautéed mixture and enough milk to produce a firm consistency when blended.

Stuff potato shells with mixture, pressing lightly. Place stuffed shells, skin down, on a baking dish. Sprinkle with cheese. Then sprinkle lightly with paprika. Bake in preheated 220°C/425°F/Gas mark 7 oven for 10 minutes. Then place under grill for 2-3 minutes, or until lightly browned.

Yield: Serves 4

CAL	F	P:S	SOD	CAR	CHO
119	7	3.9:1	31	21	8

RICH SAUTÉ POTATOES

Start with neatly cut potatoes, add a generous sprinkling of herbs and spices, sauté until golden brown and you'll produce greaseless potatoes, the likes of which you've never tasted before. Adds a new zest to chops, steaks and roasts.

	Metric	Imperial	American
Large potatoes, peeled	2	2	2
Corn oil	3 tbsp	3 tbsp	3 tbsp
Cloves garlic, finely chopped	3	3	3
Large shallot, finely chopped	1	1	1
Stick celery, finely chopped	1	1	1
Large onion, thinly sliced	1	1	1
Dried thyme leaves, crushed	½ tsp	½ tsp	½ tsp
Dried oregano leaves, crushed	⅛ tsp	⅛ tsp	⅛ tsp
Cayenne pepper	4 pinches	4 pinches	4 pinches
Mild paprika	¼ tsp	¼ tsp	¼ tsp
Freshly chopped parsley and dill or freshly chopped basil			

Wash peeled potatoes. Slice carefully into 5-mm/¼-inch thick rounds. Fill a large saucepan with water and bring to boil. Add potatoes and boil for 13 minutes. Drain in colander. Place under slow-running cold water for several minutes until cooled. Transfer to bowl. Cover and refrigerate for at least 2 hours.

Heat 1 tablespoon oil in large heavy frying pan until hot. Sauté garlic, shallot, celery and onion until lightly browned. Remove from frying pan and set aside.

Lay cooled potatoes on paper towels. Pat dry, taking care not to break slices. Heat 1 tablespoon oil in same pan until hot. Lay as many potatoes in pan as will fit in a single layer. Combine dry herbs, cayenne and paprika, blending well. Sprinkle a third of spicy mixture over potatoes, and top with spread of sautéed ingredients. Cover with rest of sliced potatoes in a single layer. Sprinkle with another third of spicy mixture. Press gently with spatula and sauté, without turning, until browned. Add remaining oil to frying pan. Turn with spatula. Add rest of spicy mixture. Press gently with spatula, and sauté until brown. Continue to turn and brown until all potatoes are well browned (about 30 minutes).

Serve immediately sprinkled with freshly chopped herbs.

Yield: Serves 4

CAL	F	P:S	SOD	CAR	CHO
163	10	4.5:1	32	16	0

POTATO PANCAKES

'Potato pancakes! They're so fattening. I can't eat them!' Oh, yes, you can. You can eat them as a side dish, as a luncheon treat or—rolled up and secured with wooden cocktail sticks—as an hors d'oeuvre. The calorie count per dinner serving is not much more than that of a glass of orange juice.

	Metric	Imperial	American
Medium-sized baking potatoes	4	4	4
Large onion, grated	1	1	1
Shallot, grated	1	1	1
Large clove garlic, finely chopped	1	1	1
Dried thyme leaves, crushed	¼ tsp	¼ tsp	¼ tsp
Egg, whites and ½ yolk from large eggs	2	2	2
Cayenne pepper	3 pinches	3 pinches	3 pinches
Low-sodium baking powder	½ tsp	½ tsp	½ tsp
Unbleached flour	3 tbsp	3 tbsp	3 tbsp
Oil for coating non-stick frying pan	1 tsp	1 tsp	1 tsp

Peel potatoes and pat dry. Medium-grate immediately into bowl. Pour off any excess water. Grate onion and shallot into potatoes. Add garlic, thyme, eggs, cayenne, baking powder and flour. Stir to blend.

Brush non-stick frying pan lightly with oil and heat until very hot. Drop a good tablespoon of mixture into pan and spread to form pancake. Make three pancakes at the same time. Brown well. Turn and brown on other side. Brush heated pan with oil before each batch of pancakes are made.

Yield: 12 pancakes, serves four

Note: A thermostatically controlled non-stick frying pan (which is excellent for crêpes) doesn't work. You must have a continual high heat to produce crispness.

CAL	F	P:S	SOD	CAR	CHO
140	2	2.6:1	35	30	31

BAKED MASHED SWEET POTATOES

Use this dish as a complement to turkey, chicken, beef or veal.

	Metric	Imperial	American
Sweet potatoes (about 700 g/1½ lb)	4	4	4
Corn oil	2 tbsp	2 tbsp	2 tbsp
Shallot, finely chopped	1	1	1
Ground ginger	1 tsp	1 tsp	1 tsp
Ground mace	1 tsp	1 tsp	1 tsp
Unsweetened orange juice	2 tbsp	2 tbsp	2 tbsp
Orange zest (see method)	1 tsp	1 tsp	1 tsp
Cayenne pepper	3 pinches	3 pinches	3 pinches
Egg whites	3	3	3
Corn oil to oil soufflé dishes	½ tsp	½ tsp	½ tsp
Ground cinnamon	3-4 pinches	3-4 pinches	3-4 pinches
Honey to taste (optional)			

Bake sweet potatoes in 180°C/350°F/Gas mark 4 oven for 1 hour, or until tender when given a gentle squeeze. Remove from skins and mash in small bowl while still warm. Add oil, shallot, ginger, mace, orange juice, zest and cayenne. Blend. (To make orange zest, peel off outer coloured skin of orange with potato peeler. Be sure not to include bitter pulpy rind. Chop into small pieces.)

Beat egg whites until almost stiff. Do this by continuing to beat for a few moments after soft peaks form. Fold into mashed sweet potato mixture. Folding is done by making a down motion with the spoon, and then a scooping up and folding over motion.

Spoon into 4 individual soufflé dishes which have been lightly oiled. Sprinkle with cinnamon. Place in preheated 200°C/400°F/Gas mark 6 oven until lightly puffed on top (about 15 minutes). Serve immediately.

Yield: Serves 6

Variation: For a particularly festive occasion, try baking the sweet potato mixture in orange shells. You'll need one orange per person. Cut off oranges 2.5 cm / 1 inch from top. Scoop out pulp and reserve for fruit salad. Fill shells with mixture. Place on lightly oiled baking sheet. Bake in preheated 200°C/400°F/Gas mark 6 oven for 15 minutes ot until heated through.

CAL	F	P:S	SOD	CAR	CHO
176	3	4.5:1	53	32	0

Note: Honey has 62 calories and 1.5 mg sodium per tablespoon.

EXTRAORDINARY KASHA

The key to retaining the bright nutlike taste of the oats is to keep the cooking time short. Bathed in your homemade stock and coddled by herbs and spices, kasha (buckwheat oats) can ascend to culinary heights.

	Metric	Imperial	American
Stock, veal, beef, or chicken to match your main course (Pages 8 to 11) (If serving fish, use chicken stock)	450 ml	¾ pt	2 cups
Kasha (buckwheat oats)	175 g	6 oz	1 cup
Shallot, finely chopped	1	1	1
Freshly chopped parsley and dill	2 tbsp	2 tbsp	2 tbsp
Dried tarragon, oregano or basil leaves, crushed	½ tsp	½ tsp	½ tsp
Cayenne pepper	3 pinches	3 pinches	3 pinches

Bring stock to boil in heavy-bottomed saucepan. Add kasha and bring to boil again. Reduce heat to simmering point. Stir well. Simmer, uncovered, for 8 minutes exactly, adding more stock if necessary. All liquid should be absorbed and each kernel should remain separate. Add remainder of ingredients, tossing well. Serve immediately.

Yield: Serves 4

Variation: Add the following to cooked mixture, toss and serve:

	Metric	Imperial	American
Small onion, finely chopped	½	½	½
Fresh mushrooms, washed, sliced and sautéed	100 g	4 oz	¼ lb

Note: This full-grained dish and its variation are suitable for stuffing chicken and turkey. For a kasha (buckwheat) with a pâté-like texture suitable for stuffing veal, see page 78.

CAL	F	P:S	SOD	CAR	CHO
With chicken stock					
44	0	—	2	8	0
With veal stock					
49	0	—	14	8	0
With beef stock					
48	0	—	23	8	0
Variation add					
7	0	—	3	0	0

BAKED BARLEY CASSEROLE

Here's a nutritious alternate to rice and potatoes. It's an excellent main dish for your meatless, fishless, poultryless days—and it's marvellous with a green salad. Smaller portions make an impeccable side dish too.

	Metric	Imperial	American
Corn oil	2 tbsp	2 tbsp	2 tbsp
Large clove garlic, finely chopped	1	1	1
Shallot, finely chopped	1	1	1
Small onion, finely chopped	1	1	1
Green pepper, finely chopped	½	½	½

Wine vinegar	1 tsp	1 tsp	1 tsp
Pearl barley, washed and drained	175 g	6 oz	¾ cup
Chicken or veal stock (Pages 8 and 10)	450-600 ml	¾-1 pt	2¼-2½ cups
Dried thyme leaves, crushed	½ tsp	½ tsp	½ tsp
Carrot, peeled and grated	½	½	½
Cayenne pepper	2 pinches	2 pinches	2 pinches
Sodium-free soya sauce	3 dashes	3 dashes	3 dashes
Caraway seeds, lightly crushed	½ tsp	½ tsp	½ tsp
2.5-cm/1-inch sliver orange rind	1	1	1
Corn oil to oil casserole	½ tsp	½ tsp	½ tsp
Freshly chopped dill and parsley	2 tbsp	2 tbsp	2 tbsp

Heat oil in heavy frying pan until hot. Add garlic, shallot, onion and pepper, and sauté until lightly brown. Add vinegar and cook for 2 minutes. Add barley and stir to coat well with sautéed mixture. Add most of the stock, thyme, carrot, cayenne, sodium-free soya sauce and caraway seeds, and bring to simmering point. Drop in orange rind. Pour into lightly oiled 2.5-litre/4-5-pint/2-3-quart casserole, and bake, covered in preheated 190°C/375°F/Gas mark 5 oven for 45 minutes, stirring twice. Liquid should be absorbed and barley tender. If you prefer a very moist barley, add remaining hot stock at this point, and stir.

Sprinkle with fresh herbs, and serve.

Yield: Serves 4, one portion left over

Variation: For stock, substitute a mixture of half chicken or veal stock and half apple juice (no sugar added). Add 3 whole cloves to casserole.

CAL	F	P:S	SOD	CAR	CHO
153	8	4.5:1	22	6	0
With veal stock					
153	8	4.5:1	32	6	0
With chicken stock/apple juice					
156	8	4.5:1	29	7	0
With veal stock/apple juice					
156	8	4.5:1	25	7	0

MACARONI STUFFED PEPPERS

This is a beautiful luncheon entree – a rich-tasting delight devoid of butter, salt, black pepper and egg yolks. You won't believe its satisfying heartiness until you make it yourself.

	Metric	Imperial	American
Whole wheat elbow macaroni, no salt or egg added	175 g	6 oz	1 cup
Large green peppers, parboiled for 1 minute and cooled under cold running water	2	2	2
Corn oil	2 tbsp	2 tbsp	2 tbsp
Large onion, finely chopped	1	1	1
Large cloves garlic, finely chopped	3	3	3
Shallot, finely chopped	1	1	1
Dry Vermouth or white wine	60 ml	2 fl oz	¼ cup
Tomato purée, no salt added	120 ml	4 fl oz	½ cup
Cayenne pepper	3 pinches	3 pinches	3 pinches
Dried mint leaves, crushed	¼ tsp	¼ tsp	¼ tsp
Dried oregano leaves, crushed	½ tsp	½ tsp	½ tsp
Dried rosemary leaves, crushed	½ tsp	½ tsp	½ tsp
Chicken stock (Page 8)	120 ml	4 fl oz	½ cup
Bread crumbs (Page 145)	25 g	1 oz	½ cup
Egg white, lightly beaten with fork	1	1	1
Corn oil to coat baking dish	½ tsp	½ tsp	½ tsp
Sharp low-fat cheese, grated (Page 6)	75 g	3 oz	½ cup
Tomato juice, no salt added	4 tbsp	4 tbsp	4 tbsp
Chopped fresh parsley and dill			

Bring large saucepan of water to boil. Add macaroni and cook, partially covered, for 10 minutes. Drain and set aside.

Cut parboiled green peppers in half, removing seeds and pulp. Set aside.

Heat oil in non-stick frying pan until hot. Sauté onion, garlic and shallot until softened (about 3 minutes). Add wine and cook for 1 minute. Add tomato purée, cayenne, dried herbs and stock, and simmer, partially covered, for 10 minutes.

Transfer cooked macaroni to large bowl. Add bread crumbs and egg white, blending well. Then add cooked mixture, stirring well.

Shape 4 pieces of foil into boats to hold each half of green pepper in such a way that foil will catch any overflow of macaroni as it's added. Fill each half of pepper with mixture, pressing gently. Place on lightly oiled baking dish. Cover loosely with foil.

Place filled dish into a large baking tin to which 2.5 cm/1 inch of boiling water has been added. Bake in preheated 180°C/350°F/Gas mark 4 oven for 20 minutes. Remove from oven, uncover, and sprinkle with grated cheese. Spoon a tablespoon of tomato juice over the top of each pepper and return to oven. Bake, uncovered, for 20 minutes until pepper is cooked through when tested with sharp knife. Serve sprinkled with chopped fresh parsley and dill.

Yield: Serves 4

Note: If you're planning to freeze some of the peppers, remove from oven 10 minutes before the end of cooking time so that when reheated they will retain their firmness.

CAL	F	P:S	SOD	CAR	CHO
225	9	2.4:1	30	24	7

ORANGE-PINEAPPLE RICE

Try this exciting innovative dish, and you'll never go back to just plain rice again. Serve with steamed or baked fish.

	Metric	Imperial	American
Corn oil	2 tbsp	2 tbsp	2 tbsp
Onion, finely chopped	1	1	1
Cloves garlic, finely chopped	2	2	2
Shallot, finely chopped	1	1	1
Stick celery with leaves, finely chopped	1	1	1
Large fresh mushrooms, washed, trimmed and sliced	5	5	5
Rice, washed and drained	175 g	6 oz	1 cup
Unsweetened orange juice	120 ml	4 fl oz	½ cup
Unsweetened pineapple juice	120 ml	4 fl oz	½ cup
Water	240 ml	8 fl oz	1 cup
Dried sage leaves, crushed	¼ tsp	¼ tsp	¼ tsp
Dried thyme leaves, crushed	¼ tsp	¼ tsp	¼ tsp
Cayenne pepper	3 pinches	3 pinches	3 pinches

Heat oil in large non-stick frying pan until hot. Sauté onion, garlic, shallot and celery until softened. Push vegetables to the side of the pan and add mushrooms. Sauté 2 minutes, stirring constantly. Mix together all ingredients in pan. Add rice, turn and stir to coat. Cook for 1 minute. Add combined juices, water, herbs and cayenne. Bring to boil. Pour into 2-litre/3.5-pint/2-qt lightly oiled casserole. Cover and bake in preheated 200°C/400°F/Gas mark 6 oven for 30-35 minutes or until all liquid is absorbed and rice is tender.

Yield: Serves 4, one portion left over

Note: This dish will stay hot for 30 minutes if left covered on top of warm stove.

CAL	F	P:S	SOD	CAR	CHO
223	3	4.5:1	32	30	0

SPAGHETTI WITH TOMATO AND MUSHROOM SAUCE

If you've never had whole wheat spaghetti made without eggs or sugar or salt, you'll be surprised at its delicious taste and texture. Top it with my slightly spicy tomato and mushroom sauce.

	Metric	Imperial	American
Corn oil	2 tbsp	2 tbsp	2 tbsp
Large onion, finely chopped	1	1	1
Large cloves garlic, finely chopped	3	3	3
Stick celery, finely chopped	1	1	1
Shallots, finely chopped	2	2	2
Large green pepper, finely chopped	1	1	1
Dry Vermouth or white wine	60 ml	2 fl oz	¼ cup
Fresh ripe tomatoes, cored, skinned and drained, or canned tomatoes, no salt added	680 g	1½ lb	3 cups
Tomato paste, no salt added	2 tbsp	2 tbsp	2 tbsp
Chicken stock (Page 8)	180 ml	6 fl oz	¾ cup
Dried oregano leaves, crushed	½ tsp	½ tsp	½ tsp
Dried thyme leaves, crushed	½ tsp	½ tsp	½ tsp
Dried basil leaves, crushed	½ tsp	½ tsp	½ tsp
Cayenne pepper	4 pinches	4 pinches	4 pinches
Bouquet garni made up of 3 sprigs parsley, ½ teaspoon fennel and 1 bay leaf tied together in muslin	1	1	1
Fresh mushrooms, washed, trimmed and sliced	225 g	8 oz	½ lb
Whole wheat spaghetti, without eggs or salt	350 g	12 oz	¾ lb
Freshly chopped parsley			

Heat oil in heavy frying pan until very warm. Sauté onion, garlic, celery and shallots until softened (about 3 minutes). Add green pepper and sauté for 2 minutes. Add wine. Bring to boil. Reduce heat and cook, uncovered, for 2 minutes. Add tomatoes, tomato paste, stock, dried herbs, cayenne and bouquet garni. Cover and simmer for 25 minutes. Add mushrooms. Stir well. Bring to simmering point. Cover and simmer for 35 minutes. Remove bouquet garni.

Fifteen minutes before sauce is ready, bring large pan of water to the boil. Ease spaghetti gently into boiling water without breaking pieces, and boil for 12-15 minutes. You will find that the whole wheat spaghetti will remain *al dente* (firm to the bite) which is the way spaghetti should be cooked. Drain well in colander. Transfer to heated serving dish, and top with hot sauce. Sprinkle with chopped parsley and serve.

Yield: Serves 6

Variations:
1. Serve with a sprinkling of grated low-fat cheese (Page 6).
2. If you like your spaghetti with meat balls, try my recipe (Page 93).

CAL	F	P:S	SOD	CAR	CHO
263	3	4.5:1	29	59	0
Sprinkled with cheese					
267	3+	4.4:1	29	59+	0

RISOTTO (RICE, PEAS AND MUSHROOMS)

This is an Italian-inspired side dish that you'll want to repeat often because it's compatible with just about every meat, poultry or fish course.

	Metric	Imperial	American
Fresh peas, shelled	225 g	8 oz	½ lb
Chicken, veal or beef stock to match your main course (Pages 8 and 10) (If serving fish, use chicken stock)	240 ml	8 fl oz	1 cup
Water	240 ml	8 fl oz	1 cup
White rice, washed and drained	175 g	6 oz	1 cup
Corn oil	2 tbsp	2 tbsp	2 tbsp
Fresh mushrooms, washed, trimmed and sliced	225 g	8 oz	½ lb
Cloves garlic, finely chopped	2	2	2
Shallots, finely chopped	2	2	2
Cider vinegar	2 tsp	2 tsp	2 tsp
Dried oregano leaves, crushed	¼ tsp	¼ tsp	¼ tsp
Dried marjoram leaves, crushed	¼ tsp	¼ tsp	¼ tsp
Cayenne pepper	3 pinches	3 pinches	3 pinches
Freshly chopped parsley	1 tbsp	1 tbsp	1 tbsp

In this recipe, rice, peas and mushrooms are cooked separately, then assembled.

Boil peas briskly in water to cover for 15 minutes or until tender. Drain and set aside.

Bring stock and water to boil. Add rice and cook, partially covered, for 15 minutes. All liquid should be absorbed.

Heat ¾ tablespoon of oil in large non-stick frying pan until hot. Add half of the mushrooms and sauté until lightly browned, turning often (about 3-4 minutes). Transfer with slotted spoon to bowl. Add ¾ tablespoon oil to frying pan and sauté rest of mushrooms. Transfer to bowl.

Heat remaining oil in same pan until hot. Add garlic and shallots and sauté until lightly browned. Add vinegar and cook for 1 minute. Add cooked rice, peas, mushrooms, dried herbs and cayenne, and toss gently until heated through. Transfer to heated serving dish, and serve immediately, sprinkled with freshly chopped parsley.

Yield: Serves 4, one portion left over

Notes:

1. Mushrooms must be cooked in small batches so that they don't touch each other. This produces a tasty non-watery mushroom which fully retains its character when mixed with other ingredients.

2. Brown rice 175 g/6 oz/1 cup may be substituted for white rice in this recipe. The short-grain organic variety is preferable to the starchy variety. Soak rice for 1 hour in 450 ml/¾ pt/2 cups liquid. Bring to boil, cover and simmer for 25 minutes.

CAL	F	P:S	SOD	CAR	CHO
With chicken stock					
177	9	4.5:1	16	28	0
With veal stock					
181	9	4.5:1	28	28	0
With beef stock					
180	9	4.5:1	37	28	0

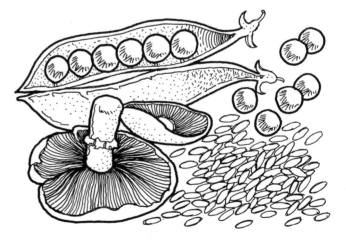

CHINESE RESTAURANT SPICED RICE

There isn't a Chinese ingredient other than rice in this surprising dish. But the well married herbs and spices and the exceptional cooking procedure make it taste as if it came from your favourite Chinese restaurant.

	Metric	Imperial	American
Water	240 ml	8 fl oz	1 cup
Chicken stock (Page 8)	240 ml	8 fl oz	1 cup
Rice, washed and drained	175 g	6 oz	1 cup
Corn oil	2 tbsp	2 tbsp	2 tbsp
Onion, finely chopped	1	1	1
Large cloves garlic, finely chopped	2	2	2
Large spring onion, finely chopped	1	1	1
Medium-sized green pepper, parboiled and cut into slivers	1	1	1
Dried marjoram leaves, crushed	¼ tsp	¼ tsp	¼ tsp
Dried tarragon leaves, crushed	¼ tsp	¼ tsp	¼ tsp
Freshly chopped parsley and dill	2 tbsp	2 tbsp	2 tbsp
Ground ginger	½ tsp	½ tsp	½ tsp
Cayenne pepper	3 pinches	3 pinches	3 pinches
Sodium-free soya sauce	4 dashes	4 dashes	4 dashes

Bring water and stock to boil in heavy-bottomed saucepan. Add rice. Bring to boil again. Reduce heat and cook, partially covered, for 12-15 minutes, or until all water is absorbed and rice is tender but firm.

Heat oil in heavy frying pan until hot. Add onion, garlic, spring onion and pepper, and sauté until lightly browned, turning frequently (5-7 minutes). Add rice to pan and turn to coat with sautéed mixture. Sprinkle with herbs, sprices and sodium-free soya sauce. Stir. Cover tightly and place in preheated 230°C/450°F/Gas mark 8 oven for 5 minutes. Serve immediately.

Yield: Serves 4, one portion left over

CAL	F	P:S	SOD	CAR	CHO
212	3	4.5:1	10	28	0

29

SOUPS

CREAMY ASPARAGUS SOUP

What can be lovelier than a meal enriched with the luxurious flavour of asparagus? Here that flavour is captured in an emerald-green soup, and enhanced with touches of herbs and spices.

	Metric	Imperial	American
Chicken stock (Page 8)	450 ml	¾ pt	2 cups
Water	350 ml	12 fl oz	1½ cups
Fresh asparagus	680 g	1½ lb	1½ lb
Thin slice orange	1	1	1
Dried tarragon leaves, crushed	1 tsp	1 tsp	1 tsp
Arrowroot, dissolved in 1 tbsp water	2 tsp	2 tsp	2 tsp
Corn oil	1 tbsp	1 tbsp	1 tbsp
Small onion, finely chopped	1	1	1
Clove garlic, finely chopped	1	1	1
Shallot, finely chopped	1	1	1
Low-fat milk	120 ml	4 fl oz	½ cup
Low-fat yogurt	3 tbsp	3 tbsp	3 tbsp

In a 1-litre/1¾-pint/2-pint saucepan, bring stock and water to boil.

Meanwhile, cut away tough bottom sections of asparagus stalks. Holding each stalk cut end up, peel downwards towards tips to remove skin. Cut each peeled stalk into 2.5-cm/1-inch pieces. Reserve tips. Place rest of cut asparagus into boiling liquid. Add orange slice and tarragon. Bring to simmering point. Turn heat down, and simmer, partially covered, for 10 minutes. Add reserved asparagus tips and stir in sufficient arrowroot mixture to thicken. Cover and simmer another 7 minutes. Turn off heat. Uncover, remove orange slice, and let soup cool in pot.

Heat oil in small frying pan until hot. Add onion, garlic and shallot, and sauté until softened. Set aside.

When soup has cooled down, remove 4 teaspoons

asparagus, picking out as many tips as you can. Set aside for garnish. Pour remainder of soup, together with sautéed mixture into blender. Blend for 1 minute.

Return to saucepan. Add milk and stir. Whisk in yogurt. Finally, add reserved tips. Reheat over very low heat, taking care not to boil.

Yield: 4 ample portions

CAL	F	P:S	SOD	CAR	CHO
113	4	3.8:1	29	12	1

CREAMY MUSHROOM SOUP

Tender fresh mushrooms, lightly sautéed with vegetables, then gently simmered in rich stock, are the basis of this delicately creamy soup. Make a lunch of it with my crispy French Bread (Page 135) and a slice of low-fat cheese (Page 6) or serve it as a light first course at your evening meal.

	Metric	Imperial	American
Corn oil	2 tbsp	2 tbsp	2 tbsp
Fresh mushrooms, washed, trimmed and coarsely chopped	350 g	12 oz	¾ lb
Small onion, finely chopped	1	1	1
Shallot, finely chopped	1	1	1
Stick celery, finely chopped	½	½	½
Cloves garlic, finely chopped	2	2	2
Dry sherry	1 tbsp	1 tbsp	1 tbsp
Chicken stock (Page 8)	450 ml	¾ pt	2 cups
Water	240 ml	8 fl oz	1 cup
Dried tarragon leaves, crushed	½ tsp	½ tsp	½ tsp
Freshly chopped dill and parsley	2 tbsp	2 tbsp	2 tbsp
Cayenne pepper	2 pinches	2 pinches	2 pinches
Honey	½ tsp	½ tsp	½ tsp
1.5-cm/½-inch sliver orange rind	1	1	1

	Metric	Imperial	American
Low-fat milk prepared from powder by using 1/3 less water than called for by instructions	180 ml	6 fl oz	3/4 cup
Arrowroot, dissolved in 1 tbsp water	2 tsp	2 tsp	2 tsp

Heat 1½ tablespoons oil until hot in non-stick frying pan. Sauté mushrooms until lightly browned, turning frequently with spoon. Take out 2 tablespoons mushrooms and reserve for garnish. Transfer rest of mushrooms to medium sized heavy-bottomed saucepan.

Heat remaining oil in frying pan. Add onion, shallot, celery and garlic. Sauté until lightly browned. Add sherry and cook for 1 minute. Pour into saucepan with mushrooms. Add stock and water. Stir to blend. Add tarragon, 1 tablespoon chopped parsley and dill, and cayenne. Heat to simmering point. Add honey and orange rind. Cover partially, and simmer for 25 minutes.

Remove orange rind. Pour into blender and blend until smooth. Pour back into saucepan. Add milk and sufficient arrowroot mixture to thicken. Heat to simmering point, stirring constantly. Serve hot, sprinkled with reserved mushrooms and rest of chopped parsley and dill.

Yield: Serves 4, with one portion left over

CAL	F	P:S	SOD	CAR	CHO
100	6	4.5:1	40	6	0

CLEAR VEGETABLE CONSOMMÉ

This fresh broth is as nutritious as it is delicious. The secret is simple: fresh vegetables and herbs simmered gently to extract their natural flavours.

	Metric	Imperial	American
Carrots, peeled and thinly sliced	3	3	3
Sticks celery, diced	3	3	3
Large onions, cut into eighths	2	2	2
Large cloves garlic, coarsely chopped	3	3	3
Large shallots, coarsely chopped	2	2	2
Swede, peeled and diced	75 g	3 oz	1/2 cup
Fresh mushrooms, trimmed and coarsely chopped	100 g	4 oz	1/4 lb
Small parsnip, peeled and thinly sliced	1	1	1
Whole leeks, well washed and coarsely chopped	2	2	2
Green cabbage, sliced	75 g	3 oz	1/2 cup
Green beans, cut into 1.5-cm/1/2-inch slices	450 g	1 lb	1 lb
Fresh tomatoes, cored and coarsely chopped	4	4	4
Whole cloves	3	3	3
Water	900 ml	1½ pt	1 qt
Sodium-free soya sauce	1/4 tsp	1/4 tsp	1/4 tsp

Place all ingredients except the sodium-free soya sauce in a saucepan, preferably stainless steel. Bring to boil. Remove scum that rises to top. Add soya sauce. Reduce heat and simmer, partially covered, for 30 minutes. Let cool, covered, in pan.

Pour into a sieve, placing a bowl underneath, and press to remove all consommé. Reserve vegetables for leftover purée. Transfer consommé to freezerproof containers. Cover tightly, and refrigerate sufficient quantity for immediate needs, and freeze remainder.

Yield: Serves 4

Note: After soup is drained from vegetables, pour vegetables into blender, and purée, adding small amount of consommé. Serve as a side dish.

CAL	F	P:S	SOD	CAR	CHO
74	0	—	98	14	0
Purée					
92	0	—	100	35	0

TWELVE-VEGETABLE BEEF SOUP

A dozen kinds of fresh vegetables plus lean beef give this soup a rich, hearty flavour. With a food processor, you can make it very quickly. But if you prefer to mince and chop by hand, double the recipe, freeze the left-over soup and you have an instant dish the next time around. Serve with French Herb Bread (Page 135).

	Metric	Imperial	American
Lean beef, cut into 5-cm/2-inch cubes	225 g	8 oz	½ lb
Large beef or veal bone	1	1	1
Water	1.2 l	2 pt	5 cups
Bouquet garni	1	1	1
Dried broad beans, soaked overnight and drained	50 g	2 oz	¼ cup
Carrots, peeled and finely diced	2	2	2
Stick celery, finely diced	1	1	1
Onions, cut into eighths	2	2	2
Large pieces dried mushrooms, or 6 fresh mushrooms, washed, trimmed and sliced	2	2	2
Small potato, peeled and diced	1	1	1
Green beans, cut into 1.5-cm/½-inch slices	175 g	6 oz	1 cup
Swede, peeled and diced	75 g	3 oz	½ cup
Small green pepper, diced	1	1	1
Fresh tomatoes, skinned, cored and chopped	2	2	2
Large shallot, finely chopped	1	1	1
Large cloves garlic, finely chopped	3	3	3
Dried thyme leaves, crushed	½ tsp	½ tsp	½ tsp
Dried rosemary leaves, crushed	½ tsp	½ tsp	½ tsp
Brown beef stock (Page 11)	3 tbsp	3 tbsp	3 tbsp
Tomato paste, no salt added	2 tbsp	2 tbsp	2 tbsp
Whole cloves	4	4	4
Medium barley	2 tbsp	2 tbsp	2 tbsp
Cayenne pepper	6 pinches	6 pinches	6 pinches
Wine vinegar	1 tbsp	1 tbsp	1 tbsp
Fresh shelled peas	75 g	3 oz	½ cup

Trim away any fat from meat. Place meat, bone, water and bouquet garni in large saucepan. Add drained beans. Bring to boil. Cover and simmer for 1 hour, removing scum that rises to top.

Add all vegetables (except peas), garlic, herbs, stock, tomato paste, cloves, barley, cayenne and vinegar. Bring to boil. Reduce heat, partially cover, and simmer for another hour. Add peas and continue to simmer for a further 30 minutes.

Let soup cool in pan for at least 1 hour. Remove bone and bouquet garni. Remove meat, cutting into small pieces, and return to pan. Reheat and serve.

Yield: Serves 6

Note: Here are some substitutions you can make.
Fresh broad beans for dried beans, split peas for fresh peas, and turnip for swede.

CAL	F	P:S	SOD	CAR	CHO
183	2	1:1	57	14	27
With fresh broad beans					
150	2	1:1	57	19	27
With split peas					
239	2	1:1	51	23	27
With turnip					

No appreciable difference

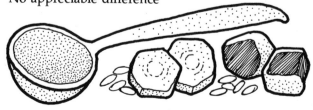

tomato soup—see page 33

CUCUMBER-TOMATO SOUP

This extremely tasty rose-hued soup is equally as delicious served hot or cold. Appetite-stimulating, and certainly not filling, it's a perfect first course.

	Metric	Imperial	American
Large fresh tomatoes, skinned, cored and coarsely chopped (see method)	3	3	3
Corn oil	1 tbsp	1 tbsp	1 tbsp
Mixed chopped leeks (white part only), garlic and shallots, finely chopped	75 g	3 oz	1/3 cup
Wine vinegar	1 tbsp	1 tbsp	1 tbsp
Medium-sized cucumbers, peeled and diced	2	2	2
Chicken stock (Page 8)	600 ml	1 pt	2 1/2 cups
Water	240 ml	8 fl oz	1 cup
Cayenne pepper	4 pinches	4 pinches	4 pinches
Dried dill weed	1/2 tsp	1/2 tsp	1/2 tsp
Freshly chopped dill	1 tsp	1 tsp	1 tsp
Low-fat plain yogurt	60-80 ml	4-5 tbsp	1/4 |1/2 cup
Arrowroot, dissolved in 1 tbsp cold water (optional)	2 tsp	2 tsp	2 tsp

Drop tomatoes in boiling water for 1 minute. Remove skin and core.

Heat oil in saucepan, preferably stainless steel, until very warm. Sauté shallots, leeks and garlic until just softened but not brown. Add vinegar and cook for 2 minutes. Add cucumbers, tomatoes, stock, water, cayenne and dill. Bring to boil. Reduce heat and simmer, partially covered, for 25 minutes. Cool.

Pour into blender and liquidize for 1 minute. Then pour through fine sieve. Rinse out pan in which soup was cooked. Pour puréed soup back into pan. Add yogurt and whisk well. Reheat over low heat (do not boil), and serve.

If you prefer a thicker soup, before adding yogurt, reheat soup to simmering point, and add dissolved arrowroot mixture, a little at a time, whisking until the desired thickness is achieved. Then add yogurt, whisking well.

Yield: Serves 4

Note: This soup is also delicious served cold.

CAL	F	P:S	SOD	CAR	CHO
90	5	3.2:1	28	9	1
Thickened					
102	5	3.2:1	28	11	1

FRESH TOMATO SOUP

This soups gourmet flavour derives from fresh tomatoes, gently simmered in rich stock, herbed with basil, and creamed with just a hint of yogurt. A perfect light first course.

	Metric	Imperial	American
Corn oil	1 tbsp	1 tbsp	1 tbsp
Small onion, coarsely chopped	1	1	1
Shallot, finely chopped	1	1	1
Large cloves garlic, finely chopped	2	2	2
Stick celery, coarsely chopped	1/2	1/2	1/2
Leek, white part only, washed and coarsely chopped	1	1	1
Chicken stock (Page 8)	450 ml	3/4 pt	2 cups
Water	450 ml	3/4 pt	2 cups
Large tomatoes, cored and quartered	4	4	4
Tomato paste, no salt added	1 tbsp	1 tbsp	1 tbsp
Dried basil leaves, crushed	1/2 tsp	1/2 tsp	1/2 tsp
Dried tarragon leaves, crushed	1/2 tsp	1/2 tsp	1/2 tsp
Carrot, peeled and diced	1/2	1/2	1/2

vegetable fruit salad—see page 102

Cayenne pepper	4 pinches	4 pinches	4 pinches
Bouquet garni	1	1	1
Plain low-fat yogurt	1½ tbsp	1½ tbsp	1½ tbsp
Freshly chopped basil or dill	1 tbsp	1 tbsp	1 tbsp

Heat oil in heavy-bottomed saucepan. Add onion, shallot, garlic, celery and leek. Sauté until softened. Add stock, water, tomatoes, tomato paste, dried herbs, carrot, cayenne and bouquet garni. Bring to simmering point. Partially covered and simmer for 20 minutes.

Remove bouquet garni and pour into blender. Liquidize for 1 minute. Pour through fine sieve directly into saucepan. Whisk in yogurt. Reheat to just below simmering point. Do not boil. Serve hot sprinkled with freshly chopped basil or dill.

Yield: Serves 4

Note: This soup is also delicious served cold. Just pour into container and refrigerate. Sprinkle with basil or dill when ready to serve.

CAL	F	P:S	SOD	CAR	CHO
110	4	4.2:1	29	16	0

TOMATO-WATERCRESS SOUP

Take advantage of tomatoes when in season, and enjoy this light, compatible combination of watercress and tomatoes. It's equally delicious served piping hot or icy cold.

	Metric	Imperial	American
Corn oil	1 tbsp	1 tbsp	1 tbsp
Small onion, finely chopped	1	1	1
Large cloves garlic, finely chopped	2	2	2
Leek, white part only, well washed, and finely chopped	1	1	1
Small shallot, finely chopped	1	1	1
Wine vinegar	1 tsp	1 tsp	1 tsp
Chicken stock (Page 8)	900 ml	1½ pt	3½ cups
Water	120 ml	4 fl oz	½ cup
Tomato paste, no salt added	1 tbsp	1 tbsp	1 tbsp
Ripe fresh tomatoes, cored and chopped	3	3	3
Fresh watercress, leaves only, washed and chopped	½ bunch	½ bunch	½ bunch
Cayenne pepper	4 pinches	4 pinches	4 pinches
Bouquet garni, including ¼ tsp fennel seeds, ½ tsp thyme leaves, ¼ tsp basil leaves, tied together in muslin	1	1	1

Heat oil in large heavy-bottomed saucepan. Sauté onion, garlic, leek and shallot until softened but not brown. Add vinegar and cook 2 minutes longer. Add chicken stock, water, tomato paste, tomatoes, chopped watercress (reserving 2 tbsp for garnish), cayenne and bouquet garni. Bring to simmering point, partially cover, and simmer for 20 minutes. Let cool, covered, in saucepan. Remove bouquet garni.

Pour into blender and liquidize for 1 minute. Then pour through fine sieve. Serve reheated or chilled, sprinkled with reserved chopped watercress.

Yield: Serves 6

Variations: If serving cold, try whisking in 4 tbsp/¼ cup low-fat yogurt before serving. It thickens soup and makes it creamier.

CAL	F	P:S	SOD	CAR	CHO
129	4	4.5:1	22	14	0
With yogurt					
132	4	4.4:1	26	14+	0

GAZPACHO

Fresh vegetables, puréed to perfection and gently spiced, are the basis of my version of the traditional dish from Spanish Andalusia. It's a perfect prelude to a main fish course. Or make a whole luncheon of it accompanied by my French Bread (Page 134).

	Metric	Imperial	American
Tomato juice, no salt added	240 ml	8 fl oz	1 cup
Onions, finely chopped	2	2	2
Large cloves garlic, finely chopped	2	2	2
Green peppers, finely chopped	2	2	2
Shallot, finely chopped	1	1	1
Cucumber, peeled and chopped	1	1	1
Corn oil	1 tbsp	1 tbsp	1 tbsp
Freshly chopped parsley and dill	2 tbsp	2 tbsp	2 tbsp
Wine vinegar	2 tbsp	2 tbsp	2 tbsp
Oregano leaves, crushed	½ tsp	½ tsp	½ tsp
Paprika	½ tsp	½ tsp	½ tsp
Cayenne pepper	8 pinches	8 pinches	8 pinches
Sodium-free soya sauce	3 dashes	3 dashes	3 dashes

Combine 60 ml/4 tbsp/¼ cup tomato juice, onions, garlic, green peppers, shallot and cucumber in blender. Blend until puréed, adding more juice if mixture is too thick to blend. Add oil, 1 tbsp chopped parsley and dill, vinegar, oregano, paprika, cayenne and sodium-free soya sauce. Blend again on high speed for 30 seconds. Add remainder of tomato juice. Pour into glass jar and refrigerate for 2-3 hours before serving. Sprinkle with rest of parsley and dill, and serve.

Yield: Serves 4

Note: If you're using a food processor, coarsely chop vegetables and proceed with recipe.
Variation: You may substitute any of the following for oregano: tarragon, basil or curry powder.

CAL	F	P:S	SOD	CAR	CHO
70	4	4.5:1	15	10	0

FRENCH ONION SOUP

When a hungry Louis XV returned from a hunting trip to find no provisions in his lodge other than onions, champagne and butter, he mixed them together, so the story goes, and invented French onion soup. Here's a spicy, slimming version of this regal delight.

	Metric	Imperial	American
Corn oil	2 tbsp	2 tbsp	2 tbsp
Large onions, thinly sliced	4	4	4
Large clove garlic, finely chopped	1	1	1
Large shallot, finely chopped	1	1	1
Unbleached flour	2 tbsp	2 tbsp	2 tbsp
Beef stock (Page 10)	750 ml	1¼ pt	3 cups
Water	240 ml	8 fl oz	1 cup
Dried thyme leaves, crushed	¼ tsp	¼ tsp	¼ tsp
Cayenne pepper	4 pinches	4 pinches	4 pinches
Wine vinegar	2 tsp	2 tsp	2 tsp
Thick slices My French Bread (Page 134)	4	4	4
Sharp low-fat cheese, grated (Page 6)	4 tbsp	4 tbsp	4 tbsp

Heat oil in heavy-bottomed 2-litre/3.5-pint/2-quart saucepan until hot. Add onions, garlic and shallot and sauté until golden brown, turning constantly (about 10-12 minutes). Sprinkle with flour and continue cooking another 5 minutes, or until mixture is golden brown. Gradually add stock and water, stirring well. Add thyme and cayenne. Bring to boil. Reduce heat and simmer, covered, for 20 minutes. Add vinegar and stir.

Lightly toast bread slices. Pour soup into individual serving dishes, and float one slice of bread on top of each serving. Sprinkle with cheese, and serve.

Yield: Serves 4

CAL	F	P:S	SOD	CAR	CHO
214	8	4.8:1	59	20	3

CHINESE SWEET AND PUNGENT SOUP

This is a happy marriage of contrasting flavours and textures, which is what Chinese cooking is all about. This lovely-to-look-at soup is simple to make, authentic tasting and makes a satisfying light meal starter.

	Metric	Imperial	American
Corn oil	2 tsp	2 tsp	2 tsp
Cloves garlic, finely chopped	2	2	2
Fresh ginger, peeled and cut into thin slivers	1½ tsp	1½ tsp	1½ tsp
Chicken stock (Page 8)	750 ml	1¼ pt	3 cups
Water	240 ml	8 fl oz	1 cup
Eye of centre cut pork chop, cut into thin slivers	25 g	1 oz	1 oz
Large fresh mushrooms, washed, trimmed and coarsely chopped	4	4	4
Piece bean curd, 5-7.5 cm/2-3 inches square, diced	1	1	1
Chinese cabbage, shredded	175 g	6 oz	¾ cup
Cayenne pepper	3 pinches	3 pinches	3 pinches
Spring onion, cut into 1.5-cm/½-inch pieces	1	1	1
Honey	1 tsp	1 tsp	1 tsp
Wine vinegar	1 tbsp	1 tbsp	1 tbsp
White vinegar	1 tbsp	1 tbsp	1 tbsp
Dry sherry	2 tsp	2 tsp	2 tsp
Sodium-free soya sauce	1 tsp	1 tsp	1 tsp

Heat oil in heavy-bottomed saucepan until hot. Add garlic and ginger. Sauté for 1 minute. Add stock, water and pork. Bring to boil. Reduce heat and simmer, uncovered, for 10 minutes, removing scum that rises to top. Add mushrooms, bean curd, cabbage, cayenne and spring onion, and simmer for another 5 minutes.

Turn heat down very low. Add honey, vinegars and sherry. Stir well. Bring to just under simmering point. Stir in sodium-free soya sauce. Serve immediately.

Yield: Serves 4

CAL	F	P:S	SOD	CAR	CHO
189	6	4.3:1	28	4	5

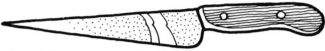

VICHYSSOISE

Although most people think this soup is so French, it was actually originated by the chef at the Ritz-Carlton in New York.

	Metric	Imperial	American
Corn oil	1 tbsp	1 tbsp	1 tbsp
Leeks, white part only, well washed and thinly sliced	2	2	2
Medium onion, finely chopped	1	1	1
Large cloves garlic, finely chopped	2	2	2
Sticks celery, finely chopped	2	2	2
Dry Vermouth or white wine	3 tbsp	3 tbsp	3 tbsp
Chicken stock (Page 8)	450 ml	¾ pt	2 cups
Water	240 ml	8 fl oz	1 cup
Medium-sized potatoes, peeled and thinly sliced	2	2	2
Finely chopped carrot	1 tbsp	1 tbsp	1 tbsp
Sprigs parsley	3	3	3
Powdered thyme	½ tsp	½ tsp	½ tsp
Cayenne pepper	6 pinches	6 pinches	6 pinches
Wine vinegar	2 tsp	2 tsp	2 tsp
Low-fat milk	240 ml	8 fl oz	1 cup
Freshly chopped dill and parsley	1 tbsp	1 tbsp	1 tbsp
Low-fat plain yogurt	1 tbsp	1 tbsp	1 tbsp
Freshly chopped chives or spring onion	2 tbsp	2 tbsp	2 tbsp

Heat oil in heavy-bottomed saucepan until fairly hot. Add leeks, onion, garlic and celery. Sauté until softened. Add Vermouth or wine, and cook over high heat for 2 minutes. Add stock, water, potatoes, carrot, parsley sprigs, thyme and cayenne pepper. Bring to simmering point. Partially cover and simmer for 20 minutes. Add vinegar and stir. Let cool in pan, partially covered.

Put through food mill. Add milk, chopped parsley and dill, and blend. Whisk in yogurt.

Serve hot or cold sprinkled with chopped chives or chopped spring onion.

Yield: Serves 4, one portion left over

Variations:

1. Do not use food mill, and serve hot with vegetables left whole.

2. If you prefer a smoother textured soup, use a blender instead of food mill. Blend 1 minute, then pour through fine sieve.

CAL	F	P:S	SOD	CAR	CHO
156	3	3.9:1	79	23	1

MEATLESS LENTIL SOUP

A steaming bowl of this thick soup is ideal on a chilly winter day. Enjoy it as a first or main course. You can also reduce the liquid and serve it as a deliciously different vegetable side dish.

	Metric	Imperial	American
Lentils, washed	350 g	12 oz	1½ cups
Corn oil	1 tbsp	1 tbsp	1 tbsp
Onion, finely chopped	1	1	1
Cloves garlic, finely chopped	3	3	3
Leek, white part only, washed and finely chopped	1	1	1
Stick celery, finely chopped	½	½	½
Cider vinegar	2 tsp	2 tsp	2 tsp
Small carrot, peeled and diced	1	1	1
Chicken stock (Page 8)	750 ml	1¼ pt	3 cups
Water, enough to cover lentils	450 ml	¾ pt	2 cups
Cayenne pepper	4 pinches	4 pinches	4 pinches
Dried thyme leaves, crushed	½ tsp	½ tsp	½ tsp
Dried tarragon leaves, crushed	½ tsp	½ tsp	½ tsp
Tomato paste, no salt	2 tsp	2 tsp	2 tsp
Bouquet garni	1	1	1
Arrowroot, dissolved in 2 tbsp water (optional)	2 tbsp	2 tbsp	2 tbsp

Soak lentils in water to cover until all water is absorbed (about 3 hours). Heat oil in saucepan, preferably stainless steel, until hot. Add onion, garlic, leek and celery. Sauté until softened but not brown. Add vinegar and cook over high heat for 1 minute. Add remainder of ingredients, except arrowroot, and bring to boil. Reduce heat and simmer, partially covered, for 1½ hours.

If you want to thicken soup, sprinkle arrowroot mixture into simmering soup, stirring constantly, until it reaches desired consistency. Remove bouquet garni. Serve hot.

Yield: Serves 6

Variation: To convert into an interesting side dish, reduce the liquid by cooking, uncovered, over medium-high heat, stirring constantly, until quite thick.

CAL	F	P:S	SOD	CAR	CHO
145	2	4.5:1	28	20	0
Thickened					
153	2	4.5:1	28	22	0

SPLIT PEA SOUP

Even in days of zooming inflation, dried peas won't put a strain on your budget. And they're so rich in protein and taste so meaty, that they make an admirable alternative to expensive meats. Here are two versions of the soup; one with meat and one without.

	Metric	Imperial	American
Veal bones, cracked and well washed under running water	3	3	3
Corn oil	1 tbsp	1 tbsp	1 tbsp
Large onion, finely chopped	1	1	1
Large cloves garlic, finely chopped	3	3	3
Large shallot, finely chopped	1	1	1
Split peas, washed	225 g	8 oz	1¼ cups
Small carrots, peeled and diced	2	2	2
Chicken or veal stock (Pages 8 and 10)	450 ml	¾ pt	2 cups
Water	240 ml	8 fl oz	1 cup
Cayenne pepper	3 pinches	3 pinches	3 pinches
Dried marjoram leaves, crushed	¼ tsp	¼ tsp	¼ tsp
Dried thyme leaves, crushed	¼ tsp	¼ tsp	¼ tsp
Dried basil leaves, crushed	¼ tsp	¼ tsp	¼ tsp
Large bouquet garni (optional)	1	1	1

Place bones in 3-litre/5-pint/3-quart saucepan. Add water to cover. Bring to boil and cook for 10 minutes. Pour into colander and drain. Wash bones under cold running water.

Rinse out pan and dry. Add oil and heat until very warm. Add onion, garlic and shallot, and sauté until softened. Add remainder of ingredients. Bring to simmering point. Turn heat off and cover. Let stand for 1 hour.

Reheat to simmering point, and cook, partially covered, for 45 minutes. Let soup cool in pan. Remove bones and bouquet garni. Pour into blender and purée for 1 minute. Reheat and serve.

Yield: Serves 4, one portion left over

Variation: Split Pea Soup Without Bones. Basic ingredients are the same except for the following increased amounts:

	Metric	Imperial	American
Shallots	2	2	2
Thyme leaves	½ tsp	½ tsp	½ tsp
Basil leaves	½ tsp	½ tsp	½ tsp

CAL	F	P:S	SOD	CAR	CHO
170	3	4.5:1	35	18	0

Without bones
No appreciable difference

HEARTY CABBAGE SOUP

There's nothing as welcome as a steaming plate of thick cabbage soup on a winter's day. It's instant warmth, and packs all the nutrition you've come to expect from the main meal of the day. Serve it with my crusty heated French Bread (Page 135).

	Metric	Imperial	American
Water	1.2 l	2 pt	5 cups
Bouquet garni, including 1 sprig dill, 1 sprig parsley and 4 whole cloves, tied together in muslin	1	1	1
Veal bone	1	1	1
Lean beef	225 g	8 oz	½ lb
Corn oil	2 tbsp	2 tbsp	2 tbsp
Large cloves garlic, finely chopped	3	3	3
Stick celery, diced	1	1	1
Carrot, peeled and diced	1	1	1
Swede, peeled and diced	50 g	2 oz	¼ cup
Large fresh mushrooms, washed, trimmed and coarsely chopped	3	3	3

	Metric	Imperial	American
Large onion, finely chopped	1	1	1
Small head green cabbage, sliced 5 mm/ ¼-inch thick and 5 cm/2 inches long	680 g	1½ lb	1½ lb
Cider vinegar	1 tbsp	1 tbsp	1 tbsp
Fresh lemon juice	3 tbsp	3 tbsp	3 tbsp
Honey	1 tbsp	1 tbsp	1 tbsp
Brown beef stock (Page 11)	60 ml	4 tbsp	¼ cup
Canned tomatoes, no salt added	225 g	8 oz	8 oz
Tomato paste, no salt added	1 tbsp	1 tbsp	1 tbsp
Dried thyme leaves, crushed	¾ tsp	¾ tsp	¾ tsp
Caraway seeds	1 tsp	1 tsp	1 tsp

Pour 750 ml/1¼ pt/3 cups water into a large saucepan. Add bouquet garni, veal bone and meat. Bring to boil. Reduce heat and cook for 2 minutes. Remove scum that rises to top. Cover partially and simmer for 1 hour.

While meat is cooking, prepare all the vegetables. Then heat oil in a large heavy frying pan until very warm. Add garlic and all vegetables except tomatoes and cabbage. Brown lightly, continually turning with large spoon. Add cabbage, half at a time, and continue to cook until cabbage browns lightly. (Volume will reduce after 5 minutes of cooking and turning.) Add vinegar, lemon juice and honey, stirring well. Then add brown stock, tomatoes, tomato paste, thyme and caraway seeds. Cook for 5 minutes.

Pour vegetable mixture into meat which has cooked for 1 hour, and add 450 ml/¾ pt/2 cups water. Bring to boil. Simmer, partially covered, for 1 hour, stirring from time to time.

Cool in pan, covered. Remove bouquet garni. If using the same day reheat and serve.

Yield: Serves 6

CAL	F	P:S	SOD	CAR	CHO
172	7	3.5:1	74	18	27
Thickened					
176	7	3.5:1	74	19	27

MUSHROOM AND BARLEY SOUP

You won't believe the hearty flavour of this thick, bracing soup until you try it. Crisp firm cloves of garlic make all the difference. Be certain the garlic is chopped finely rather than crushed, and you'll never taste it. Serve steaming hot either as a first course (small portion, please) or as a one-dish meal accompanied by French Bread (Page 134).

	Metric	Imperial	American
Corn oil	1 tbsp	1 tbsp	1 tbsp
Spring onion, finely chopped, or ½ leek, white section only, well washed and finely chopped	1	1	1
Small onion, finely chopped	1	1	1
Cloves garlic, finely chopped	3	3	3
Large shallot, finely chopped	1	1	1
Small stick celery, finely chopped	1	1	1
Chicken stock (Page 8)	450 ml	¾ pt	2 cups
Small carrot, peeled and diced	1	1	1
Dried mushrooms, soaked and finely chopped	15 g	½ oz	½ oz
Medium barley, washed and drained	50 g	2 oz	¼ cup
Water	450 ml	¾ pt	2 cups
Dried tarragon leaves, crushed	½ tsp	½ tsp	½ tsp
Dried basil leaves, crushed	½ tsp	½ tsp	½ tsp
Cider vinegar	2 tsp	2 tsp	2 tsp
Cayenne pepper	4 pinches	4 pinches	4 pinches
Large bouquet garni	1	1	1

Heat oil in medium sized saucepan until very warm. Add spring onion, onion, garlic, shallot and celery, and sauté until vegetables and garlic are softened (about 5 minutes over a medium heat). Add chicken stock and remainder of ingredients. Bring to slow boil. Reduce heat, partially cover and simmer for 45 minutes, stirring from time to time to prevent ingredients from sticking to bottom of pan. Taste. You may want to add a little more cayenne. Re-cover and continue simmering for another 20 minutes. Remove from heat and let soup cool, covered for 1 hour before serving. Remove bouquet garni.

To serve, reheat over a low flame.

Yield: Serves 4

Note: This soup improves in flavour if it is prepared a day ahead, stored in a glass container in the refrigerator, and slowly reheated at serving time.
Variation: At end of cooking time, when soup has cooled down, add 2 heaped tablespoons low-fat plain yogurt and blend. Reheat over very low flame, taking care that soup does not boil.

CAL	F	P:S	SOD	CAR	CHO
116	4	4.5:1	44	20	0
With yogurt					
123	2	3.2:1	52	22	1

BRACING FISH SOUP

Fresh fish, cooked to perfection with a delicate blend of herbs and spices, comes to the table as a subtle but far from bland thick soup.

	Metric	Imperial	American
Corn oil	1 tbsp	1 tbsp	1 tbsp
Medium onions, halved and sliced	2	2	2
Cloves garlic, finely chopped	2	2	2
Large shallot, finely chopped	1	1	1
Stick celery, diced	1	1	1
Small potatoes, peeled and diced	2	2	2
Carrot, peeled and diced	½	½	½
Fish stock (Page 9)	240 ml	8 fl oz	1 cup
Water	240 ml	8 fl oz	1 cup
Powdered cloves	2 pinches	2 pinches	2 pinches
Dried tarragon leaves, crushed	½ tsp	½ tsp	½ tsp
Bay leaf	1	1	1
Cayenne pepper	4-5 pinches	4-5 pinches	4-5 pinches
Fresh haddock or cod fillets, cut into 5-cm/2-inch pieces	450 g	1 lb	1 lb
Sprigs watercress leaves only, chopped	2	2	2
Low-fat milk, warmed	360 ml	12½ fl oz	1½ cups
Freshly chopped parsley			

Heat oil in heavy-bottomed 2-litre/3.5-pint/2-quart saucepan until warm. Add onions, garlic, shallot and celery. Sauté over medium heat for 3 minutes, turning constantly. Add potatoes, carrot, stock, water, cloves, tarragon, bay leaf and cayenne. Bring to simmering point. Partially cover and simmer for 10 minutes.

Add fish and watercress. Simmer until fish flakes easily (about 15 minutes). Add warm milk and stir well. Pour into heated soup dishes. Sprinkle with freshly chopped parsley. Serve with my French Herb Bread (Page 135).

Yield: Serves 4

CAL	F	P:S	SOD	CAR	CHO
Haddock					
209	4	4.4:1	160	23	80
Cod					
209	4	4.4:1	170	23	80

FISH

POACHED FLOUNDER OR SOLE WITH SAVOURY SAUCE

Flounder is one of those simple fish that needs a deft touch in the kitchen to achieve gourmet status. Here it's tenderly poached in a flavoursome court bouillon and served with a creamy pungent sauce.

	Metric	Imperial	American
For the court bouillon:			
Leek, white part only, well washed, split lengthwise and coarsely chopped	1	1	1
Large cloves garlic, coarsely chopped	2	2	2
Large shallots, coarsely chopped	2	2	2
Onion, sliced	½	½	½
Stick celery, cut into 2.5-cm/1-inch slices	1	1	1
Carrot, peeled and thinly sliced	1	1	1
Thin slice lemon	1	1	1
Water	1 l	1¾ pt	4 cups
Cayenne pepper	4 pinches	4 pinches	4 pinches
Whole cloves	4	4	4
Dried thyme leaves	¼ tsp	¼ tsp	¼ tsp
Dry Vermouth or white wine	360 ml	12½ fl oz	1½ cups
Fish stock or water (Page 9)	120 ml	4 fl oz	½ cup
Bouquet garni, including ½ tsp fennel, tied together in muslin	1	1	1

	Metric	Imperial	American
For the sauce:			
Fish stock, room temperature (Page 9)	180 ml	6 fl oz	¾ cup
Dry Vermouth or white wine	2 tbsp	2 tbsp	2 tbsp
Large fresh mushrooms, washed, trimmed and coarsely chopped	4	4	4
Small onion, finely chopped	1	1	1
Stick celery, coarsely chopped	½	½	½
Large clove garlic, finely chopped	1	1	1
Shallot, finely chopped	1	1	1
Low-fat dry milk	1 tbsp	1 tbsp	1 tbsp
Chicken stock (Page 8)	120 ml	4 fl oz	½ cup
Large sprigs fresh watercress, leaves only, washed and coarsely chopped	4	4	4
Duxelles (see method)	1 tbsp	1 tbsp	1 tbsp
Low-fat plain yogurt	1 tbsp	1 tbsp	1 tbsp

	Metric	Imperial	American
For the fish:			
Flounder or sole fillets, cut into serving pieces	680 g	1½ lb	1½ lb
Freshly chopped parsley	1 tbsp	1 tbsp	1 tbsp

Prepare the court bouillon first. Place all ingredients in a large saucepan. Bring to boil. Reduce heat, cover, and simmer for 20 minutes. Court bouillon is now ready for poaching.

For sauce, you will need duxelles (see recipe below). Note: the quantity this recipe makes is more than you will need, but the surplus can be kept in the freezer and used for other dishes.

	Metric	Imperial	American
For the duxelles:			
Corn oil	3 tbsp	3 tbsp	3 tbsp
Large clove garlic, finely chopped	1	1	1
Large shallots, finely chopped	2	2	2

		Metric	Imperial	American
Fresh mushrooms, washed and trimmed		225 g	8 oz	½ lb
Dried tarragon leaves, crushed		½ tsp	½ tsp	½ tsp
Cayenne papper		3 pinches	3 pinches	3 pinches
Freshly chopped parsley		1 tsp	1 tsp	1 tsp

Heat oil in large heavy frying pan until hot. Add garlic and shallots and cook turning constantly for 1 minute. Add mushrooms, spreading smoothly over pan. Cook for 2 minutes. Turn over with large spoon, and smooth out in frying pan. Continue turning over and smoothing out in frying pan until all liquid is evaporated (about 8-10 minutes). Sprinkle with tarragon, cayenne and chopped parsley. Stir to blend.

Yield: 175 g/6 oz/1 cup

Combine fish stock, wine, mushrooms, onion, celery, garlic and shallot in a heavy-bottomed saucepan, and heat to simmering point. Reduce heat and continue cooking for 7 minutes, partially covered, stirring from time to time.

Whisk dry milk into chicken stock until blended. Add to hot mixture and simmer for 2 minutes. Add watercress and duxelles and simmer for another minute. Uncover and let stand while poaching fish.

If you have a poacher, bring court bouillon to simmering point. Pat fish dry with paper towels. Place fish on rack and lower into court bouillon. Bring to simmering point again. Reduce heat and simmer, covered, for 12-15 minutes depending upon the thickness of fish.

If you don't have a poacher, arrange fish on double piece of muslin. Fold muslin around fish. Tie ends securely with white thread. Gently lower into simmering court bouillon and continue according to directions given for poacher.

Pour prepared sauce mixture into blender and purée for 1 minute. Pour back into saucepan. Whisk in yogurt. Reheat over very low heat, taking care that mixture doesn't boil.

Remove fish from court bouillon and drain. Serve on heated individual plates. Pour sauce over fish and serve, sprinkled with freshly chopped parsley.

Yield: Serves 4

Note: Court bouillon can be frozen.

CAL	F	P:S	SOD	CAR	CHO
77	0	—	90	5	61
Sauce					
50	2	1.9:1	35	4	0

STUFFED SOLE ROLL-UPS

This dish is a delightfully refreshing departure from high-calorie fried fillets.

	Metric	Imperial	American
Wine vinegar	60 ml	4 tbsp	¼ cup
Small sole fillets (8 fillets)	680 g	1½ lb	1½ lb
Corn oil	1 tbsp	1 tbsp	1 tbsp
Cloves garlic, finely chopped	2	2	2
Shallots, finely chopped	2	2	2
Small green pepper, finely chopped	1	1	1
My French Herb Bread for stuffing (Page 135)	75 g	3 oz	1½ cups
Cayenne pepper	4 pinches	4 pinches	4 pinches
Freshly chopped parsley and dill	2 tbsp	2 tbsp	2 tbsp
Fish stock (Page 9)	120 ml	4 fl oz	½ cup
Chicken stock (Page 8)	60 ml	4 tbsp	¼ cup
Ground ginger	½ tsp	½ tsp	½ tsp
Sodium-free soya sauce	3 dashes	3 dashes	3 dashes

Pour vinegar into medium-sized bowl. Add fillets and marinate at room temperature for 1 hour, turning once.

Now prepare stuffing. Heat oil in small frying pan and sauté garlic, shallots and green pepper until softened but not brown. Reserve half sautéed mixture for sauce, and transfer remainder to bowl. Break up bread for stuffing into small pieces. Add to half of sautéed mixture and toss together with 2 pinches cayenne and 1 tablespoon freshly chopped parsley and dill.

In a small saucepan, heat combined stocks until warm. Then add just enough bread mixture to dampen bread and make it spreadable (about 2 tablespoons).

Remove fillets from marinade, reserving marinade. Dry well with paper towels. Lay each fillet flat. Spoon a tablespoon of stuffing mixture on top of each fillet, and spread evenly. Roll up and secure with wooden cocktail sticks. Place in lightly oiled casserole large enough to hold fillets in one layer.

Reheat stock. Add 2 tablespoons reserved marinade, rest of sautéed mixture, ginger, sodium-free soya sauce and remaining cayenne. Stir to blend. Pour over roll-ups. Cover and bake in preheated 200°C/400°F/Gas mark 6 oven for 10 minutes. Remove cover and baste fillets. Return to oven and bake uncovered for another 10 minutes.

Transfer roll-ups to heated serving platter. Cover to keep warm. Pour cooking liquid and vegetables into blender and blend for 1 minute. Reheat and pour over fish. Sprinkle roll-ups with fresh parsley and dill, and serve.

Yield: Serves 4

CAL	F	P:S	SOD	CAR	CHO
215	5	3.4:1	201	10	61

BAKED PIKE WITH MUSTARD SAUCE

How do you make an ordinary fish extraordinary? Bake it with flavour-enriching vegetables and herbs, and then bathe it in a creamy white sauce accented with the sharp edge of mustard.

	Metric	Imperial	American
For the fish:			
Pike, cleaned, head left on	1.5 kg	3 lb	3 lb
Cayenne pepper	2 pinches	2 pinches	2 pinches
Dried thyme leaves, crushed	1/4 tsp	1/4 tsp	1/4 tsp
Fennel seeds, crushed	1/4 tsp	1/4 tsp	1/4 tsp
Dill sprigs	2	2	2
Parsley sprigs	2	2	2
Corn oil	1 tbsp	1 tbsp	1 tbsp
Small onion, finely chopped	1	1	1
Large cloves garlic, finely chopped	2	2	2
Shallots, finely chopped	2	2	2
Corn oil to coat baking dish	1/2 tsp	1/2 tsp	1/2 tsp
For the sauce:			
Corn oil	1 1/2 tbsp	1 1/2 tbsp	1 1/2 tbsp
Shallot, finely chopped	1	1	1
Unbleached flour	1 1/2 tbsp	1 1/2 tbsp	1 1/2 tbsp
Dry Vermouth or white wine	2 tbsp	2 tbsp	2 tbsp
Fish stock, warmed (Page 9)	120 ml	4 fl oz	1/2 cup
Low-fat milk, warmed	300 ml	1/2 pt	1 1/4 cups
Dry mustard, dissolved in 2 tsp water	2 tsp	2 tsp	2 tsp
Cayenne pepper	2 pinches	2 pinches	2 pinches
Ground cloves	1/8 tsp	1/8 tsp	1/8 tsp
Freshly chopped parsley	1 tbsp	1 tbsp	1 tbsp

Wash fish inside and out under cold running water. Dry well with paper towels. Make 4-5 diagonal slashes across fish on each side. Combine cayenne, thyme and fennel. Rub cavity and skin with mixture. Stuff cavity with herb sprigs. Secure with skewers. Cover and let stand at room temperature for 1 hour before baking.

Heat oil in non-stick frying pan until hot. Sauté onion, garlic and shallots until softened. Spoon over both sides of fish, pressing into cuts. Bake, uncovered, in preheated 200°C/400°F/Gas mark 6 oven for 15 minutes. Baste. Cover and bake for 15-20 minutes, or until fish flakes easily. Transfer to warm serving dish.

While fish is baking, prepare the sauce. Heat oil in heavy-bottomed saucepan until hot. Add shallot and sauté until softened. Add flour and cook for 2 minutes, stirring constantly. Stir in wine and cook for 1 minute. Add stock and blend with whisk. Stir in milk, mustard, cayenne and cloves, whisking until thickened. Add parsley and stir. Serve immediately (do not reheat) in sauceboat with fish.

Yield: Serves 4

CAL	F	P:S	SOD	CAR	CHO
117	5	3.7:1	68	2	66
Sauce					
48	5	4.5:1	24	5	0

SIMPLE SAUTÉED FILLET OF LEMON SOLE 1

Lemon sole is so firmly textured that it can be turned in the pan and successfully sautéed. Enjoy it *au naturel* (this recipe) or lightly coated with flour (the next).

	Metric	Imperial	American
Lemon sole, cut into serving pieces	680 g	1½ lb	1½ lb
Combined dried tarragon, basil and parsley leaves, crushed	½ tsp	½ tsp	½ tsp
Combined dill and fennel seeds, crushed	¼ tsp	¼ tsp	¼ tsp
Corn oil	2 tbsp	2 tbsp	2 tbsp
Shallots, finely chopped	2	2	2
Cloves garlic, finely chopped	3	3	3
Wine vinegar	1 tbsp	1 tbsp	1 tbsp
Sodium-free soya sauce	½ tsp	½ tsp	½ tsp

Dry fish with paper towels. An hour before cooking, sprinkle with herbs and seeds. Press gently into fish on both sides. Cover and set aside at room temperature.

Cook fish in two batches as follows: Heat half of the oil in non-stick frying pan until hot. Add half the shallots and garlic and sauté for 2 minutes. Spread evenly over pan. Place half of the fish over sautéed mixture and cook over medium-high heat for 5 minutes. Turn carefully with spatula and cook on second side for 3 minutes. Add half the vinegar and cook for 1 minute. Add half the sodium-free soya sauce and cook for a further minute, tilting pan so that liquid is equally distributed. Transfer to heated serving platter.

Add remainder of ingredients to pan and cook second batch of fish in the same way. Transfer to heated serving platter and serve immediately.

Yield: Serves 4

Note: Excellent served on my crisp, heated French Bread (Page 134).

CAL	F	P:S	SOD	CAR	CHO
113	8	4.3:1	52	2	92

SIMPLE SAUTÉED FILLET OF LEMON SOLE 2

	Metric	Imperial	American
Unbleached flour	50 g	2 oz	½ cup
Combined dried tarragon, basil and parsley leaves, crushed	½ tsp	½ tsp	½ tsp
Combined dill and fennel seeds, lightly crushed	¼ tsp	¼ tsp	¼ tsp
Cayenne papper	4 pinches	4 pinches	4 pinches
Fillet of lemon sole, cut into serving pieces	680 g	1½ lb	1½ lb
Low-fat milk	80 ml	3 fl oz	⅓ cup
Corn oil	2 tbsp	2 tbsp	2 tbsp
Cloves garlic, finely chopped	2	2	2
Shallots, finely chopped	2	2	2
Freshly chopped chives or spring onions	1 tbsp	1 tbsp	1 tbsp
Lemon wedges			

Combine flour with dried herbs, seeds and cayenne. Dry fish with paper towels. Dip into milk and then into flour mixture, coating well. Place on plate in one layer, cover and refrigerate for 1 hour before cooking.

Cook fish in two batches as follows: Heat half the oil in large non-stick frying pan until hot. Add half of the garlic and shallots and sauté for 2 minutes. Spread evenly over pan. Place half the fish over sautéed mixture and cook over medium heat for 5 minutes. Turn carefully with spatula and cook on second side until lightly browned. Don't overcook. Transfer to heated serving platter and keep warm.

Add remainder of ingredients to pan and cook second batch of fish in the same way. Transfer to heated serving platter. Sprinkle with chives or spring onions, garnish with lemon wedges and serve.

Yield: Serves 4

Note: Fillet of flounder may be substituted successfully for fillet of sole.

CAL	F	P:S	SOD	CAR	CHO
218	8	4.3:1	58	13	92

Flounder
No appreciable difference

WHITING BAKED IN RED WINE

Whiting is one of those misunderstood fish that's usually breaded and deep-fried. But once you get to know the sweetness and delicate texture of this favourite of true fish lovers, you'll never want to disguise its charms again. Try this simple recipe for a surprising treat.

	Metric	Imperial	American
Whitings, 680 g/1½ lb each, cleaned, heads left on	2	2	2
Dried thyme leaves, crushed	½ tsp	½ tsp	½ tsp
Rosemary leaves, crushed	½ tsp	½ tsp	½ tsp
Cayenne pepper	4 pinches	4 pinches	4 pinches
Carrot, peeled and finely diced	1	1	1
Parsley sprigs	4	4	4
Dill sprigs	4	4	4
Corn oil	1 tbsp	1 tbsp	1 tbsp
Onion, finely chopped	1	1	1
Stick celery, finely chopped	1	1	1
Cloves garlic, finely chopped	2	2	2
Shallots, finely chopped	2	2	2
Water	60 ml	4 tbsp	¼ cup
Red wine	240 ml	8 fl oz	1 cup
Bay leaf	1	1	1

Wash fish inside and out. Dry well. Make 3-4 slashes on each side of fish. Rub well with dried herbs. Sprinkle with cayenne. Cover and let stand at room temperature for 1 hour.

When ready to cook, fill cavities of fish with equal amounts of carrot, parsley and dill sprigs. Close with thin skewers.

Heat oil in small frying pan until hot. Sauté onion, celery, garlic and shallots until softened but not brown. Add water, wine and bay leaf. Bring to boil. Reduce heat and simmer, uncovered, for 3 minutes.

Line a rectangular pan, large enough to hold fish flat, with foil. Place fish on foil. Pour hot vegetable-wine mixture over fish.

Cover with another piece of foil and bake in pre-heated 200°C/400°F/Gas mark 6 oven for 10 minutes. Remove from oven, baste, cover and return to oven for 10-12 minutes. Transfer fish carefully to heated serving platter. Spoon with cooking liquid and vegetables, and serve.

Yield: Serves 4

CAL	F	P:S	SOD	CAR	CHO
181	7	3.0:1	126	4	73

COD IN COURT BOUILLON

Cod has a special crunchiness that is preserved by poaching (the boiling point, which can create havoc with the texture of a fish, is never reached). This sweet-fleshed fish, with its flavour enhanced by court bouillon, emerges from the poacher firm and resistant to crumbling. Serve as it is or turn into delicious fish cakes.

	Metric	Imperial	American
Cod, cut into 4 pieces	900 g	2 lb	2 lb
Stick celery and leaves, coarsely chopped	1	1	1
Large onion, quartered	1	1	1
Fish stock (Page 9)	240 ml	8 fl oz	1 cup
Water	450 ml	¾ pt	2 cups
Dry Vermouth or white wine	80 ml	3 fl oz	⅓ cup
Carrot, peeled and sliced	1	1	1
Vegetable concentrate	½ tsp	½ tsp	½ tsp
Freshly chopped dill or ½ tsp dill weed	1 tsp	1 tsp	1 tsp
Cayenne pepper	4 pinches	4 pinches	4 pinches
Small bouquet garni	1	1	1
Arrowroot, dissolved in 2 tsp water (optional)	2 tsp	2 tsp	2 tsp

Place fish in saucepan, preferably stainless steel, wide enough to hold 4 pieces of fish in one layer. Add rest of ingredients except arrowroot. Bring to simmering point. Partially cover and simmer for 15 minutes, or until fish flakes easily. Do not overcook.

Remove cover and let fish cool in liquid. When ready to serve, reheat. Remove fish from liquid with slotted spoon and keep warm. Discard bouquet garni.

Reduce liquid by half over high heat. Pour contents of pan into blender and purée for 1 minute. Reheat to simmering point. Sauce is now ready to serve. If you prefer a thickened sauce, sprinkle arrowroot mixture into simmering sauce, adding only enough to reach desired consistency.

Yield: Serves 4

CAL	F	P:S	SOD	CAR	CHO
77	0	—	94	5	61
Thickened					
81	0	—	94	6	61

QUENELLES WITH MUSHROOM SAUCE

These lighter-than-air dumplings are a combination of minced fish with my version of pate-a-choux (a seasoned egg-flour-oil mixture), subtly accented with herbs and spices, and gently simmered in an herb-enriched stock. Served under a blanket of velvety mushroom sauce, they are a special treat.

	Metric	Imperial	American
For the quenelles:			
Large eggs, using half of 1 yolk and both whites	2	2	2
Unbleached flour	50 g	2 oz	½ cup
Cayenne pepper	3 pinches	3 pinches	3 pinches
Ground nutmeg	¼ tsp	¼ tsp	¼ tsp
Corn oil	3 tbsp	3 tbsp	3 tbsp
Low-fat milk, prepared by using ⅓ less water than called for by instructions	240 ml	8 fl oz	1 cup
Dried tarragon leaves, crushed	½ tsp	½ tsp	½ tsp
Fillet of lemon sole or pike, cut into 2.5-cm/1-inch pieces	570 g	1¼ lb	1¼ lb
Shallots, finely chopped	2	2	2
Powdered thyme	¼ tsp	¼ tsp	¼ tsp
Freshly chopped parsley and dill	2 tsp	2 tsp	2 tsp
Corn oil to oil baking dish	½ tsp	½ tsp	½ tsp
Water	1.2 l	2 pt	5 cups
Bay leaf	1	1	1

For the sauce:

Corn oil	2 tbsp	2 tbsp	2 tbsp
Fresh mushrooms, washed, trimmed and thinly sliced	100 g	4 oz	¼ lb
Shallot, finely chopped	1	1	1
Dry Vermouth or white wine	120 ml	4 fl oz	½ cup
Unbleached flour	1½ tbsp	1½ tbsp	1½ tbsp
Fish stock (Page 9)	120 ml	4 fl oz	½ cup
Chicken stock (Page 8)	120 ml	4 fl oz	½ cup
Cayenne pepper	2 pinches	2 pinches	2 pinches
Dried tarragon leaves, crushed	¼ tsp	¼ tsp	¼ tsp
Low-fat milk	240 ml	8 fl oz	1 cup

Prepare quenelles first. In a heavy-bottomed saucepan combine egg yolk, flour, 2 pinches cayenne and nutmeg. Whisk well. Add oil and whisk again. Warm 180 ml/6 fl oz/¾ cup milk and pour into saucepan, whisking constantly. Add tarragon and cook over medium heat, continuing to whisk until mixture is very thick (about 5 minutes). Let cool, partially covered.

Mince fish with shallots, remaining cayenne, thyme and balance of milk, using mincer or food processor. Turn into bowl of mixing machine. Add cooled mixture in small amounts at a time, beating well after each addition. Add egg whites, parsley and dill, and beat well.

Lightly oil an oblong baking dish 43 × 27 × 5 cm/ 17 × 11 × 2 inches. Shape fish into 12 balls, using 2 spoons moistened continually with hot water to prevent sticking, arranging balls in four rows in pan. Cover lightly with greaseproof paper and refrigerate for 1 hour.

To cook quenelles in simmering water, first remove greaseproof paper. Place quenelles on top of stove. Bring 1.2 l/2 pt/5 cups water to boil in saucepan. Add bay leaf and boil for 2 minutes. Gently pour water around quenelles—never directly on them (they're fragile and break easily). Turn heat on under pan and bring to simmering point. Continue to simmer, very gently, for 12 minutes, basting twice. Quenelles will puff up.

Start to prepare sauce while quenelles are simmering. Heat 1 tablespoon oil in non-stick frying pan until hot. Add mushrooms and shallot, and sauté until lightly browned. Add wine, and cook over medium-high heat for 3 minutes. Set aside.

In heavy-bottomed saucepan, heat remaining oil until hot. Add flour and whisk well. Cook for 2 minutes over medium heat. Add stocks, cayenne and tarragon, whisking continually. Pour in sautéed mixture and stir. Finally, add milk and cook over low heat, stirring frequently, for 10 minutes. Sauce should not boil.

Transfer quenelles with slotted spoon to heated individual plates. Gently spoon sauce over quenelles, and serve immediately.

Yield: Serves 4 for main course; serves 6 for starter

CAL	F	P:S	SOD	CAR	CHO
Starter					
155	9	4.1:1	115	7	61
Sauce					
72	4	4.5:1	27	5	0
Main course					
233	13	4.1:1	172	10	91
Sauce					
108	6	4.5:1	40	7	0

SAUTÉED COD FISH CAKES

	Metric	Imperial	American
Recipe Cod in Court Bouillon, including puréed sauce, blended but unthickened (Page 46)	1	1	1
Corn oil	2½ tbsp	2½ tbsp	2½ tbsp
Large cloves garlic, finely chopped	2	2	2
Shallots, finely chopped	2	2	2
Large potatoes, either baked and mashed with fork, or peeled, cut, boiled and mashed with fork	3	3	3
Bread crumbs (Page 145)	25 g +1 tbsp	1 oz +1 tbsp	½ cup +1 tbsp
Dried tarragon leaves, crushed	½ tsp	½ tsp	½ tsp
Freshly chopped parsley	1½ tsp	1½ tsp	1½ tsp
Dry mustard, dissolved in ½ tsp water	½ tsp	½ tsp	½ tsp
Cayenne papper	3 pinches	3 pinches	3 pinches
Dry sherry	1 tsp	1 tsp	1 tsp
Egg white, lightly beaten with fork	1	1	1
Low-fat milk	1 tbsp	1 tbsp	1 tbsp
Lemon wedges (optional)			

Reheat cod in court bouillon. Remove fish from bones and place in bowl. Combine 80 ml/3-4 fl oz/ ⅓-½ cup puréed sauce with fish and mash with fork. Set aside.

Heat 1 tablespoon oil in non-stick frying pan until hot. Sauté garlic and shallots until softened. Combine mashed potatoes with ½ tablespoon oil, together with 1 tablespoon crumbs, herbs, mustard, cayenne, sherry and egg white. Add potato mixture to mashed fish, together with sautéed garlic and shallots. Add just enough milk to make mixture smooth. Shape into 8 round cakes.

Dip each cake into remaining crumbs, coating evenly. Place on plate in one layer. Cover with clingfilm and refrigerate for at least 1 hour.

Heat remaining oil in non-stick frying pan until hot. Sauté cakes on both sides until golden brown. Drain on paper towels. Serve with lemon wedges or with rest of heated blended sauce.

Yield: Serves 4

CAL	F	P:S	SOD	CAR	CHO
208	9	4.1:1	49	10	61

GRILLED COD FISH CAKES

	Metric	Imperial	American
Recipe Sautéed Cod Fish Cakes, using only 1 tbsp bread crumbs, cakes not breaded (Page 48)	1	1	1
Fresh lemon or lime juice	2 tsp	2 tsp	2 tsp
Corn oil	1½ tbsp	1½ tbsp	1½ tbsp
Shallots, finely chopped	2	2	2
Sodium-free soya sauce	2 dashes	2 dashes	2 dashes
Corn oil to oil dish	½ tsp	½ tsp	½ tsp
Lemon or lime wedges			

Sprinkle fish cakes on both sides with lemon or lime juice. Heat 1½ tablespoons oil in non-stick frying pan until hot. Sauté shallots until softened but not brown. Add sodium-free soya sauce, blending well. Spread half of mixture over one side of fish cakes.

Arrange in lightly oiled flameproof baking dish in one layer. Grill 4 cm/1½ inches from heat until lightly browned. Turn. Spread with remaining mixture and grill until browned. Serve with lemon or lime wedges.

Yield: Serves 4

CAL	F	P:S	SOD	CAR	CHO
248	13	4.4:1	50	4	61

saute fillet lemon sole—see page 44

GRILLED HALIBUT WITH DILL SAUCE

Halibut is one of the more delicious denizens of the cold waters of the North Sea. Here it is grilled simply, with just a soupçon of seasoning to accentuate its clear, meaty flavour. Enjoy it straight from the grill, or spoon over my delicate dill sauce.

	Metric	Imperial	American
For the fish and marinade:			
Slices halibut, cut into 4 serving pieces (about 500 g/1¼ lb)	2	2	2
Shallots, finely chopped	2	2	2
Onion, finely chopped	½	½	½
Cloves garlic, finely chopped	2	2	2
Cayenne pepper	4 pinches	4 pinches	4 pinches
Wine vinegar	1 tsp	1 tsp	1 tsp
Corn oil	1 tbsp	1 tbsp	1 tbsp
For the dill sauce:			
Corn oil	1 tbsp	1 tbsp	1 tbsp
Unbleached flour	1 tbsp	1 tbsp	1 tbsp
Chicken or fish stock (Pages 8 and 9)	120 ml	4 fl oz	½ cup
Low-fat milk	120- 180 ml	4- 6 fl oz	½- ¾ cup
Cayenne pepper	3 pinches	3 pinches	3 pinches
Fresh dill, finely chopped	3 tbsp	3 tbsp	3 tbsp

First prepare marinade by combining all ingredients, except fish, in a bowl and blending well. Place fish in marinade, turning to coat. Let stand, covered, for 1 hour.

Place coated fish in shallow baking tin. Grill 5 cm/2 inches from heat for 10 minutes. Turn carefully, baste and grill on second side for 5-10 minutes, or until fish flakes easily when tested with fork. Serve immediately with lemon wedges or dill sauce.

Prepare the sauce while fish is grilling. Heat oil in heavy-bottomed saucepan until hot but not smoking. Add flour and beat with whisk for 2 minutes while mixture bubbles. Pour in stock, whisking constantly as mixture thickens. Add 120 ml/4 fl oz/½ cup milk and cayenne, whisking well for 1 minute. Add dill and continue cooking over very low heat for 5 minutes, stirring constantly. If too thick, thin with a little more milk. Pour over fish and serve immediately. Do not reheat.

Yield: Serves 4

CAL	F	P:S	SOD	CAR	CHO
149	5	3.0:1	48	2	82
Sauce					
72	6	4.5:1	22	4	0

BAKED RIVER TROUT

This simply prepared dish gets its flavour from the natural sweetness of the river trout itself, and by herbs and tasty homemade bread crumbs. Served with lemon wedges, this is a real treat for the fish lover, and an eye-opener to those who don't like fish unless it's dressed up.

	Metric	Imperial	American
River trout, about 350 g/12 oz/¾ lb each	4	4	4
Fresh lemon juice	1 tbsp	1 tbsp	1 tbsp
Bread crumbs (Page 145)	25 g	1 oz	½ cup
Dried rosemary leaves, crushed	½ tsp	½ tsp	½ tsp
Dried sage leaves, crushed	½ tsp	½ tsp	½ tsp
Garlic powder, no salt added	½ tsp	½ tsp	½ tsp
Cayenne pepper	3 pinches	3 pinches	3 pinches
Low-fat milk	60 ml	4 tbsp	¼ cup
Large sprigs dill	4	4	4
Large fresh mushrooms, washed, trimmed and sliced	4	4	4
Corn oil	1½ tbsp	1½ tbsp	1½ tbsp
Lemon wedges			

chinese steamed sea bass—see page 50

Wash fish thoroughly. Dry with paper towels inside and out. Make 3 diagonal slashes on each side of fish. Sprinkle inside and out with lemon juice. Cover and refrigerate for 2 hours.

Combine crumbs with crushed herbs, garlic powder and cayenne pepper. Pat fish dry with paper towels. Brush fish with milk, using pastry brush. Dip fish into herbed crumbs, coating well. Tuck one dill sprig into cavity of each fish, together with equal amounts of mushrooms.

Choose baking dish large enough to accommodate 4 fish in one layer. Brush bottom of dish with ½ tablespoon oil. Arrange trout in dish and sprinkle with remaining oil. Bake, uncovered, in preheated 220°C/425°F/Gas mark 7 oven until cooked (25-30 minutes). Fish should be lightly browned, and flake easily. Discard dill sprigs.

Serve on heated individual plates, garnished with cooked mushrooms and lemon wedges.

Yield: Serves 4

CAL	F	P:S	SOD	CAR	CHO
234	9	3.0:1	94	4	92

CHINESE STEAMED SEA BASS

Sea bass is a Chinese favourite, and deservedly so. It's a sweet firm-textured fish, remarkably suited to steaming. It's simple to prepare, makes use of only a handful of ingredients, and produces a delightful tangy flavour.

	Metric	Imperial	American
Sea bass, cleaned and left whole	1.3-1.5kg	3-3½ lb	3-3½ lb
Corn oil	60 ml	4 tbsp	¼ cup
Dry Vermouth or white wine	3 tbsp	3 tbsp	3 tbsp
Fresh ginger, peeled and cut into thin slivers	2 tsp	2 tsp	2 tsp
Spring onions, thinly sliced for cooking	3	3	3
Large cloves garlic, cut into quarters	2	2	2
Sodium-free soya sauce	1 tbsp	1 tbsp	1 tbsp
Spring onions, thinly sliced for garnish	2	2	2

Use a steamer or devise your own, using very large pan with a tight fitting cover, and a slightly narrower and shorter steaming bowl. Pour 4-5 cm/1½-2 inches water into pan. Insert bowl. Be sure there is enough room between sides of bowl and pan so that steam can circulate freely.

Rinse fish inside and out, and dry with paper towels. Make about 6 diagonal slashes on each side. Brush with oil to coat fish lightly. Lay whole fish in steaming bowl. If it doesn't fit, cut in half. Spoon Vermouth over both sides letting overflow drip into bowl. Sprinkle with ginger and spring onion. Bring water to boil, cover pan and steam for 30 minutes.

Transfer fish to heated serving platter. Heat oil in small heavy-bottomed saucepan until very hot and smoking. Add garlic to oil and cook for 15 seconds, then remove with slotted spoon. Pour hot oil over entire fish. Spoon with sodium-free soya sauce. Finally, sprinkle with rest of spring onions. Serve immediately.

Yields: 4

CAL	F	P:S	SOD	CAR	CHO
281	18	4.1:1	107	4	80

BAKED TUNA WITH BROCCOLI

Broccoli with complimentary herbs, spices, and wine, transform an ordinary can of tuna into a delectable one-dish meal.

	Metric	Imperial	American
Canned tuna packed in water, no salt added	180 g	6½ oz	6½ oz
Fresh lemon juice	1 tbsp	1 tbsp	1 tbsp
Corn oil	2 tbsp	2 tbsp	2 tbsp
Spring onions, finely chopped	2	2	2
Cloves garlic, finely chopped	2	2	2
Shallot, finely chopped	1	1	1
Large fresh mushrooms, washed, trimmed and sliced	4	4	4
Unbleached flour	2 tbsp	2 tbsp	2 tbsp
Fish stock or chicken stock (Pages 9 and 8)	120 ml	4 fl oz	½ cup
Dry mustard, dissolved in 1 tsp water	½ tsp	½ tsp	½ tsp
Dry Vermouth or white wine	3 tbsp	3 tbsp	3 tbsp
Low-fat milk	240 ml	8 fl oz	1 cup
Dried tarragon leaves, crushed	½ tsp	½ tsp	½ tsp
Freshly chopped dill and parsley	1 tbsp	1 tbsp	1 tbsp
Tomato paste, no salt added	1 tsp	1 tsp	1 tsp
Corn oil for coating casserole	½ tsp	½ tsp	½ tsp
Cooked broccoli (see recipe)	450 g	1 lb	2 cups
Bread crumbs (Page 145)	15 g	½ oz	¼ cup

Drain tuna. Place in bowl together with lemon juice. Flake coarsely with fork and set aside.

Heat 1 tablespoon oil in non-stick frying pan until hot. Sauté spring onions, garlic and shallot until softened. Add mushrooms and sauté for 1 minute, stir-ring constantly. Sprinkle flour into pan, stirring well. Cook for 1 minute. Add stock, mustard and wine, blending well. Add milk, herbs and tomato paste, and continue stirring while mixture thickens. Cook over very low heat for 3 minutes.

Prepare broccoli as for Broccoli Magic (Page 17), breaking broccoli into florets and cutting stalks into dice. Fill a large pan with water and bring to boil. Drop cubed stalks into water and boil, partially covered, for 4 minutes. Drop the florets into the same boiling water, and when returned to boil, cook for 5 minutes. Colour should remain bright green. Do not overcook! Drain in colander and rinse immediately under cold water to stop the cooking action.

Lightly oil a 2-litre/3.5-pint/2-quart covered casserole. Arrange broccoli and flaked tuna in alternate layers. Pour hot sauce over mixture. Sprinkle with bread crumbs and sprinkle rest of oil. Bake in preheated 200°C/400°F/Gas mark 6 oven for 20 minutes or until bubbly and lightly brown on top.

Yield: Serves 4

Note: If you like an exotic flavour, substitute 1 teaspoon curry powder (no salt or pepper added) for tarragon.

CAL	F	P:S	SOD	CAR	CHO
208	7	4:1	67	16	30
With curry					
208	7	4:1	74	16	30

SALMON IN WHITE WINE

In this recipe the salmon is cooked in one of my versions of a French court bouillon. Result: a fast-cooking easy-to-make dish that's enticingly moist and sparkling with flavour. Serve it *au naturel* or with my creamy sauce.

	Metric	Imperial	American
Small onion, finely chopped	1	1	1
Shallots, finely chopped	2	2	2
Cloves garlic, finely chopped	2	2	2
Fish stock (Page 9)	120 ml	4 fl oz	½ cup
Chicken stock (Page 8)	60 ml	4 tbsp	¼ cup
Large bay leaf	1	1	1
Dry Vermouth or white wine	180 ml	6 fl oz	¾ cup
Dried thyme leaves, crushed	½ tsp	½ tsp	½ tsp
Cayenne pepper	3 pinches	3 pinches	3 pinches
Slice salmon, 2-cm/¾-inch thick, cut into 4 pieces	680 g	1½ lb	1½ lb

Place onion, shallots, garlic, stocks, bay leaf, wine, thyme and cayenne in large iron frying pan. Bring to boil. Reduce heat, and simmer for 2 minutes. Add fish in one layer, spooning well with liquid. Cook, uncovered, for 5 minutes, turning once. Cover and place in preheated 190°C/375°F/Gas mark 5 oven for 15 minutes. Transfer fish to heated serving dish and keep warm.

Place pan with cooking liquid over medium high heat, and reduce by half. Remove bay leaf, and pour over fish. Serve immediately.

Yield: Serves 4

Variation: After fish has finished baking, place on heated serving platter. Pour cooking liquid, together with garlic and onion and 1 teaspoon low-fat dry milk into blender. Blend 1 minute. Return to saucepan and reheat over very low flame. Thicken with 1 teaspoon arrowroot that has been dissolved in 1 teaspoon water, using only enough to lightly thicken sauce. Pour over fish or serve with fish in sauceboat.

CAL	F	P:S	SOD	CAR	CHO
Salmon					
250	7	8:1	156	3	124
With sauce					
258	7	8:1	166	4	124

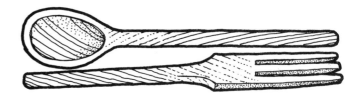

GRILLED SALMON WITH GREEN SAUCE

Salmon is regarded by gourmets everywhere as the king of fish, and rightly so. It's so basically tasty that grilled *au naturel* it's marvellous. This recipe serves the fish in a velvety sauce.

	Metric	Imperial	American
For the fish:			
Slices fresh salmon, each piece sliced in half along length of bone (about 680 g/1½ lb)	2	2	2
Corn oil	1 tbsp	1 tbsp	1 tbsp
Corn oil for coating baking dish	½ tsp	½ tsp	½ tsp
Clove garlic, finely chopped	1	1	1

Shallots, finely chopped	2	2	2
Fresh lemon juice	2 tbsp	2 tbsp	2 tbsp
Cayenne pepper	3 pinches	3 pinches	3 pinches
Dried tarragon leaves, crushed	½ tsp	½ tsp	½ tsp
For the green sauce:			
Corn oil	2 tbsp	2 tbsp	2 tbsp
Cloves garlic, finely chopped	2	2	2
Shallot, finely chopped	1	1	1
Unbleached flour	2 tbsp	2 tbsp	2 tbsp
Fish stock, warmed (Page 9)	180 ml	6 fl oz	¾ cup
Chicken stock, warmed (Page 8)	180 ml	6 fl oz	¾ cup
Dried tarragon leaves, crushed	½ tsp	½ tsp	½ tsp
Cayenne pepper	4 pinches	4 pinches	4 pinches
Low-fat milk	120-180 ml	4-6 fl oz	½-¾ cup
Very finely chopped fresh parsley	25 g	1 oz	½ cup

Prepare the fish first. Wipe dry with paper towels. Combine rest of ingredients in small bowl. Mix well. Place fish in lightly oiled flameproof baking dish. Brush half of mixture over top of fish. Grill 7.5 cm/3 inches from heat for 10 minutes. Turn carefully. Spread with remaining mixture and grill for another 7 minutes. Do not overcook. Serve on heated individual plates with green sauce spooned over.

While salmon is on the grill, prepare the sauce. Heat oil in heavy-bottomed saucepan until hot. Add garlic and shallot. Cook for 1 minute. Add flour all at once, whisking well. Cook for 2 minutes. Add combined stocks, tarragon and cayenne, blending well. Add 120 ml/4 fl oz/½ cup milk and parsley. Bring to simmering point and cook for 10 minutes over very low heat, uncovered, whisking often. Add more milk if a thinner sauce is desired. Pour over fish, and serve.

Yield: Serves 4

CAL	F	P:S	SOD	CAR	CHO
192	4	2.4:1	98	2	122
Sauce					
141	11	4.5:1	38	8	0

SAUTÉED PRAWNS

Quick cooking brings out all the natural flavour, and retains the firmness and crunchiness of these fresh shellfish. Gentle hints of herbs and seasonings make for a flavour as subtle as it is delicious.

	Metric	Imperial	American
Corn oil	1½ tbsp	1½ tbsp	1½ tbsp
Onion, sliced	1	1	1
Cloves, garlic, finely chopped	3	3	3
Shallot, finely chopped	1	1	1
Small green pepper, parboiled 1 minute, cut into slivers	1	1	1
Fresh prawns, shelled, deveined and dried	570 g	1¼ lb	1¼ lb
Cider vinegar	1 tbsp	1 tbsp	1 tbsp
Combined dried tarragon, basil and thyme leaves, crushed	½ tsp	½ tsp	½ tsp
Sodium-free soya sauce	3 dashes	3 dashes	3 dashes
Cayenne pepper	3 pinches	3 pinches	3 pinches
Freshly chopped parsley	1 tbsp	1 tbsp	1 tbsp

Heat oil in large iron frying pan until hot. Add onion, garlic and shallot and sauté 1 minute. Add green pepper and sauté 1 minute. Push to one side.

Add prawns, arranging in one layer, and sauté until lightly pink underneath (2-3 minutes). Turn and sauté 1 minute. Add vinegar and stir sautéed onions, garlic, shallot and green pepper together with shellfish. Add dried herbs, sodium-free soya sauce and cayenne. Cook for 1 minute only over high heat. Serve immediately on bed of plain boiled rice. Add parsley.

Yield: Serves 4

CAL	F	P:S	SOD	CAR	CHO
149	7	2.7:1	152	3	121
Rice					
43	0	—	0	10	0

PAELLA

Don't look for the traditional ingredients in this mini-paella. It's simply a combination of herbed rice with separately quickly cooked prawns (they retain their original crunchiness this way). Easier to make than the Spanish national dish which inspired it, my paella is light and full of rich, enticing flavours.

	Metric	Imperial	American
Corn oil	2 tbsp	2 tbsp	2 tbsp
Onion, finely chopped	1	1	1
Large cloves garlic, finely chopped	2	2	2
Shallots, finely chopped	2	2	2
Green pepper, parboiled for 1 minute, cut into thin strips	½	½	½
Rice	175 g	6 oz	1 cup
Dry Vermouth or white wine	120 ml	4 fl oz	½ cup
Fish stock (Page 9)	60 ml	2 fl oz	¼ cup
Chicken stock (Page 8)	60 ml	2 fl oz	¼ cup
Tomato purée, no salt added	120 ml	4 fl oz	½ cup
Dried tarragon leaves, crushed	1 tsp	1 tsp	1 tsp
Freshly chopped parsley	2 tsp	2 tsp	2 tsp
Tomato juice, no salt added (optional)	120 ml	4 fl oz	½ cup
Bouquet garni	1	1	1
Corn oil to oil casserole	½ tsp	½ tsp	½ tsp
Fresh prawns, shelled and deveined	450 g	1 lb	1 lb
Fresh mushrooms, washed, trimmed and sliced	100 g	4 oz	¼ lb

Heat ½ tablespoon oil in large non-stick frying pan until hot. Sauté onion, garlic and shallots for 1 minute. Add green pepper and sauté another minute. Add rice and stir well to coat. Cook for 2 minutes. Add wine. Bring to simmering point and cook for 2 minutes. Add remaining ingredients, except prawns and mushrooms, and heat to simmering point. Pour into lightly oiled 2-litre/3.5-pint/2-quart casserole. Cover and bake in preheated 200°C/400°F/Gas mark 6 oven for 15 minutes.

While rice is baking, heat 1 tablespoon oil in frying pan until hot. Add mushrooms and sauté for 2 minutes. Transfer to bowl. Heat rest of oil in pan until hot. Add prawns in one layer and cook on each side until lightly pink (about 1½ minutes on each side).

Remove casserole from oven. Add prawns and mushrooms, stirring until well distributed. Cover and return to oven for 7 minutes, or until rice is tender and moist. If too dry, add a little tomato juice, stirring well. Serve hot from casserole.

Yield: Serves 4 generously

Variation: For an unusual change of flavour, try substituting 1 teaspoon curry powder (no salt or pepper added) for tarragon.

CAL	F	P:S	SOD	CAR	CHO
353	5	2.5:1	121	49	110
With curry					
353	5	2.5:1	128	49	110
With tomato juice					
359	5	2.5:1	120	51	110

SAUTÉED PRAWNS—ITALIAN STYLE

Yield: Serves 4

CAL	F	P:S	SOD	CAR	CHO
151	7	2.7:1	158	4	121
Rice					
43	0	—	0	10	0

If you like scampi, you'll love this dish. Italian herbs and a drop of Vermouth or white wine are your passport to the *Via Veneto*.

	Metric	Imperial	American
Corn oil	1½ tbsp	1½ tbsp	1½ tbsp
Onion, thinly sliced	1	1	1
Cloves garlic, finely chopped	3	3	3
Small green pepper, parboiled 1 minute, diced	1	1	1
Fresh prawns, shelled, deveined and well dried	570 g	1¼ lb	1¼ lb
Dry Vermouth or white wine	60 ml	2 fl oz	¼ cup
Tomato juice, no salt added	80 ml	3 fl oz	⅓ cup
Dried oregano leaves, crushed	½ tsp	½ tsp	½ tsp
Dried sweet basil leaves, crushed	½ tsp	½ tsp	½ tsp
Cayenne papper	3 pinches	3 pinches	3 pinches
Sodium-free soya sauce	2 dashes	2 dashes	2 dashes
Freshly chopped parsley	1 tbsp	1 tbsp	1 tbsp

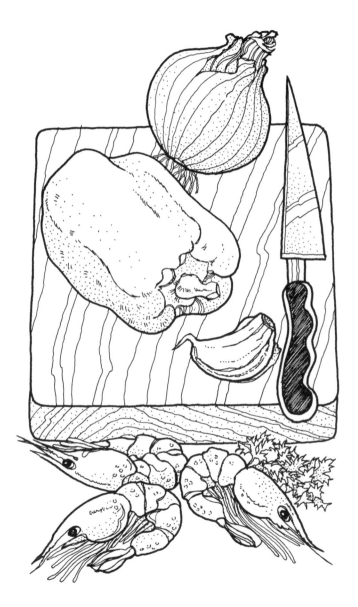

Heat 1 tablespoon oil in large heavy frying pan until hot. Add onion and garlic and sauté 1 minute. Add green pepper and sauté another minute, stirring constantly. Push vegetables to side of pan.

Add remaining oil and heat until hot. Add prawns, arranging in one layer. Sauté until lightly pink underneath (2-3 minutes). Turn and sauté 1 minute. Add wine and stir sautéed onion, garlic and green pepper together with prawns. Cook for 1 minute. Add tomato juice, dried herbs, cayenne and sodium-free soya sauce, and cook 1 minute more over high heat.

Serve immediately on a bed of plain boiled rice. Sprinkle with freshly chopped parsley.

CHICKEN AND TURKEY

POACHED CHICKEN BREASTS

This is a very simple and quick dish to prepare. Its light, mild flavour makes it adaptable to many variations, two of which follow this basic recipe. You'll easily invent more yourself.

	Metric	Imperial	American
Boneless chicken breasts, skinned and pounded to 1.5-cm/⅜-inch thickness (about 680 g/1½ lb)	4	4	4
Small carrot, peeled and diced	1	1	1
Large clove garlic, finely chopped	1	1	1
Leek, white part only, well washed and finely chopped	½	½	½
Small stick celery, finely chopped	1	1	1
Shallot, finely chopped	1	1	1
Chicken stock or enough to barely cover chicken (Page 8)	240 ml	8 fl oz	1 cup
Dry Vermouth or white wine	60 ml	2 fl oz	¼ cup
Large fresh mushrooms, washed, trimmed and sliced	3	3	3
Cayenne pepper	3 pinches	3 pinches	3 pinches
Small bouquet garni	1	1	1

Wipe chicken dry with paper towels. Arrange in one layer in heavy-bottomed saucepan. Combine remainder of ingredients and pour over chicken. Bring to slow boil. Reduce heat and simmer, covered, for 30 minutes, turning once half way through cooking. Do not overcook. Turn off heat and leave chicken in broth and vegetables for at least 30 minutes before serving. Remove bouquet garni.

Reheat and serve with boiled Parsleyed Potatoes (Page 20) as a simple lunch or dinner, or serve cold next day, immersed in cooking liquid which will have gelled.

Yield: Serves 4

CAL	F	P:S	SOD	CAR	CHO
214	4	1.8:1	112	4	98

CHICKEN BREASTS WITH CREAMY SAUCE

	Metric	Imperial	American
Recipe Poached Chicken Breasts (Page 56)	1	1	1
Arrowroot, dissolved in 2 tsp water	2 tsp	2 tsp	2 tsp
Freshly chopped parsley and dill			

Prepare Poached Chicken Breasts according to recipe. Transfer chicken to heated serving platter and keep warm.

Reduce unstrained broth by a third. Pour into blender and blend for 1 minute. Pour back into saucepan and reheat. Sprinkle arrowroot mixture into heated liquid, adding only enough to make a light, fairly thin gravy. Pour over chicken breasts and sprinkle with freshly chopped parsley and dill.

Yield: Serves 4

CAL	F	P:S	SOD	CAR	CHO
218	4	1.8:1	112	5	98

CHICKEN DIVAN

Chicken Divan consists of a bed of fresh and lightly cooked broccoli, blanketed with thinly sliced breasts of chicken, and bathed in a piquant Mornay sauce. It is a relatively inexpensive dish for two or for a party.

	Metric	Imperial	American
Fresh broccoli, slightly undercooked (see recipe)	680 g	1½ lb	3 cups
Corn oil for oiling baking dishes	½ tsp	½ tsp	½ tsp
Chicken stock (see Page 8)	360 ml	12½ fl oz	1½ cups
Fresh mushrooms, washed, trimmed and sliced	4	4	4
Arrowroot, dissolved in 1½ tbsp water	1½ tbsp	1½ tbsp	1½ tbsp
Low-fat milk	180 ml	6 fl oz	¾ cup
Combined powdered sage and thyme	¼ tsp	¼ tsp	¼ tsp
Sodium-free soya sauce	2 dashes	2 dashes	2 dashes
Cayenne pepper	3 pinches	3 pinches	3 pinches
Grated low-fat cheese (Page 6)	50 g	2 oz	¼ cup
Poached chicken breasts, thinly sliced (Page 56)	225 g	8 oz	½ lb
Freshly chopped parsley	1 tbsp	1 tbsp	1 tbsp

Prepare the broccoli as for Broccoli Magic (Page 17), breaking into florets and cutting stalks into dice. Fill a large pan with water and bring to boil. Drop cubed stalks into water and boil, partially covered, for 4 minutes. Drop the florets into the same boiling water and when returned to boil, cook for 5 minutes. Colour should remain bright green. Do not overcook! Drain in colander and rinse immediately under cold water to stop the cooking action.

Lightly oil 4 individual ovenproof baking dishes. Arrange broccoli in equal portions on bottom of each dish.

To prepare the sauce, heat stock to simmering point. Add mushrooms and cook over low heat, covered, for 5 minutes. Add arrowroot mixture a little at a time, whisking well. Slowly add milk and blend. Add powdered herbs, sodium-free soya sauce, cayenne and cheese and bring to simmering point. Spoon half the hot sauce over broccoli. Arrange sliced chicken over broccoli in equal portions, and spoon remaining sauce over each individual dish. Bake in preheated 220°C/425°F/Gas mark 7 oven for 15 minutes, or until lightly browned. Sprinkle with freshly chopped parsley, and serve.

Yield: Serves 4

Note: Sliced white meat of turkey may be substituted for chicken.

CAL	F	P:S	SOD	CAR	CHO
165	12	4.2:1	78	15	10
Turkey					
162	12	4.2:1	73	15	10

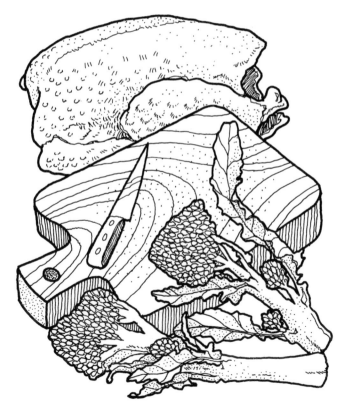

CHICKEN BOLOGNESE

This extravagant extension of my recipe for Poached Chicken Breasts is a lighter and more delicate version of the Chicken Bolognese featured in fine Italian restaurants. A superb party dish.

	Metric	Imperial	American
Recipe Poached Chicken Breasts (Page 56)	1	1	1
Corn oil	1 tbsp	1 tbsp	1 tbsp
Corn oil to coat casserole	½ tsp	½ tsp	½ tsp
Enough low-fat cheese, sliced 3-mm/⅛-inch thick, to cover chicken breasts (Page 6)			
Arrowroot, dissolved in 2 tsp water	2 tsp	2 tsp	2 tsp
Freshly chopped parsley and dill	2 tbsp	2 tbsp	2 tbsp

Prepare Poached Chicken Breasts according to recipe. Remove from liquid and pat dry. Heat oil in non-stick frying pan until hot. Sauté chicken breasts until lightly browned on both sides.

Lightly oil a flameproof casserole. Place browned chicken breasts in casserole in one layer, covering each piece with slices of cheese.

Reduce unstrained broth by a third. Pour into blender and blend for 1 minute. Return to saucepan, reheat, and thicken with only enough dissolved arrowroot to make a light gravy. Spoon half of gravy over chicken pieces and place under grill until cheese is melted and lightly browned. Transfer to serving platter and spoon rest of hot gravy over chicken. Sprinkle with freshly chopped parsley and dill.

Yield: Serves 4

CAL	F	P:S	SOD	CAR	CHO
341	15	4.3:1	143	15	109

SIMPLE GRILLED CHICKEN

The emphasis is on simple—you just marinate and grill. But it's one of the tastiest ways of preparing chicken.

	Metric	Imperial	American
Young chicken, cut into serving pieces, skinned	1.5 kg	3 lb	3 lb
Freshly chopped parsley and dill	1-2 tbsp	1-2 tbsp	1-2 tbsp
For the marinade:			
Large shallot, finely chopped	1	1	1
Freshly chopped parsley and dill	2 tbsp	2 tbsp	2 tbsp
Dried rosemary leaves, crushed, or combined dried rosemary and thyme leaves, crushed	1 tsp	1 tsp	1 tsp
Corn oil	2 tbsp	2 tbsp	2 tbsp
Cider vinegar	60 ml	2 fl oz	¼ cup
Sodium-free soya sauce	4 dashes	4 dashes	4 dashes
Cayenne pepper	2 pinches	2 pinches	2 pinches

Mix ingredients for marinade in large bowl, stirring well to blend. Place chicken in bowl just large enough to hold all chicken. Pour marinade over chicken, turning pieces to coat evenly. Cover with foil and refrigerate for 5-6 hours.

Arrange legs and breasts on racks in grill. Grill 7 cm/3 inches from heat for 8-10 minutes. Turn, add smaller chicken pieces (they require less cooking time) and grill for 8-10 minutes. Raise pan so that it is 4 cm/1½ inches from heat, and continue grilling and turning until chicken is cooked. Total cooking time is about 30-35 minutes, depending upon weight of bird. Serve immediately sprinkled with parsley and dill.

Yield: Serves 4

CAL	F	P:S	SOD	CAR	CHO
258	8	2.6:1	122	1	98

GRILLED CHICKEN PAPRIKASH

This is a grilled version without tomatoes, of one of Hungary's great contributions to the art of haute cuisine, chicken paprikash (Hungarians prefer it as a stew). It's a spicy, full-bodied dish with just a hint of sweetness.

	Metric	Imperial	American
Young chicken, cut into serving pieces, skinned	1.5 kg	3 lb	3 lb
Corn oil	1 tbsp	1 tbsp	1 tbsp
Paprika	1 tsp	1 tsp	1 tsp
Large cloves garlic, finely chopped	2	2	2
Cider vinegar	2 tsp	2 tsp	2 tsp
Cayenne pepper	2 pinches	2 pinches	2 pinches
Juice of ½ lemon			
Honey	1 tsp	1 tsp	1 tsp

Pat chicken dry with paper towels. Make a marinade by combining remaining ingredients. Spoon and spread over chicken. Cover and refrigerate for 3 hours before cooking.

Arrange legs and breasts on rack in grill. Grill 7.5 cm/3 inches from heat for 8-10 minutes. Turn, add smaller chicken pieces (they require less cooking time) and grill for 8-10 minutes. Raise pan so that it is 4 cm/1½ inches from heat, and continue grilling and turning until chicken is cooked. Total cooking time is about 30-35 minutes, depending upon weight of bird. Serve immediately.

Yield: Serves 4

Note: The spiciness of the marinade will depend upon the kind of paprika used. In this recipe I use mild paprika, which can be obtained in most shops. If you prefer a hot paprika, eliminate cayenne.

CAL	F	P:S	SOD	CAR	CHO
279	9	2.8:1	121	2	98

APPLE CHICKEN

An adventurous way to use apple juice.

	Metric	Imperial	American
Apple juice concentrate, no sugar added	½ can	½ can	½ can
Ground ginger	1 tsp	1 tsp	1 tsp
Ground cloves	¼ tsp	¼ tsp	¼ tsp
Dried marjoram leaves, crushed	¼ tsp	¼ tsp	¼ tsp
Cayenne pepper	2 pinches	2 pinches	2 pinches
Young chicken, cut into eighths, skinned, with wing tips removed	1.5 kg	3 lb	3 lb
Bread crumbs (Page 145)	40 g	1½ oz	¾ cup
Toasted wheat germ	4 tbsp	4 tbsp	¼ cup

In small bowl, combine apple concentrate with ginger, cloves, marjoram and cayenne, and blend with fork. Pat chicken dry with paper towels. Dip each piece into mixture, letting excess liquid drain off. Mix together bread crumbs and toasted wheat germ. Dip chicken pieces into crumb mixture, covering well. Refrigerate for at least 30 minutes before cooking.

Lightly oil a shallow roasting tin large enough to hold entire chicken in one layer. Place chicken in pan. Bake, uncovered, in preheated 190°C/375°F/Gas mark 5 oven for 45 minutes, turning once half way through cooking. Serve immediately. The golden crunchy crust is a feature of this dish.

Yield: Serves 4

CAL	F	P:S	SOD	CAR	CHO
419	6	1.8:1	126	39	113

SIMPLE SAUTÉED CHICKEN ROSEMARY

Rosemary—minty and fragrant—is a dominant herb in this recipe, which is very easy to make.

	Metric	Imperial	American
Young chicken, cut into serving pieces, skinned	1.5 kg	3 lb	3 lb
Corn oil	2 tbsp	2 tbsp	2 tbsp
Large cloves garlic, finely chopped	3	3	3
Small onion, finely chopped	1	1	1
Shallots, finely chopped	2	2	2
Dry Vermouth or white wine	60 ml	2 fl oz	¼ cup
Tomato juice, no salt added	120 ml	4 fl oz	½ cup
Sodium-free soya sauce	3 dashes	3 dashes	3 dashes
Chicken stock (Page 8)	80 ml	3 fl oz	⅓ cup
Cayenne pepper	3 pinches	3 pinches	3 pinches
Dried rosemary leaves, crushed	1 tsp	1 tsp	1 tsp
Carrot, peeled and grated	½	½	½
Bouquet garni	1	1	1
Freshly chopped parsley			

Pat chicken dry with paper towels. Combine ½ tablespoon oil with 2 cloves finely chopped garlic. Spoon and rub over chicken. Cover and refrigerate overnight.

Heat ½ tablespoon oil in large non-stick frying pan until hot. Add half of the chicken and sauté on both sides until lightly browned, turning carefully with spatula. Transfer to bowl. Heat ½ tablespoon corn oil until hot. Brown rest of chicken. Transfer to bowl.

Heat remaining oil in pan until hot. Add onion, shallot and remaining garlic, and sauté until lightly browned. Add wine and cook for 2 minutes. Add tomato juice, sodium-free soya sauce, stock, cayenne, rosemary and carrot. Stir. Add browned chicken, turning well to coat. Add bouquet garni. Bring to simmering point cover and cook for 45 minutes, turning twice.

Turn off heat, and let stand, covered, for 30 minutes. When ready to serve, reheat over low flame. Remove bouquet garni. Sprinkle with freshly chopped parsley and serve.

Yield: Serves 4

CAL	F	P:S	SOD	CAR	CHO
323	13	3.2:1	132	9	98

SAUTÉED CHICKEN LEGS WITH PIMENTOS

Yes, there are dark meat lovers! And if you're not one already, you probably will be when you taste this easy-to-make dish. It's spicy and a delight to the eye.

	Metric	Imperial	American
Chicken legs with thighs, skinned, leg separated from thigh (about 900 g/2 lb)	4	4	4
Cloves garlic, finely chopped	4	4	4
Wine vinegar	1 tsp	1 tsp	1 tsp
Corn oil	2 tbsp	2 tbsp	2 tbsp
Ground ginger	½ tsp	½ tsp	½ tsp
Sodium-free soya sauce	½ tsp	½ tsp	½ tsp
Large onion, sliced	1	1	1
Small green pepper, sliced into thin strips	1	1	1
Chicken stock (Page 8)	60 ml	2 fl oz	¼ cup
Dried thyme leaves, crushed	½ tsp	½ tsp	½ tsp
Cayenne pepper	4 pinches	4 pinches	4 pinches
Large pimento, no salt added, sliced	1	1	1

Pat chicken dry with paper towels. Combine garlic, vinegar, ½ tablespoon oil, ginger and sodium-free soya sauce in bowl large enough to accommodate all chicken. Add chicken, turning to coat. Cover and refrigerate for at least 6 hours.

Heat 1 tablespoon oil in large heavy frying pan until hot. Add chicken and sauté to a golden brown on both sides turning carefully with spatula. Skinned chicken must be handled carefully. Remove from pan and set aside.

Heat remaining oil until hot. Add onion, and green pepper to same pan and sauté until lightly browned. Add stock, thyme and cayenne, and cook over medium heat, scraping to loosen brown particles (about 2 minutes). Return browned chicken and juices to pan, turning well. Bring small amount of liquid in pan to simmering point. Reduce heat, cover and simmer for 20 minutes.

Turn chicken pieces and add pimento. Bring to simmering point, re-cover and simmer for 20 minutes, stirring and turning once. Turn off heat and leave, covered, for 30 minutes before serving.

At serving time, reheat over very low flame and serve piping hot.

Yield: Serves 4

Variation: The marinated chicken may be grilled.

CAL	F	P:S	SOD	CAR	CHO
277	15	3.1:1	91	5	83
Grilled					
256	15	3.1:1	80	2	83

HERB-FLAVOURED ROAST CHICKEN

Roast chicken can be, and generally is, pretty dull. But just glance over the ingredients for this luscious, herb-flavoured chicken and you'll agree, chicken can be exciting.

	Metric	Imperial	American
Freshly chopped parsley and dill	2 tbsp	2 tbsp	2 tbsp
Large shallot, finely chopped	1	1	1
Dried rosemary leaves, crushed, or combined dried rosemary and thyme leaves, crushed	1 tsp	1 tsp	1 tsp
Corn oil	2 tbsp	2 tbsp	2 tbsp
Cider vinegar	60 ml	2 fl oz	¼ cup
Sodium-free soya sauce	½ tsp	½ tsp	½ tsp
Cayenne pepper	2 pinches	2 pinches	2 pinches
Young chicken	1.5 kg	3 lb	3 lb

Combine all ingredients, except chicken, in large bowl. Blend well to make marinade.

Lay chicken on its back. Lift skin by gently pushing your finger under skin of breast and then to the thigh and leg. Gently spoon a portion of marinade under skin as far as it will go. Press skin down and skewer in place. With a sharp-pronged fork, prick the skin of wings and back, and spoon with remaining marinade. Turn to coat. Cover with foil and refrigerate overnight. Remove from refrigerator 1 hour before roasting.

Place bird on rack in roasting tin. Pour half the marinade over bird. Place in preheated 180°C/350°F/ Gas mark 4 oven and roast uncovered for 30 minutes. Pour rest of marinade over bird and roast for 45 minutes. Remove from oven and loosely cover with greaseproof paper. Let stand for 5 minutes before slicing.

Yield: Serves 4

Variation: Stuffed Herbed Chicken: Follow stuffing instructions in recipe for Orange-Pineapple Chicken (Page 64) truss, and roast, uncovered. Cooking time 1½ hours.
Note: This marinade is delicious for veal and pork roasts as well.

CAL	F	P:S	SOD	CAR	CHO
351	18	2.7:1	125	1	98
Stuffing					
142	0	—	32	28	16

CHICKEN TANDOORI

This dish and the one that follows, are unmistakably Indian dishes that are wonderfully light, subtle-tasting, and far from alien to the European palate. Here's where East meets West!

	Metric	Imperial	American
Young chicken, skinned and left whole	1.5 kg	3 lb	3 lb
Cayenne pepper	¼ tsp	¼ tsp	¼ tsp
Mild paprika	1 tsp	1 tsp	1 tsp
Fresh lime juice	6 tbsp	6 tbsp	6 tbsp
Wine vinegar	6 tbsp	6 tbsp	6 tbsp
Corn oil	1 tbsp	1 tbsp	1 tbsp
Dried rosemary leaves, crushed	¼ tsp	¼ tsp	¼ tsp
Dried thyme leaves, crushed	⅛ tsp	⅛ tsp	⅛ tsp
Larve clove garlic, very finely chopped	1	1	1
Fresh ginger, cut into thin slices	½ tbsp	½ tbsp	½ tbsp
Onion, finely chopped	1	1	1
Stick celery, finely chopped	½	½	½
Large pimento, no salt added, diced	1	1	1
Low-fat plain yogurt	240 ml	8 fl oz	1 cup

Here's how to skin a whole chicken. Start by slipping knife under skin at bottom of breast bone and cutting skin up toward the centre of the bird to the neck. Peel skin back from either side of breast, using the knife only to assist the separation of skin from the meat. Skin can be removed from back and legs in a similar manner; cut the skin down the backbone and along the thighs, and peel back with one hand assisted by the knife in the other. Skinning the wings is more difficult and not essential, so prick them instead with a sharp-pronged fork.

Wash out cavity of chicken. Pat entire bird dry with paper towels. Combine cayenne, paprika, lime juice and vinegar. Mix well. Pour this marinade over chicken and rub in and around entire bird. Cover, and refrigerate for 3-4 hours.

Combine 1 teaspoon oil, dried herbs and garlic. Remove chicken from marinade. Drain and discard excess. Rub with herb-garlic mixture and return, covered, to refrigerator for a further 3-4 hours.

Combine ginger, onion, celery and pimento. Add yogurt and blend well. Coat chicken all over with mixture. Place chicken on rack in shallow roasting tin. Roast, uncovered in preheated 200°C/400°F/Gas mark 6 over for 30 minutes. Brush with 1 teaspoon oil. Roast 15 minutes and brush with remaining oil. Roast 15 minutes. Total cooking time 1 hour.

Cut into serving pieces, and serve.

Yield: Serves 4

Note: Typical Chicken Tandoori recipes call for roasting until bird is quite dry. My timetable produces a moister bird.

CAL	F	P:S	SOD	CAR	CHO
340	16	2.8:1	152	8	99

MOGUL CHICKEN WITH MUSHROOMS

	Metric	Imperial	American
Cloves garlic, very finely chopped	3	3	3
Fresh lime juice or 1 tbsp fresh lemon juice	3 tbsp	3 tbsp	3 tbsp
Mild paprika	¼ tsp	¼ tsp	¼ tsp
Water	240 ml	8 fl oz	1 cup
Ground turmeric	1½ tsp	1½ tsp	1½ tsp
Fresh mushrooms, washed, trimmed and thickly sliced	225 g	8 oz	½ lb

Whole chicken legs (including thighs) and 1 whole chicken breast, skinned (about 900 g/2 lb total)	2	2	2
Corn oil	2 tbsp	2 tbsp	2 tbsp
Seeds of 4 cardamom pods crushed or ¼ tbsp ground cardamom			
Freshly chopped chives or parsley	1 tbsp	1 tbsp	1 tbsp

Combine garlic with 3 tablespoons water. Set aside. Combine lime juice with paprika, and set aside. Combine 240 ml/8 fl oz/1 cup water with turmeric. Add mushrooms to soak, and set aside.

Pat chicken dry with paper towels. Heat oil in large heavy frying pan until hot. Add chicken and sauté on both sides until lightly browned (about 15 minutes). Sprinkle with cardamom and continue sautéeing for 5 minutes. Transfer to bowl and cover to keep warm.

Drain mushrooms and add to frying pan. Cook over high heat, uncovered, for 2 minutes. Return warm chicken to pan and sauté with mushrooms over medium-high heat until all liquid evaporates (about 10 minutes).

In small saucepan, bring garlic and water to boil. Pour over chicken and turn rapidly to coat. Bring lime juice and paprika to boil, and pour over chicken, turning to coat. Sprinkle with chopped chives or parsley, and serve immediately.

Yield: Serves 4

CAL	F	P:S	SOD	CAR	CHO
210	11	3.2:1	86	1	87

NEAR-EAST CHICKEN

Many Near-east recipes call for buttermilk as an ingredient for their meat and poultry marinades. The liaison of this lean milk product with exotic herbs not only adds an admirable pungency, but also tenderizes the food.

	Metric	Imperial	American
For the chicken:			
Young chickens, (1.25 kg/2½ lb each), skinned, cut into eighths; backbones, giblets and wing tips reserved to make rich gravy	2	2	2
Corn oil to coat baking tin	1 tsp	1 tsp	1 tsp
For the marinade:			
Buttermilk, no salt added	180 ml	6 fl oz	¾ cup
Small onion, grated	1	1	1
Shallot, finely chopped	1	1	1
Cloves garlic, finely chopped	3	3	3
Stick celery, finely chopped	1	1	1
Dried sage leaves, crushed	¼ tsp	¼ tsp	¼ tsp
Dried thyme leaves, crushed	¼ tsp	¼ tsp	¼ tsp
Cayenne pepper	3 pinches	3 pinches	3 pinches
Freshly chopped parsley	1 tbsp	1 tbsp	1 tbsp
For the sauce:			
Reserved backs, wings, and giblets (except heart)			
Water, enough to barely cover chicken pieces	450 ml	¾ pt	2 cups
Small onion, coarsely chopped	1	1	1
Large clove garlic, finely chopped	1	1	1

Large shallot, finely chopped	1	1	1
Carrot, peeled and sliced	½	½	½
Stick celery with leaves, coarsely chopped	½	½	½
Dried sage leaves	½ tsp	½ tsp	½ tsp
Dried thyme leaves	½ tsp	½ tsp	½ tsp
Small bouquet garni	1	1	1
Fresh mushrooms, washed, trimmed and quartered	4	4	4
Cayenne pepper	2 pinches	2 pinches	2 pinches
Freshly chopped parsley	1 tbsp	1 tbsp	1 tbsp
For the breading:			
Bread crumbs, preferably made from My French Bread (Page 134)	40 g	1½ oz	¾ cup
Toasted wheat germ, no sugar added	4 tbsp	4 tbsp	¼ cup

First prepare marinade by combining all ingredients in large bowl. Stir to blend. Add chicken, turning to coat well. Cover and refrigerate for at least 6 hours, or overnight.

Now prepare stock for sauce. Place reserved chicken pieces in heavy-bottomed saucepan. Add water. Bring to boil. Cook, uncovered, for 5 minutes, removing scum that rises to top. Add onion, garlic, shallot, carrot, celery, dried herbs and bouquet garni. Partially cover and simmer for 45 minutes. Remove from heat and let stand, covered, for 1 hour. Skim off fat that rises to the top. Add mushrooms. Bring to simmering point, cover and cook for 15 minutes.

Remove chicken pieces from broth with slotted spoon. Reserve for a light lunch. Remove bouquet garni. This stock can be prepared up to this point a day ahead and reheated if liked.

Now prepare and bake the chicken. An hour before baking chicken, remove from marinade. Combine crumbs and wheat germ, and blend. Dip each piece of chicken into crumbs, turning well to coat. Place all breaded pieces of chicken on a platter. Cover with cling film and refrigerate for 1 hour. Discard marinade.

When ready to cook, arrange chicken in lightly oiled baking tin large enough to hold all chicken in one layer. Bake in preheated 180°C/350°F/Gas mark 4 oven for 45 minutes, turning carefully with spatula. Chicken will now be ready to serve.

Ten minutes before chicken is done, finish preparation of sauce. Pour stock and vegetables into blender and blend for 2 minutes. Reheat sauce over low flame, adding cayenne and freshly chopped parsley. Stir. Serve in sauceboat with chicken.

Yield: Serves 6

Note: Don't purée the chicken broth and vegetables until 10 minutes before chicken has finished baking. This light, frothy sauce has no thickener and will collapse if prepared in advance of serving time.

CAL	F	P:S	SOD	CAR	CHO
366	6	1.8:1	165	21	108
Sauce					
19	0	—	19	3	0

ORANGE-PINEAPPLE CHICKEN

This is a grand dish made with a delicious herbaceous stuffing, and served with a sweet and pungent sauce.

	Metric	Imperial	American
For the chicken:			
Young chicken, with giblets	1.5 kg	3 lb	3 lb
Corn oil	1 tbsp	1 tbsp	1 tbsp
For the marinade:			
Unsweetened orange juice	120 ml	4 fl oz	½ cup
Unsweetened pineapple juice	60 ml	2 fl oz	¼ cup
Juice of 1 large lemon			
Cloves garlic, finely chopped	2	2	2
Shallot, finely chopped	1	1	1

chicken divan—see page 57

Small onion, thinly sliced	1	1	1
Dried sage leaves, crushed	½ tsp	½ tsp	½ tsp
Dried thyme leaves, crushed	½ tsp	½ tsp	½ tsp
Small bay leaf	1	1	1
Cayenne pepper	2 pinches	2 pinches	2 pinches
For the stuffing:			
Corn oil	1 tbsp	1 tbsp	1 tbsp
Cloves garlic, finely chopped	2	2	2
Shallot, finely chopped	1	1	1
Onion, finely chopped	1	1	1
Chicken liver, diced	1	1	1
French Bread (Page 134), cubed, for stuffing (see recipe)	100 g	4 oz	2 cups
Dried sage leaves, crushed	½ tsp	½ tsp	½ tsp
Dried thyme leaves, crushed	½ tsp	½ tsp	½ tsp
Freshly chopped parsley	2½ tbsp	2½ tbsp	2½ tbsp
Egg white, lightly beaten with fork	1	1	1
Chicken stock, as much as needed to lightly moisten bread cubes (Page 8)	180 ml	6 fl oz	¾ cup
Cayenne pepper	2 pinches	2 pinches	2 pinches
Low-fat milk	1 tbsp	1 tbsp	1 tbsp
For the sauce:			
Chicken stock (Page 8)	60 ml	2 fl oz	¼ cup
Large fresh mushrooms, washed, trimmed and sliced	3	3	3
Remaining marinade, after chicken is braised, and fat skimmed			
Cider vinegar or white vinegar	1 tbsp	1 tbsp	1 tbsp
Honey	1 tbsp	1 tbsp	1 tbsp
Julienne strips of ½ orange (see method)			
Arrowroot, dissolved in 1 tsp water (optional)	1 tsp	1 tsp	1 tsp

Mix all ingredients for marinade. Wipe chicken well inside and out with paper towels. Prick skin with sharp-pronged fork. In a bowl large enough to fit bird, pour marinade over chicken, spooning some into the cavity. Cover with foil and refrigerate overnight.

To prepare the stuffing: cut about ½ loaf of my French Bread into 1.5-cm/½-inch slices, and then into cubes. Spread cubes on baking tray in one layer. Bake in preheated 220°C/425°F/Gas mark 7 oven for 10 minutes, turning cubes with spatula after 5 minutes. Cool. Heat oil until hot in small heavy frying pan. Sauté garlic, shallot and onion until lightly browned. Add chicken liver and brown. In a large bowl pour sautéed mixture over bread cubes. Stir. Add herbs, egg white, chicken stock and cayenne, mixing well. Add milk and mix. If necessary, add a little more milk.

To prepare the chicken: remove chicken from marinade, reserving excess marinade. Wipe bird dry. Stuff cavity and truss bird. With pastry brush, lightly oil the entire bird. Brown in flameproof casserole.

Pour off any oil left in casserole and discard. Pour reserved marinade over bird, cover tightly, and place in preheated 180°C/350°F/Gas mark 4 oven. Bake for 30 minutes. Remove cover and bake for 45 minutes, basting twice. Remove from casserole and keep warm.

Julienne strips: Peel off skin from half orange, cutting away white part. Slice skin into very thin slivers and drop into boiling water for 3 minutes. Drain and rinse under cold water. Set aside.

To prepare the sauce: heat chicken stock with mushrooms. Simmer for 3 minutes. Pour into blender together with cooked marinade from which fat has been skimmed. Add vinegar and honey. Blend well. Return to saucepan. Pour juices that have dripped from chicken into saucepan. Reheat and add julienne strips. If you prefer a slightly thicker sauce, sprinkle tiny amounts of arrowroot mixture into sauce.

Cut chicken into serving pieces and place on serving platter with stuffing in centre. Spoon small amount of sauce over chicken and sprinkle with parsley.

Yield: Serves 4

CAL	F	P:S	SOD	CAR	CHO
278	9	2.6:1	121	9	98
Stuffing					
142	0	—	32	28	16
Sauce					
16	0	—	3	3	0

baked herbed veal chops—see page 80

SAUTÉED CHICKEN WITH APPLES

The best gourmet dishes are made of high quality local ingredients blended with imagination and care. The ingredients produce a distinctive and unforgettable flavour—such as this one.

	Metric	Imperial	American
Young chicken, cut into serving pieces, skinned	1.5 kg	3 lb	3 lb
Dried sage leaves, crushed	¼ tsp	¼ tsp	¼ tsp
Dried thyme leaves, crushed	¼ tsp	¼ tsp	¼ tsp
Corn oil	2 tbsp	2 tbsp	2 tbsp
Large cloves garlic, finely chopped	2	2	2
Large shallot, finely chopped	1	1	1
Dry Vermouth or white wine	60 ml	2 fl oz	¼ cup
Unsweetened apple juice	120 ml	4 fl oz	½ cup
Chicken stock (Page 8)	120 ml	4 fl oz	½ cup
Dry mustard, dissolved in 1 tsp water	¼ tsp	¼ tsp	¼ tsp
Fresh lemon juice	1 tsp	1 tsp	1 tsp
Sodium-free soya sauce	½ tsp	½ tsp	½ tsp
Ground ginger	¾ tsp	¾ tsp	¾ tsp
Cayenne pepper	3 pinches	3 pinches	3 pinches
Sweet, crisp apples, peeled, cored and diced	2	2	2
Sesame seeds, toasted (see note)	2 tsp	2 tsp	2 tsp

Wipe chicken dry with paper towels. Rub with herbs. Heat 1 tablespoon oil in large non-stick frying pan until hot. Sauté half the chicken on both sides until lightly browned, taking care in turning. Remove from pan and set aside. Heat remaining oil until hot, and brown rest of chicken. Return first browned batch to pan. Add garlic and shallot. Brown with chicken for 5 minutes, turning twice. Add wine and cook for 2 minutes, turning chicken to coat.

Combine apple juice, stock, mustard, lemon juice, sodium-free soya sauce and ginger. Pour over chicken. Sprinkle with cayenne. Heat to simmering point, cover and simmer for 30 minutes. Add apples. Re-cover, and cook for 10 minutes. Remove from heat and leave chicken in liquid for 30 minutes before serving.

When ready to serve, reheat, uncovered, over medium flame until simmering, turning chicken pieces once. Transfer chicken and apples to heated serving dish, using slotted spoon for apples. Cover to keep warm. Boil gravy over high heat to reduce by half. Pour over chicken. Sprinkle with sesame seeds and serve.

Note: How to toast sesame seeds: heat small heavy frying pan until hot. Sprinkle seeds into pan and cook over heat for about 2 minutes, shaking pan often, until seeds are very lightly browned.

Yield: Serves 4

CAL	F	P:S	SOD	CAR	CHO
331	13	2.7:1	151	8	98

CHICKEN À L'ORANGE

Juicy sweet-and-tart navel oranges are the secret ingredient that transforms a simple unadorned bird into an exquisitely dressed fowl.

	Metric	Imperial	American
Dried thyme leaves, crushed	¼ tsp	¼ tsp	¼ tsp
Dried tarragon leaves, crushed	½ tsp	½ tsp	½ tsp
Dried marjoram leaves, crushed	½ tsp	½ tsp	½ tsp
Unbleached flour	50 g	2 oz	½ cup
Young chicken, cut into serving pieces, skinned	1.5 kg	3 lb	3 lb
Corn oil	2 tbsp	2 tbsp	2 tbsp
Large cloves garlic, finely chopped	2	2	2
Small green pepper, finely chopped	1	1	1

Large shallot, finely chopped	1	1	1
Small onion, finely chopped	1	1	1
Carrot, peeled and finely chopped	½	½	½
Small stick celery, finely chopped	1	1	1
Cider vinegar	2 tbsp	2 tbsp	2 tbsp
Chicken stock (Page 8)	120 ml	4 fl oz	½ cup
Brown beef stock (Page 11)	2 tbsp	2 tbsp	2 tbsp
Unsweetened orange juice	120 ml	4 fl oz	½ cup
Freshly chopped parsley	1 tbsp	1 tbsp	1 tbsp
Sodium-free soya sauce	1 tsp	1 tsp	1 tsp
Fresh watercress sprigs	3	3	3
Cayenne pepper	2 pinches	2 pinches	2 pinches
Silver orange rind	1	1	1
Unsweetened orange juice for sauce	60 ml	2 fl oz	¼ cup
Orange, peeled, sliced; each slice quartered	1	1	1

Combine dried herbs with flour and blend. Dry chicken well with paper towels. Dredge lightly in flour-herb mixture, shaking off excess. Heat ½ tablespoon oil in large non-stick frying pan until hot. Add half the chicken and brown lightly. Transfer to flameproof casserole. Heat ½ tablespoon oil in pan and brown remaining chicken. Transfer to casserole.

Heat rest of oil in pan and add garlic and vegetables with the exception of watercress. Brown lightly. Add vinegar and cook for 1 minute. Add stock and 120 ml/4 fl oz/½ cup orange juice, together with parsley, sodium-free soya sauce, watercress, cayenne and orange rind. Heat to simmering point, and cook uncovered, for 2 minutes. Pour over chicken. Cover tightly and bake for 50 minutes in preheated 180°C/350°F/Gas mark 4 oven, turning once halfway through cooking.

With slotted spoon, transfer chicken to covered serving dish. Skim off any fat from gravy. Add 60 ml/2 fl oz/¼ cup orange juice. Pour into blender and blend on high speed for 1 minute. Reheat to simmering point. Pour over chicken. Garnish with orange and serve.

Yield: Serves 4

Note: If you're very calorie conscious, you can leave out the flour. Just rub dried chicken with crushed combined herbs and refrigerate for 4 hours before cooking. Then proceed with recipe. Gravy will be unthickened.

CAL	F	P:S	SOD	CAR	CHO
409	12	3.2:1	156	26	26
Unthickened					
359	12	3.2:1	156	14	26

BRUNSWICK STEW

Sparkling vegetables enriching tender chicken.

	Metric	Imperial	American
Unbleached flour	25 g	1 oz	¼ cup
Dried thyme leaves, crushed	¾ tsp	¾ tsp	¾ tsp
Dried rosemary leaves, crushed	¾ tsp	¾ tsp	¾ tsp
Young chicken, cut into serving pieces, skinned	1.5 kg	3 lb	3 lb
Corn oil	2 tbsp	2 tbsp	2 tbsp
Large onion, thinly sliced	1	1	1
Large cloves garlic, finely chopped	3	3	3
Stick celery, diced	1	1	1
Shallot, finely chopped	1	1	1
Leek, white part only, well washed and finely chopped	½	½	½
Small green pepper, finely chopped	1	1	1
Wine vinegar	2 tsp	2 tsp	2 tsp
Fresh tomatoes, cored, skinned and chopped, or 225 g/8 oz canned tomatoes, no salt added	3	3	3
Chicken stock (Page 8)	240 ml	8 fl oz	1 cup

Dry mustard, dissolved in 1 tsp water	½ tsp	½ tsp	½ tsp
Cayenne pepper	4 pinches	4 pinches	4 pinches
Sodium-free soya sauce	1 tsp	1 tsp	1 tsp
Large fresh mushrooms, washed, trimmed and thickly sliced	4	4	4
Carrots, peeled and diced	2	2	2
Swede, peeled and diced	75 g	3 oz	⅓ cup
Potatoes, peeled and diced	2	2	2
Sliver orange peel	1	1	1
Bouquet garni	1	1	1
Fresh corn on the cob, kernels removed	1	1	1
Fresh broad beans, shelled	225 g	8 oz	½ lb

Mix flour with herbs. Pat chicken dry with paper towels. Dredge lightly in flour mixture, shaking off excess. Heat ½ tablespoon oil in non-stick frying pan. Brown half the chicken on both sides, turning carefully with spatula. Transfer to flameproof casserole. Add half tablespoon oil to frying pan and brown rest of chicken. Transfer to casserole. Heat balance of oil in pan until hot. Add onion, garlic, celery, shallot, leek and green pepper. Sauté for 3 minutes. Add vinegar and cook 1 minute. Add tomatoes, stock, mustard, cayenne, sodium-free soya sauce, mushrooms, carrots, swede, potato orange peel and bouquet garni. Bring to boiling point. Pour over chicken. Cover and bake in preheated 180°C/350°F/Gas mark 4 oven for 40 minutes.

Uncover and add corn and broad beans. Simmer on top of stove, re-cover and cook for 15 minutes. Remove orange and bouquet garni, and serve.

Yield: Serves 6

Note: Fresh peas may be substituted for broad beans.

CAL	F	P:S	SOD	CAR	CHO
324	9	3.2:1	129	31	65
With peas					
317	9	3.2:1	129	30	65

CHICKEN CACCIATORE

No chicken cacciatore was ever prepared this way before. In my version, the chicken is sautéed until brown, then baked with rosy, tender tomatoes, snow-white crunchy mushrooms and the spicy herbs of Italy.

	Metric	Imperial	American
Young chicken, cut into serving pieces, skinned	1.5 kg	3 lb	3 lb
Combined dried oregano and basil leaves, crushed	1 tbsp	1 tbsp	1 tbsp
Unbleached flour	40 g	1½ oz	⅓ cup
Corn oil	1½ tbsp	1½ tbsp	1½ tbsp
Large onion, quartered and thinly sliced	1	1	1
Large cloves garlic, finely chopped	3	3	3
Green pepper, finely chopped	½	½	½
Shallots, finely chopped	2	2	2
Wine vinegar	1 tbsp	1 tbsp	1 tbsp
Cider vinegar	1 tbsp	1 tbsp	1 tbsp
Fresh tomatoes, cored, skinned, drained and chopped	2	2	2
Tomato paste, no salt added	1½ tbsp	1½ tbsp	1½ tbsp
Chicken stock (Page 8)	80 ml	3 fl oz	⅓ cup
Cayenne pepper	4 pinches	4 pinches	4 pinches
Bouquet garni	1	1	1
Fresh mushrooms, washed, trimmed and sliced	225 g	8 oz	½ lb
Freshly chopped parsley			

Pat chicken dry with paper towels. Rub with dried herbs. Cover and refrigerate for 2 hours before cooking. When ready to cook, dredge chicken lightly in flour.

Heat 1 tablespoon oil in large heavy frying pan until hot. Add chicken and brown on both sides, turning gently with spatula. Transfer to flameproof casserole.

Add remaining oil to frying pan and heat. Add onion, garlic, green pepper and shallots. Sauté until lightly browned. Add vinegars and cook for 2 minutes. Combine tomatoes with tomato paste. Add to pan together with stock, cayenne and bouquet garni. Bring to simmering point and pour over browned chicken. Cover tightly and bake in preheated 180°C/350°F/Gas mark 4 oven for 20 minutes. Add mushrooms. Re-cover and bake for 25 minutes. Remove from oven. Let casserole stand, covered, for 30 minutes. Remove bouquet garni.

Reheat over low flame. Turn into heated dish and sprinkle with freshly chopped parsley.

Yield: Serves 4

CAL	F	P:S	SOD	CAR	CHO
395	15	3.5:1	146	19	98

MIRACLE CHICKEN

This dish doesn't taste like chicken—and that's a miracle.

	Metric	Imperial	American
Young chicken, cut into serving pieces, skinned	1.5 kg	3 lb	3 lb
Cloves garlic, finely chopped	3	3	3
Corn oil	2 tbsp	2 tbsp	2 tbsp
Dried thyme leaves, crushed	½ tsp	½ tsp	½ tsp
Aubergine, peeled and diced	225 g	8 oz	1 cup
Small leek, white part only, well washed and finely chopped	1	1	1
Onion, finely chopped	1	1	1
Large shallot, finely chopped	1	1	1
Stick celery, finely chopped	1	1	1
Green pepper, finely chopped	½	½	½
Wine vinegar	2 tsp	2 tsp	2 tsp
Chicken stock (Page 8)	240 ml	8 fl oz	1 cup
Brown beef stock (Page 11)	2 tbsp	2 tbsp	2 tbsp
Curry powder, no salt or pepper added	¾ tsp	¾ tsp	¾ tsp
Carrot, peeled and grated	½	½	½
Sliver orange peel	1	1	1
Freshly chopped parsley and dill	2 tbsp	2 tbsp	2 tbsp

Pat chicken dry with paper towels and place in bowl. Mix garlic with 1 tablespoon oil and thyme. Coat chicken with mixture and refrigerate for 4-6 hours.

Heat non-stick frying pan until hot. Add half of the garlic-coated chicken, and sauté until lightly browned on both sides. Transfer to casserole. Brown remaining chicken. Transfer to casserole.

In same frying pan, heat rest of oil until hot. Sauté aubergine until lightly browned, turning constantly. Sprinkle over chicken. In same pan, sauté all vegetables, except carrot, until lightly browned. Add vinegar and cook for 2 minutes. Add stocks, curry and carrot. Heat to simmering point. Cook for 2 minutes, stirring well. Pour over browned ingredients in casserole. Add orange peel, parsley and dill, cover, and bake in preheated 190°C/375°F/Gas mark 5 oven for 30 minutes. Remove from oven, baste and re-cover. Let stand on top of stove without cooking for 10 minutes. Increase oven temperature to 200°C/400°F/Gas mark 6, return casserole to oven, uncovered, and bake for 5 minutes. Turn chicken and baste. Bake uncovered for another 5 minutes. Liquid will have reduced and chicken will have an all-over-brown colour. Remove orange peel, and serve.

Yield: Serves 4

CAL	F	P:S	SOD	CAR	CHO
345	12	3.2:1	159	8	98

CHICKEN MARENGO

At Marengo, two victories were won by Napoleon—one on the battlefield, and the other in the kitchen. The results of the battlefield victory are long forgotten, but the culinary triumph still stirs our hearts—and appetites—today. It's Chicken Marengo, that marvellous stew improvized by Napoleon's chef from whatever he had on hand that day. Here's my version of the dish.

	Metric	Imperial	American
Dried tarragon leaves, crushed	½ tsp	½ tsp	½ tsp
Dried rosemary leaves, crushed	½ tsp	½ tsp	½ tsp
Unbleached flour	50 g	2 oz	½ cup
Young chicken, cut into serving pieces, skinned	1.5 kg	3 lb	3 lb
Corn oil	2 tbsp	2 tbsp	2 tbsp
Small onion, finely chopped	1	1	1
Large cloves garlic, finely chopped	2	2	2
Shallot, finely chopped	1	1	1
Dry Vermouth or white wine	120 ml	4 fl oz	½ cup
Fresh tomatoes, cored, skinned and chopped, or 225 g/8 oz canned tomatoes, no salt added, drained	4	4	4
Chicken stock (Page 8)	120 ml	4 fl oz	½ cup
Sodium-free soya sauce	2 dashes	2 dashes	2 dashes
Carrot, peeled and diced	½	½	½
Cayenne pepper	4 pinches	4 pinches	4 pinches
Sliver orange peel	1	1	1
Small bouquet garni	1	1	1
Fresh mushrooms, washed, trimmed and thickly sliced	100 g	4 oz	¼ lb
Arrowroot, dissolved in 1 tbsp water (optional)	1 tbsp	1 tbsp	1 tbsp
Freshly chopped parsley	1 tbsp	1 tbsp	1 tbsp

Mix dried herbs with flour. Pat chicken dry with paper towels. Dredge chicken in flour mixture, shaking off excess. Heat ½ tablespoon oil in large non-stick frying pan until hot. Add half the chicken and brown lightly on each side. Transfer to flameproof casserole. Heat ½ tablespoon oil in pan until hot. Brown rest of chicken. Transfer to casserole.

Sauté onion, garlic and shallot in ½ tablespoon of oil until softened (about 3 minutes). Add wine and cook for 2 minutes, scraping pan gently, if necessary, to remove browned particles. Add tomatoes, stock, sodium-free soya sauce, carrot and cayenne. Bring to simmering point, and cook for 2 minutes. Pour over chicken. Add orange sliver and bouquet garni. Cover tightly and bake in preheated 180°C/350°F/Gas mark 4 oven for 30 minutes.

Meanwhile wash out frying pan. Heat remaining oil until hot. Add sliced mushrooms and sauté for 3 minutes, turning constantly. Add to chicken when baked for 30 minutes. Re-cover and return chicken to oven for 15 minutes, or until tender.

Remove chicken with slotted spoon and keep warm in covered serving dish. Remove bouquet garni and orange peel, and discard. Place casserole over medium high heat and bring to boil. Reduce heat and simmer for 1 minute. For a slightly thicker gravy, add arrowroot mixture, a little at a time, to hot gravy, stirring constantly. Pour over chicken. Sprinkle with freshly chopped parsley and serve.

Yield: Serves 4

CAL	F	P:S	SOD	CAR	CHO
399	10	2.8:1	144	22	98
Thickened					
405	10	2.8:1	144	23	98

TURKEY SUPREME

There are always leftovers when you serve turkey. Here's a way to use them to make a highly original dish that may become more popular in your household than the turkey itself.

	Metric	Imperial	American
Corn oil	2 tbsp	2 tbsp	2 tbsp
Onion, finely chopped	1	1	1
Large cloves garlic, finely chopped	2	2	2
Large shallot, finely chopped	1	1	1
Small green pepper, finely chopped	1	1	1
Dry Vermouth or white wine	120 ml	4 fl oz	½ cup
Rice	75 g	3 oz	½ cup
Chicken or veal stock (Page 8)	750 ml	1¼ pt	3 cups
Tomato paste, no salt added	2 tbsp	2 tbsp	2 tbsp
Curry powder, no salt or pepper added	1½ tsp	1½ tsp	1½ tsp
Small bouquet garni	1	1	1
Corn oil to oil casserole	½ tsp	½ tsp	½ tsp
Fresh mushrooms, washed, trimmed and quartered	100 g	4 oz	¼ lb
Cooked turkey, diced	680 g	1½ lb	3 cups
Fresh peas, shelled and cooked	225 g	8 oz	½ lb
Freshly chopped parsley	1 tbsp	1 tbsp	1 tbsp

Heat 1 tablespoon oil in non-stick frying pan until hot. Add onion, garlic, shallot and green pepper, and sauté until tender (about 5 minutes). Add wine. Cook and stir over high heat for 1 minute. Add rice and stir well to coat. Add stock, tomato paste, curry and bouquet garni. Bring to simmering point. Pour into lightly oiled 2-litre/3.5-pint/2-quart casserole. Cover and bake in preheated 200°C/400°F/Gas mark 6 oven for 25 minutes.

Meanwhile wipe out frying pan. Heat remaining oil until hot. Add mushrooms and sauté for 2 minutes, turning constantly. Add turkey and sauté only until heated through. After rice mixture has been cooking for 25 minutes, add turkey-mushroom mixture, stirring well. Return casserole to oven, covered, and bake 10 minutes, or until rice is tender and all liquid is absorbed. Uncover, remove bouquet garni, and stir in cooked peas, distributing evenly. Sprinkle with freshly chopped parsley and serve.

Yield: Serves 4

Note: Start to cook peas 15 minutes before you are ready to take casserole from oven. In that way they will not wrinkle and will retain their bright green colour.

CAL	F	P:S	SOD	CAR	CHO
265	6	3.7:1	57	39	17

STUFFED ROAST TURKEY WITH GIBLET GRAVY

This succulent bird is lower in saturated fats than chicken, and it's economical because you can use leftovers in so many intriguing ways.

	Metric	Imperial	American
For the turkey:			
Whole fresh turkey	2.75 kg	6 lb	6 lb
Dried sage leaves, crushed	1 tsp	1 tsp	1 tsp
Dried thyme leaves, crushed	1 tsp	1 tsp	1 tsp
Dried rosemary leaves, crushed	½ tsp	½ tsp	½ tsp
Several pinches cayenne pepper			
Recipe for stuffing, doubled (Page 65)			
Corn oil	1 tbsp	1 tbsp	1 tbsp
For the giblets:			
Giblets from turkey, except heart. Set liver aside for stuffing			

Small whole onion, peeled	1	1	1
Cloves garlic, finely chopped	2	2	2
Dried thyme leaves, crushed	½ tsp	½ tsp	½ tsp
Carrot, peeled	½	½	½
Stick celery, cut in half	½	½	½
Bouquet garni, made with 2 sprigs parsley, ½ bay leaf and ½ teaspoon fennel, tied together in muslin	1	1	1
Chicken stock (Page 8)	240 ml	8 fl oz	1 cup
Water	240 ml	8 fl oz	1 cup
For the gravy:			
Chopped cooked giblets			
Jellied liquid, fat removed			
Chicken stock	450 ml	¾ pt	2 cups
Corn oil	2 tbsp	2 tbsp	2 tbsp
Unbleached flour	1½ tbsp	1½ tbsp	1½ tbsp
Low-fat milk	60 ml	2 fl oz	¼ cup
Cayenne pepper	3-4 pinches	3-4 pinches	3-4 pinches
Sodium-free soya sauce	3 dashes	3 dashes	3 dashes
Combined powdered sage and thyme	½ tsp	½ tsp	½ tsp

Remove giblets from cavity. Wash and set aside. Wash turkey inside and out. Dry well with paper towels. Prick skin all over with sharp-pronged fork. Rub with combined herbs. Sprinkle with cayenne. Cover with foil while stuffing is prepared.

Prepare stuffing by doubling recipe. Stuff cavity, packing loosely. Secure with skewers. Truss bird. Place on rack in roasting tin. Dip pastry brush in oil and brush turkey on all sides. Cover with heavy duty foil. Place in centre of preheated 180°C/350°F/Gas mark 4 oven, and roast for 1½ hours. Remove foil and roast for 45 minutes. Brush again with oil. Roast for an additional 30-45 minutes. Brush again with oil. Roast for an additional 30-45 minutes. Test to see if it's cooked in the following way: prick turkey near bottom of thigh; juices should not run pink. If they do, return to oven for another 15 minutes. Let stand for 20 minutes, covered, before carving. Serve with stuffing and giblet gravy.

Cook giblets the day before turkey is roasted so that all fat can be removed. Place giblets in heavy-bottomed saucepan. Add 250 ml/8 fl oz/1 cup water. Bring to boil. Reduce heat and simmer, uncovered, for 5 minutes, removing scum that rises to top. Add remaining ingredients. Bring to simmering point. Cover partially and simmer for 2 hours, adding more water, if necessary, so that giblets are barely covered throughout cooking time. Remove giblets with slotted spoon to small bowl. Strain liquid into jar, discarding vegetables and bouquet garni. Cover the giblet and liquid and refrigerate overnight. Next day remove fat that rises to top of liquid. Liquid and giblets are now ready for gravy.

For the gravy, chop up soft section of gizzard and discard remainder. Pull off meat from neck and chop. Reheat jellied liquid and set aside. Heat corn oil in heavy-bottomed saucepan until hot but not smoking. Add flour and beat with wire whisk. Turn heat down and cook for 1 minute. Add reheated liquid to roux (flour and oil) a little at a time, using whisk to blend. Add milk, cayenne, sodium-free soya sauce, sage and thyme. Finally, add chopped giblets and simmer, uncovered, for 5 minutes. Serve in sauceboat.

Yield: Turkey serves 8; gravy yields about 450 ml/¾ pt/2 cups; allow 2 tablespoons per serving.

Notes:

1. Say no to frozen birds that are injected with butter or other fat, salt and other ingredients, you prefer to avoid.

2. Substitute turkey for chicken in the following recipes: Chicken Divan (Page 57), Chef Salad (Page 101) and Bombay Chicken Balls (Page 116). Turkey Supreme is also made from leftovers (see Page 71).

CAL	F	P:S	SOD	CAR	CHO
229	12	2.5:1	186	0	89
Gravy					
56	3	4.5:1	32	6	0
Stuffing					
142	0	—	32	28	16

MEAT

BEEF BOURGUIGNON

Here's my version of this classic French gourmet masterpiece which is safe for weight watchers. You'll find it as authentic in appearance as it is in taste. For true lovers of French food.

	Metric	Imperial	American
Beef topside, cut into 7.5-cm/3-inch chunks	680 g	1½ lb	1½ lb
Unbleached flour	3-4 tbsp	3-4 tbsp	3-4 tbsp
Corn oil	2 tbsp	2 tbsp	2 tbsp
Onions, finely chopped	2	2	2
Large cloves garlic, finely chopped	3	3	3
Large shallot, finely chopped	1	1	1
Dry sherry	2 tbsp	2 tbsp	2 tbsp
Tomato paste, no salt added	2 tbsp	2 tbsp	2 tbsp
Beef stock (Page 10)	360 ml	12½ fl oz	1½ cups
Brown beef stock (Page 11)	3 tbsp	3 tbsp	3 tbsp
Burgundy wine	180 ml	6 fl oz	¾ cup
Dried thyme leaves, crushed	½ tsp	½ tsp	½ tsp
Dried rosemary leaves, crushed	½ tsp	½ tsp	½ tsp
Small bouquet garni	1	1	1
Fresh mushrooms, washed, trimmed and thickly sliced	225 g	8 oz	½ lb

Wipe meat well with paper towels. Dredge in flour, shaking off excess. Heat ½ tablespoon oil in large non-stick frying pan until very hot but not smoking. Brown half the meat on all sides. Transfer to flame-proof casserole. Add ½ tablespoon oil to frying pan, and brown remaining meat. Transfer to casserole.

Add onions, garlic and shallot to pan and sauté until lightly browned, adding a drop or two more oil if necessary. Add sherry, and scrape pan to loosen browned particles. Blend tomato paste with beef stock and brown beef stock and add to pan. Pour in Burgundy wine and stir. Add herbs and bring to simmering point. Pour over browned meat in casserole and add bouquet garni. Simmer, uncovered, on top of stove for 5 minutes, stirring well so that meat does not stick.

Cook meat in centre of preheated 120°C/250°F/Gas mark ½ oven, covered, for 1¼ hours. Uncover and stir. If liquid is thickening too fast at this point, add a little water. Re-cover and bake for another 1½ hours, adding more water halfway through cooking if necessary.

While meat is in the oven, wipe out pan and add rest of oil, heating until hot. Sauté mushrooms until lightly browned. after meat has cooked a total of 2½ hours, uncover and add mushrooms. Return covered casserole to oven and bake 15-30 minutes, or until meat is tender, taking care that meat does not stick to casserole. Remove bouquet garni.

Serve immediately with Parsleyed Potatoes (Page 20) or rice, flecked with a sprinkling of chopped fresh parsley.

Yield: Serves 4 with one portion left over

CAL	F	P:S	SOD	CAR	CHO
294	12	3.2:1	113	10	81
Rice					
43	0	—	0	10	0

STEAK PIZZAIOLA

Start with one of the leanest of all beef cuts, sirloin; brush with a light garlic marinade, and grill to perfection—that's my version of one of the most delectable of Italian dishes. Serve with a Risotto (Page 28) and salad.

	Metric	Imperial	American
Sirloin steak including fillet, sliced 2.5-cm/1-inch thick	1.5 kg	3 lb	3 lb
Large shallot, finely chopped	1	1	1
Large cloves garlic, finely chopped	2	2	2
Corn oil	1 tbsp	1 tbsp	1 tbsp
Dried thyme leaves, crushed	½ tsp	½ tsp	½ tsp
Freshly chopped parsley	1 tbsp	1 tbsp	1 tbsp
Cayenne pepper	5 pinches	5 pinches	5 pinches
Wine vinegar	½ tsp	½ tsp	½ tsp
Sodium-free soya sauce	⅛ tsp	⅛ tsp	⅛ tsp

Let steak stand at room temperature for 30 minutes before grilling. Wipe dry with paper towels. For the marinade, combine remaining ingredients in a small bowl and blend well.

Preheat grill. Brush half marinade over one side of steak. Place under grill 4 cm/1½ inches from flame and grill for 7 minutes. Turn and spread rest of marinade over second side. Grill another 7 minutes. Turn again, basting with marinade, and grill for 10 minutes, 5 minutes on each side. The steak will be medium rare. Serve immediately.

Yield: Serves 6

CAL	F	P:S	SOD	CAR	CHO
314	12	1.6:1	126	0	135

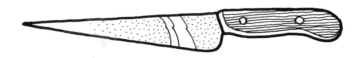

SWISS STEAK

In this dish, herbed slices of lean beef are bathed in a mushroom-enriched gravy. It is made to order for contemporary living for it freezes well and is as delicious the second time around.

	Metric	Imperial	American
Beef, rump or topside	1.25 kg	2½ lb	2½ lb
Unbleached flour	4 tbsp	4 tbsp	4 tbsp
Corn oil	2 tbsp	2 tbsp	2 tbsp
Onions, finely chopped	2	2	2
Large cloves garlic, finely chopped	3	3	3
Large shallot, finely chopped	1	1	1
Water	2 tbsp	2 tbsp	2 tbsp
Dry Vermouth or white wine	60 ml	2 fl oz	¼ cup
Dried oregano leaves, crushed	½ tsp	½ tsp	½ tsp
Dried basil leaves, crushed	½ tsp	½ tsp	½ tsp
Large fresh tomatoes, cored and skinned, or 225 g/8 oz canned tomatoes, no salt added	2	2	2
Tomato paste, no salt added	1 tbsp	1 tbsp	1 tbsp
Tomato juice, no salt added	120 ml	4 fl oz	½ cup
Beef stock (Page 10)	60 ml	2 fl oz	¼ cup
Brown beef stock (Page 11)	2 tbsp	2 tbsp	2 tbsp
Cayenne pepper	4 pinches	4 pinches	4 pinches
Carrot, peeled and grated	½	½	½
Caraway seeds, lightly crushed	1 tsp	1 tsp	1 tsp
Large bouquet garni	1	1	1
Large fresh mushrooms, washed, trimmed and sliced	6	6	6
Freshly chopped parsley	1 tbsp	1 tbsp	1 tbsp

Wipe meat dry with paper towels. Cut into 1-cm/⅜-inch slices. There should be 8 slices in all. (Cutting suggestion: To facilitate easier slicing, freeze uncooked meat. The night before using, remove from freezing compartment and place in refrigerator. Next day, remove from refrigerator and leave at room temperature for 1 hour. Slice.) Dredge lightly in flour, shaking off excess. Heat enough oil to lightly coat bottom of large non-stick frying pan. Add meat and brown two to three slices at a time, on both sides, until golden brown, turning carefully with spatula so that coating does not separate from meat. If necessary, add more oil for browning second and third batch. Transfer browned meat to flameproof casserole. (Do not use glass as meat sticks to it.)

Add a few drops oil to frying pan. Brown onions, garlic and shallot. Add water and scrape around pan to loosen browned particles. Add wine and cook over high heat for 2 minutes. Add herbs, tomatoes, tomato paste, tomato juice, stocks, cayenne, carrot, caraway seeds and bouquet garni. Simmer for 5 minutes. Pour over meat and cover tightly. Place in preheated 180°C/350°F/Gas mark 4 oven and bake for 1 hour, removing from oven once to move pieces of meat around casserole to prevent sticking. Remove from oven and add sliced mushrooms. Re-cover and bake for another 25 minutes.

Remove from oven and let stand on top of stove, covered, for 15 minutes. Place meat on serving platter without gravy, removing slices with slotted spoon or spatula. Whisk gravy around casserole until well blended. pour over meat. sprinkle liberally with freshly chopped parsley.

Yield: Serves 6

CAL	F	P:S	SOD	CAR	CHO
339	14	2.2:1	139	9	133

SWEET AND SAUERBRATEN

In my version of this traditional German dish, lean tender beef is marinated in pickling spices, lemon juice and apple juice. It's served in a cream sauce that's as tangy as it's smooth. Preparation is simple, so if you want to show off your mastery of Teutonic cooking effortlessly, this is the recipe for you.

	Metric	Imperial	American
Pickling spices, no salt added	50 g	2 oz	¼ cup
Large sprigs parsley, washed and dried	4	4	4
Corn oil	2 tbsp	2 tbsp	2 tbsp
Large cloves garlic, finely chopped	2	2	2
Onion, coarsely chopped	225 g	8 oz	1 cup
Sticks celery, finely chopped	2	2	2
Carrot, peeled and diced	½	½	½
Unsweetened apple juice	450 ml	¾ pt	2 cups
Cayenne pepper	5 pinches	5 pinches	5 pinches
Thyme leaves, crushed	½ tsp	½ tsp	½ tsp
Juice of 2 lemons			
Grated lemon rind	1 tsp	1 tsp	1 tsp
Beef, rump or topside	1.5 kg	3 lb	3 lb
Enough boiling water to cover meat			

In preparing marinade, check pickling spices to see if it includes bay leaf and cloves. If not, add 1 bay leaf and 8 cloves. Tie spices in small piece of muslin. Tie parsley sprigs with white thread in a separate bunch. Set both bunches aside.

Heat 1 tablespoon oil in non-stick frying pan until hot. Add garlic, onions, celery and carrot. Sauté until lightly browned. Add apple juice and bring to boil. Add cayenne, thyme, lemon juice, rind and pickling spices. Reduce heat and simmer for 5 minutes.

Wipe meat dry with paper towels. Trim away all fat. Place meat in deep, narrow container (stainless steel or glass, not plastic). Pour hot marinade over meat. Add enough boiling water to cover meat. (The narrower the pot the less diluted the marinade.) Cover and refrigerate for 3 days, turning once daily.

When ready to cook, remove meat from marinade, reserving liquid. Wipe meat dry. Heat remaining oil in flameproof casserole until hot. Brown meat well on all sides. Pour off any excess oil. Measure out 450 ml/ ¾ pt/2 cups marinade and vegetables and add to casserole. Add bunch parsley. Heat to boiling point on top of stove, skimming off scum that rises to top. Cover, and bake in preheated 160°C/325°F/Gas mark 3 oven for 2½-3 hours. (There should be about 350 ml/12 fl oz/1½ cups liquid in casserole at all times. If not, add some reserved marinade.) Test with long-pronged fork to see if it's cooked. Meat should be very tender.

Remove meat from casserole and slice with very sharp knife. Transfer to heated serving dish and keep warm. Discard parsley. Pour contents of casserole into blender and purée until smooth. Pour back into a saucepan and reheat. Pour heated gravy over sliced meat, and serve.

Yield: Serves 6

Variations:

1. Dissolve 1 tablespoon arrowroot in 1 tablespoon water. Sprinkle into hot gravy, whisking constantly until thickened to desired consistency. Pour over meat.

2. Add 3 tablespoons low-fat yogurt to gravy, whisking well. Bring to simmering point, and pour over meat.

CAL	F	P:S	SOD	CAR	CHO
321	14	1.3:1	198	3	135
Thickened					
325	14	1.3:1	198	4	135
With yogurt					
327	14+	1.2:1	198	4	135

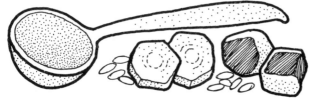

SAUTÉED ESCALOPES OF VEAL

Veal escalopes are thin slices (2-cm/¾-inch thick) cut from the fillet—the most expensive cut of veal. So if you're in an extravagant mood, treat your family or friends to this delicious dish.

	Metric	Imperial	American
Veal escalopes (about 500 g/1¼ lb)	8	8	8
Unbleached flour	2 tbsp	2 tbsp	2 tbsp
Corn oil	2 tbsp	2 tbsp	2 tbsp
Large cloves garlic, finely chopped	2	2	2
Stick celery, finely chopped	½	½	½
Large shallot, finely chopped	1	1	1
Dry Vermouth or white wine	60 ml	2 fl oz	¼ cup
Grated carrot	1 tsp	1 tsp	1 tsp
Veal or chicken stock (Pages 10 and 8)	150 ml	¼ pt	⅔ cup
Tomato paste, no salt added	1 tsp	1 tsp	1 tsp
Dried rosemary leaves, crushed	½ tsp	½ tsp	½ tsp
Large sprig parsley	1	1	1
Slice orange peel	1	1	1
Cayenne pepper	4 pinches	4 pinches	4 pinches
Sodium-free soya sauce	4 dashes	4 dashes	4 dashes
Freshly chopped parsley			

Wipe meat dry with paper towels. Dredge with flour, shaking off excess. Heat oil in large heavy frying pan until hot. Add veal and sauté on both sides until lightly browned (about 8 minutes). Add garlic, celery and shallot, and sauté for 1 minute. Add wine. Cook for 1 minute. Add remaining ingredients, except chopped parsley. Cover and simmer until tender (about 25 minutes), turning twice. Discard orange peel and parsley sprig.

Place meat on heated individual plates, and spoon over sauce. Sprinkle with chopped parsley, and serve. Delicious accompanied by Parsleyed Potatoes (Page 20) and any green vegetables.

Yield: Serves 4

CAL	F	P:S	SOD	CAR	CHO
299	15	1.5:1	117	3	103
With veal stock					
299	15	1.5:1	129	3	103

BRAISED BONED AND ROLLED LEG OF VEAL

Serve this delicious dish in three ways. Hot, cold in thin slices, or as a tasty Veal Salad (Page 99).

	Metric	Imperial	American
Piece of leg of veal, boned, rolled and tied	1.25 kg	2½ lb	2½ lb
Unbleached flour	2 tbsp	2 tbsp	2 tbsp
Corn oil	2 tbsp	2 tbsp	2 tbsp
Onion, thinly sliced	1	1	1
Shallots, finely chopped	2	2	2
Cloves garlic, finely chopped	3	3	3
Stick celery, finely chopped	1	1	1
Carrot, peeled and thinly sliced	1	1	1
Small green pepper, finely chopped	1	1	1
Cayenne pepper	6 pinches	6 pinches	6 pinches
Dried rosemary leaves, crushed	½ tsp	½ tsp	½ tsp
Dried thyme leaves, crushed	½ tsp	½ tsp	½ tsp
Tomato, cored and coarsely chopped	1	1	1
Small bouquet garni	1	1	1
Veal stock (Page 10)	120 ml	4 fl oz	½ cup
Tomato juice, no salt added	180 ml	6 fl oz	¾ cup
Dry Vermouth or white wine	60 ml	2 fl oz	¼ cup

Wipe meat dry with paper towels. Dredge lightly with flour, shaking off excess. Heat oil in large flame-proof casserole until hot. Add meat and brown on all sides. Remove from casserole.

Arrange onion, shallots, garlic, celery, carrot and green pepper over bottom of casserole in one layer. Place browned meat on top of vegetable mixture. Sprinkle with cayenne and dried herbs. Add chopped tomato and bouquet garni. Pour stock and 120 ml/ 4 fl oz/½ cup tomato juice over meat. Bring to simmering point. Cover and bake in preheated 160°C/325°F/ Gas mark 3 oven for 1 hour. Remove from oven and baste, adding more juice if liquid has evaporated. There should be 180 ml/6 fl oz/¾ cup liquid in casserole at all times. Return to oven and bake for another hour, basting halfway through cooking, and adding more juice if necessary. Test to see if it's cooked by inserting long-pronged fork into middle of roast. Meat should be tender yet firm. Place meat on platter and cover to keep warm.

Pour remaining contents of casserole into measuring cup or jug. Add enough tomato juice to make 250 ml/8 fl oz/1 cup. Return to casserole together with wine. Bring to boil. Reduce heat and simmer until liquid is reduced to 180 ml/6 fl oz/¾ cup. Pour into blender and purée for 1 minute. Reheat over low flame.

Slice meat thinly and serve sauce in a sauceboat. Spoon over meat. Serve with Risotto or a selection from my recipe for Broccoli Magic (Pages 28 and 17).

Yield: Serves 6

CAL	F	P:S	SOD	CAR	CHO
201	10	2.8:1	107	7	134

STUFFED VEAL

This lowest-calorie of all veal cuts is delicious when it's bathed in a herbed marinade and stuffed with full-kernelled kasha. A sumptuous looking dish, it more than satisfies the heartiest appetite.

	Metric	Imperial	American
For the stuffing:			
Corn oil	1/2 tsp	1/2 tsp	1/2 tsp
Large cloves garlic, finely chopped	2	2	2
Onion, finely chopped	1	1	1
Shallot, finely chopped	1	1	1
Wine vinegar	1/2 tsp	1/2 tsp	1/2 tsp
Dry Vermouth or white wine	120 ml	4 fl oz	1/2 cup
Water	60 ml	2 fl oz	1/4 cup
Freshly chopped dill	1 tsp	1 tsp	1 tsp
Dried thyme leaves, crushed	1/4 tsp	1/4 tsp	1/4 tsp
Cayenne pepper	3 pinches	3 pinches	3 pinches
Veal stock (Page 10)	240 ml	8 fl oz	1 cup
Kasha (buckwheat oats)	230 g	8 oz	1 1/4 cups
Egg white, lightly beaten with fork	1	1	1
Carrot, peeled and grated	1/2	1/2	1/2
For the meat:			
Slices boneless veal, cut from the leg, 5-mm/1/4-inch thick, thinly beaten (about 900 g/2 lb)	3	3	3
Tomato juice, no salt added	450 ml	3/4 pt	2 cups
Veal stock (Page 10)	120 ml	4 fl oz	1/2 cup
For the marinade:			
Cider vinegar	3 tbsp	3 tbsp	3 tbsp
Corn oil	1 tbsp	1 tbsp	1 tbsp
Cloves garlic, finely chopped	3	3	3
Shallots, finely chopped	2	2	2
Freshly chopped dill	1 tsp	1 tsp	1 tsp
Dried rosemary leaves, crushed	1/2 tsp	1/2 tsp	1/2 tsp
Dried thyme leaves, crushed	1/2 tsp	1/2 tsp	1/2 tsp
Cayenne pepper	3 pinches	3 pinches	3 pinches

Prepare stuffing first. Heat oil in large non-stick frying pan until hot. Add garlic, onion and shallot, and sauté until lightly brown. Add vinegar, wine and water, and cook over medium heat for 1 minute. Add herbs, pepper, stock and kasha (buckwheat), and bring to simmering point. Cover and cook for 6-8 minutes, or until all liquid is absorbed. Uncover and let cool. Add egg white and carrot. Blend. Set aside.

Wipe meat dry with paper towels. Arrange slices of meat on board alongside each other lengthwise, overlapping edges. Pound seams to hold together. Mix marinade ingredients together and brush over meat. Spoon and spread stuffing over meat leaving bare 2.5 cm/1 inch from all edges. Roll up firmly. Tie meat securely in several places. Brush all over with marinade. Place in large flameproof casserole. Cover and refrigerate for 4-5 hours.

Remove meat from marinade and dry. Pour off marinade and discard. Heat casserole until hot. Add rolled meat and brown lightly on all sides. Add 240 ml/8 fl oz/1 cup tomato juice and veal stock. Bring to simmering point on top of stove. Cover and bake in preheated 180°C/350°F/Gas mark 4 oven for 20 minutes. Uncover, and add 120 ml/4 fl oz/1/2 cup tomato juice, and return to oven, uncovered. Bake for 40 minutes, basting from time to time, and turning once. Cover, and leave on top of stove for 20 minutes before carving. Transfer to heated serving dish and keep warm. Pour remaining contents of casserole into measuring cup or jug. Add enough tomato juice to equal 240 ml/8 fl oz/1 cup. Heat to simmering point.

Slice meat and serve with gravy spooned over each slice.

Yield: Serves 8

Note: This dish is particularly delicious served cold the next day. It can be thinly sliced and served on sandwich bread, or on a bed of lettuce, as a salad.

CAL	F	P:S	SOD	CAR	CHO
102	5	1.6:1	125	2	85
Stuffing					
80	1	4.5:1	19	15	0

BRAISED VEAL

The enjoyment of food begins when you look at a dish. And here's one dish with a palette of colours—pink veal, orange carrots, pale red sauce, and bright green peas—that's a delight to the eye.

	Metric	Imperial	American
Best end of neck veal, cut into 2.5-cm/1-inch slices, well trimmed	1.5 kg	3 lb	3 lb
Unbleached flour	2 tbsp	2 tbsp	2 tbsp
Corn oil	2 tbsp	2 tbsp	2 tbsp
Large cloves garlic, finely chopped	3	3	3
Stick celery, diced	1	1	1
Onion, finely chopped	1	1	1
Shallots, finely chopped	3	3	3
Water	180 ml	6 fl oz	¾ cup
Dry Vermouth or white wine	180 ml	6 fl oz	¾ cup
Baby carrots, each cut in half	4	4	4
Veal stock (Page 10)	120 ml	4 fl oz	½ cup
Tomato purée, no salt added	180 ml	6 fl oz	¾ cup
Tomato paste, no salt added	1½ tbsp	1½ tbsp	1½ tbsp
Cayenne pepper	3 pinches	3 pinches	3 pinches
Dried thyme leaves, crushed	¾ tsp	¾ tsp	¾ tsp
Dried basil leaves, crushed	¾ tsp	¾ tsp	¾ tsp
Bouquet garni	1	1	1
Dried mint leaves, crushed	1 tsp	1 tsp	1 tsp
Fresh peas, shelled and cooked	225 g	8 oz	½ lb
Freshly chopped parsley			

Wipe meat dry with paper towels. Dredge lightly with flour, shaking off excess. Heat 1 tablespoon oil in large non-stick frying pan until hot. Brown meat on all sides, turning carefully with spatula. Transfer meat to casserole.

Add remaining oil to frying pan, and sauté garlic, celery, onion and shallots, until lightly browned. Add water, scraping pan to loosen browned particles. Add wine and bring to simmering point. Cook for 3 minutes. Add carrots, stock, tomato purée, tomato paste, cayenne, thyme and basil, and bouquet garni. Bring to simmering point and cook for 3 minutes.

Pour over meat. Sprinkle with mint leaves. Place in centre of preheated 160°C/325°F/Gas mark 3 oven and cook for 1 hour, stirring once halfway through cooking, or until meat is tender. Remove from oven and set aside.

Cook shelled peas in rapidly boiling water to cover for 10 minutes. Colour should remain bright green. Drain and add to casserole, stirring gently. Sprinkle with freshly chopped parsley.

Yield: Serves 4

CAL	F	P:S	SOD	CAR	CHO
370	15	2.1:1	187	16	159

BAKED HERBED VEAL CHOPS

Veal, the lowest in fat of all meats, can be prepared in many simple yet exciting ways because it so readily takes on the flavours of herbs and spices. If you have an adventurous streak, there's no reason why you can't add a variety of veal dishes to your menu.

	Metric	Imperial	American
Loin veal chops, (about 680 g/1½ lb) well trimmed	4	4	4
Dried thyme leaves, crushed	½ tsp	½ tsp	½ tsp
Dried sage leaves, crushed	½ tsp	½ tsp	½ tsp
Corn oil	1 tbsp	1 tbsp	1 tbsp
Shallots, finely chopped	3	3	3
Onion, finely chopped	1	1	1
Green pepper, parboiled and finely chopped	½	½	½
Cloves garlic, finely chopped	3	3	3
Dry Vermouth or white wine	60 ml	2 fl oz	¼ cup
Veal stock (Page 10)	120 ml	4 fl oz	½ cup
Tomato paste, no salt added	1 tbsp	1 tbsp	1 tbsp
Bay leaf	1	1	1
Cayenne pepper	3 pinches	3 pinches	3 pinches
Sodium-free soya sauce	2 dashes	2 dashes	2 dashes
Freshly chopped parsley			

Wipe chops dry with paper towels. Rub with dried herbs and let stand, covered, at room temperature for 1 hour.

Heat half the oil in large heavy frying pan until hot. Brown chops lightly on both sides. Transfer to shallow roasting tin.

Heat remaining oil in pan until hot. Add vegetables and garlic and brown lightly. Add wine and cook for 2 minutes. Combine stock with tomato paste. Add to pan. Add bay leaf, cayenne and sodium-free soya sauce. Simmer for 1 minute.

Pour sauce over chops. Cover with foil and bake in preheated 180°C/350°F/Gas mark 4 oven for 45 minutes, turning once halfway through cooking, or until chops are tender.

Arrange chops on heated serving platter. Pour sauce over. Sprinkle with parsley and serve.

Yield: Serves 4

CAL	F	P:S	SOD	CAR	CHO
366	12	2.0:1	165	4	120

VEAL LOAF WITH CREAMY MUSHROOM SAUCE

The delicate mushroom sauce with its muted accents of shallot and garlic makes a happy marriage with the herb-flavoured veal.

	Metric	Imperial	American
Corn oil	2 tbsp	2 tbsp	2 tbsp
Onion, finely chopped	1	1	1
Large cloves garlic, finely chopped	2	2	2
Stick celery, finely chopped	½	½	½
Shallot, finely chopped	1	1	1
Fresh mushrooms, washed, trimmed and sliced	100 g	4 oz	¼ lb
Lean veal, minced	680 g	1½ lb	1½ lb
Bread crumbs (Page 145)	60 g	2½ oz	1¼ cups
Dried basil leaves, crushed	¼ tsp	¼ tsp	¼ tsp
Dried thyme leaves, crushed	¼ tsp	¼ tsp	¼ tsp
Dried sage leaves, crushed	¼ tsp	¼ tsp	¼ tsp

baked pears in red wine—see page 119

Freshly chopped dill and parsley	2 tbsp	2 tbsp	2 tbsp
Cayenne pepper	3 pinches	3 pinches	3 pinches
Low-fat milk	60 ml	2 fl oz	¼ cup
Egg white, beaten lightly with fork	1	1	1
Sodium-free soya sauce	2 dashes	2 dashes	2 dashes
Corn oil to oil baking dish	½ tsp	½ tsp	½ tsp

Heat oil in large heavy frying pan until very warm but not smoking. Add onion, garlic, celery and shallot, and cook for 2 minutes, turing constantly. Increase heat and add mushrooms. Shake pan until cooked through lightly (about 3 minutes). Pour into bowl and let cool.

Add veal, crumbs, herbs and cayenne to sautéed mixture and blend well. Add milk, egg white, sodium-free soya sauce and blend again.

Lightly oil a rectangular baking dish. Shape meat into loaf approximately 20 × 10 cm/8 ×4 inches, pressing together with hands. Do not use loaf tin. Bake in preheated 180°C/350°F/Gas mark 4 oven for 15 minutes. Remove from oven and pour off any fat that may have dripped from meat. Return to oven and bake for another 35 minutes. Let cool for 5 minutes.

Cut into serving slices and serve topped with creamy mushroom sauce.

	Metric	Imperial	American
Creamy mushroom sauce:			
Corn oil	2 tbsp	2 tbsp	2 tbsp
Shallots, finely chopped	2	2	2
Clove garlic, finely chopped	1	1	1
Fresh mushrooms, washed, trimmed and sliced	100 g	4 oz	¼ lb
Dry Vermouth or white wine	60 ml	2 fl oz	¼ cup
Arrowroot	1½ tbsp	1½ tbsp	1½ tbsp
Veal or chicken stock (Pages 10 and 8)	300 ml	½ pt	1¼ cups
Dried basil leaves, crushed	¼ tsp	¼ tsp	¼ tsp
Dried thyme leaves, crushed	¼ tsp	¼ tsp	¼ tsp

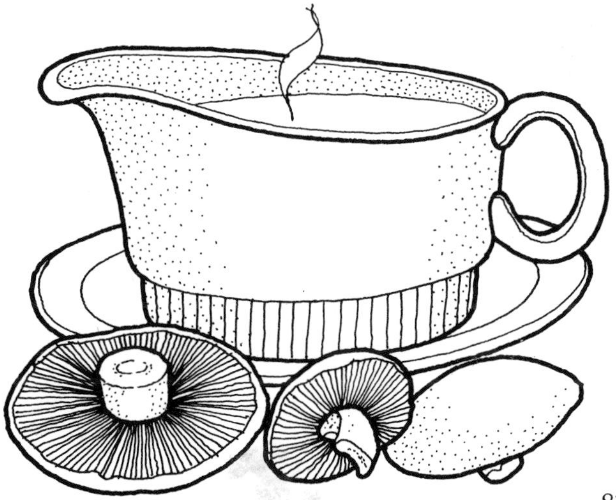

pineapple chiffon pie—see page 126

Freshly chopped dill and parsley	2 tbsp	2 tbsp	2 tbsp
Low-fat milk	240-300 ml	8-10 fl oz	1-1¼ cups

Heat 1 tablespoon oil in large non-stick frying pan until hot. Add shallots and garlic and sauté for 1 minute. Add mushrooms and sauté for 3 minutes, turning constantly. Add wine and cook over medium high heat until wine is almost evaporated. Pour into bowl and set aside.

Heat remaining oil in heavy-bottomed saucepan until hot. Add flour all at once, beating rapidly with wire whisk until well blended. Reduce heat. Add stock and continue whisking until thickened and smooth. Whisk in herbs and milk. Add sautéed mushroom mixture. Bring to simmering point, and simmer very gently for 2 minutes. Serve.

Yield: Loaf serves 6; about 600 ml/1 pt/2½ cups sauce; allow 4 tablespoons per serving. There will be leftover sauce.

Notes:

1. This sauce is adaptable to many dishes such as fish, prawns and chicken.
2. See note for Light Meat Loaf (Page 91).

CAL	F	P:S	SOD	CAR	CHO
192	4	1:1	129	9	102
Sauce					
54	0	—	22	2	0

VEAL STEW WITH TOMATOES AND MUSHROOMS

This is a light and delicate version of a hearty stew that's popular in the small auberges that dot the French countryside. It has a flavour all its own. It's an excellent dish to make when you're expecting guests because it can be prepared a day in advance and slowly reheated before dinner.

	Metric	Imperial	American
Stewing veal, cut into 2.5-cm/1-inch chunks, trimmed	1.25 kg	2½ lb	2½ lb
Corn oil	2 tbsp	2 tbsp	2 tbsp
Onion, finely chopped	1	1	1
Stick celery, finely chopped	½	½	½
Large cloves garlic, finely chopped	3	3	3
Green pepper, finely chopped	½	½	½
Large shallots, finely chopped	2	2	2
Dry Vermouth or white wine	180 ml	6 fl oz	¾ cup
Veal stock (Page 10)	80 ml	3 fl oz	⅓ cup
Dried rosemary leaves, crushed	1 tsp	1 tsp	1 tsp
Dried thyme leaves, crushed	½ tsp	½ tsp	½ tsp
Grated orange rind	2 tsp	2 tsp	2 tsp
Fresh tomatoes, cored, skinned and coarsely chopped, or 225 g/8 oz canned tomatoes, no salt added	3	3	3
Tomato paste, no salt added	2 tbsp	2 tbsp	2 tbsp
Cayenne pepper	3 pinches	3 pinches	3 pinches
Small bouquet garni	1	1	1
Large fresh mushrooms, washed, trimmed and sliced	8	8	8
Freshly chopped parsley			

Dry meat thoroughly with paper towels. Trim off fat and membranes. Heat 1 tablespoon oil in flameproof casserole until hot. Add half of the veal and brown well on all sides. Transfer to a bowl. Heat remaining oil in same casserole until hot, and brown rest of veal. Transfer to bowl.

Add onion, celery, garlic, green pepper and shallots to casserole, and sauté until lightly browned, adding a little more oil if necessary. Add wine, scraping pan with large spoon to loosen browned particles. Return browned meat to casserole, stirring well. Combine veal stock with dried herbs, orange rind, tomatoes, tomato paste and cayenne. Pour over meat. Add bouquet garni and bring to simmering point. Cover tightly. Place in preheated 160°C/325°F/Gas mark 3 oven, and bake until meat is almost tender (about 1 hour).

Remove from oven and add mushrooms, stirring well. Bring to simmering point on top of stove. Cover and return to oven for 30 minutes. Test to see if it's cooked with a long-pronged fork. Meat should be firm yet tender. If not, return to oven for another 10 minutes.

Serve on a bed of plain boiled rice, and sprinkle with freshly chopped parsley.

Yield: Serves 6

Note: I have found that the flavour of this stew is enhanced if it stands, covered, out of the oven for 30 minutes before serving. It can then be reheated briefly.

CAL	F	P:S	SOD	CAR	CHO
359	16	2.7:1	189	9	171
Rice					
43	0	—	0	10	0

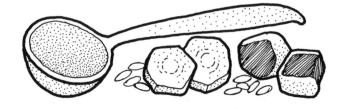

For the following two recipes you will need Duxelles. Here is the recipe.
Note: the quantity made is more than you will need, but the surplus can be frozen for use in other dishes.

	Metric	Imperial	American
Corn oil	3 tbsp	3 tbsp	3 tbsp
Large clove garlic, finely chopped	1	1	1
Large shallots, finely chopped	2	2	2
Fresh mushrooms, washed and trimmed	225 g	8 oz	½ lb
Dried tarragon leaves, crushed	½ tsp	½ tsp	½ tsp
Cayenne pepper	3 pinches	3 pinches	3 pinches
Freshly chopped parsley	1 tsp	1 tsp	1 tsp

Heat oil in large heavy frying pan until hot. Add garlic and shallots and cook, turning constantly, for 1 minute. Add mushrooms, spreading smoothly over pan. Cook for 2 minutes. Turn over with large spoon, and smooth out. Continue turning over and smoothing out until all liquid has evaporated (about 8-10 minutes). Sprinkle with tarragon, cayenne and chopped parsley. Stir to blend.

Yield: 175 g/6 oz/1 cup

CAL	F	P:S	SOD	CAR	CHO
Per tablespoon					
26	3	4.5:1	2	1	0

VEAL BIRDS

My version of this north Italian delicacy is built around a mixture of meat, herbs and bread crumbs sandwiched between thinly pounded slices of lean pink veal. Sautéed to a golden brown, then braised gently in stock, wine and vegetables, it makes an elegant dish.

	Metric	Imperial	American
For the stuffing:			
Corn oil	1 tbsp	1 tbsp	1 tbsp
Lean pork, minced	100 g	4 oz	¼ lb
Lean veal, minced	100 g	4 oz	¼ lb
Very small onion, finely chopped	1	1	1
Cloves garlic, finely chopped	2	2	2
Stick celery, finely chopped	½	½	½
Large shallots, finely chopped	2	2	2
Duxelles (see opposite)	3 tbsp	3 tbsp	3 tbsp
Drained, chopped water-chestnuts, packed in water, no salt added	3 tbsp	3 tbsp	3 tbsp
Small carrot, peeled and grated	1	1	1
Sodium-free soya sauce	3 dashes	3 dashes	3 dashes
Cayenne pepper	2 pinches	2 pinches	2 pinches
Dried thyme leaves, crushed	¼ tsp	¼ tsp	¼ tsp
Dried rosemary leaves, crushed	⅛ tsp	⅛ tsp	⅛ tsp
Freshly chopped dill and parsley	1 tbsp	1 tbsp	1 tbsp
Freshly made, very lightly toasted bread crumbs (Page 145)	40 g	1½ oz	¾ cup
Egg white	1	1	1
Low-fat milk	60 ml	2 fl oz	¼ cup
For the birds:			
Veal slices, (about 450 g/1 lb) cut from leg, thinly beaten	4	4	4
Corn oil	1½ tbsp	1½ tbsp	1½ tbsp

Ingredient	Metric	Imperial	American
Small onion, finely chopped	1	1	1
Large clove garlic, finely chopped	1	1	1
Large shallot, finely chopped	1	1	1
Stick celery, finely chopped	½	½	½
Veal stock (Page 10)	300 ml	½ pt	1¼ cups
Brown beef stock (Page 11)	1 tbsp	1 tbsp	1 tbsp
Dry red wine	80 ml	3 fl oz	⅓ cup
Freshly chopped dill and parsley	2 tbsp	2 tbsp	2 tbsp
Dried thyme leaves, crushed	¼ tsp	¼ tsp	¼ tsp
Dried rosemary leaves, crushed	⅛ tsp	⅛ tsp	⅛ tsp
Small bay leaf	1	1	1
Cayenne pepper	2 pinches	2 pinches	2 pinches
Fresh tomatoes, skinned, cored and chopped	2	2	2
Tomato paste, no salt added	2 tsp	2 tsp	2 tsp

Prepare stuffing first. Heat oil in large non-stick frying pan until hot. Sauté combined minced meat. Use large metal spoon to break up pieces while cooking. Continue sautéeing, turning often, for 4 minutes, until barely cooked through. Add onion, garlic, celery and shallots, and cook another 3 minutes, mixing well. Transfer to large bowl.

Add duxelles, water-chestnuts, carrot, sodium-free soya sauce, cayenne, herbs, bread crumbs, egg white and milk. Blend well.

Wipe veal slices dry on both sides. Cut each slice in half. Place a large mound of stuffing on top of each half, pressing to hold. Cover with another half. Secure each bird with 4 wooden cocktail sticks. Spoon any leftover stuffing into lightly oiled ovenproof dish and set aside.

Heat 1 tablespoon oil in non-stick frying pan until hot. Sauté birds until lightly brown on both sides. Transfer to casserole.

Add remaining oil to frying pan and brown onion, garlic, shallot and celery. Add stocks, wine, herbs, cayenne, tomatoes and tomato paste. Heat to simmering point. Cook for 1 minute. Pour over meat in cas-serole, reserving 2 tablespoons for leftover stuffing. Cover tightly. Bake in preheated 180°C/350°F/Gas mark 4 oven for 50 minutes, removing bay leaf when ready to serve.

Serve on 4 heated individual plates, saving leftover stuffing for another light meal.

Yield: Serves 4; 2 leftover portions stuffing

CAL	F	P:S	SOD	CAR	CHO
199	12	2.5:1	96	8	105
Stuffing					
143	4	4.5:1	96	8	61

STUFFED PORK CHOPS IN RED WINE

This is one of my most spectacular dishes. It's guaranteed to evoke a chorus of praise when you bring it to the table. A special treat for hearty eaters.

	Metric	Imperial	American
For the chops and sauce:			
Loin pork chops (570 g/1¼ lb)	4	4	4
Unbleached flour	4 tbsp	4 tbsp	4 tbsp
Dried rosemary leaves, crushed	½ tsp	½ tsp	½ tsp
Dried thyme leaves, crushed	½ tsp	½ tsp	½ tsp
Cayenne pepper	2 pinches	2 pinches	2 pinches
Corn oil	2 tbsp	2 tbsp	2 tbsp
Small onion, finely chopped	1	1	1
Large clove garlic, finely chopped	1	1	1
Shallot, finely chopped	1	1	1

Ingredient	Metric	Imperial	US
Chicken or beef stock (Pages 8 and 10)	150 ml	¼ pt	⅔ cup
Dry red wine	180 ml	6 fl oz	¾ cup
Tomato paste, no salt added	1½ tbsp	1½ tbsp	1½ tbsp
Large fresh mushrooms, washed, trimmed and sliced	2	2	2
Sliver orange rind	1	1	1
Freshly chopped parsley and dill			

For the stuffing:

Ingredient	Metric	Imperial	US
Corn oil	1 tbsp	1 tbsp	1 tbsp
Clove garlic, finely chopped	1	1	1
Shallot, finely chopped	1	1	1
Celery, finely chopped	2 tbsp	2 tbsp	2 tbsp
Onion, finely chopped	2 tbsp	2 tbsp	2 tbsp
Stuffing bread, cubed (Page 145)	50 g	2 oz	1 cup
Duxelles (Page 83)	2 tbsp	2 tbsp	2 tbsp
Dried thyme leaves, crushed	¼ tsp	¼ tsp	¼ tsp
Dried rosemary leaves, crushed	¼ tsp	¼ tsp	¼ tsp
Cayenne pepper	2 pinches	2 pinches	2 pinches
Sweet, crisp apple, peeled and chopped	75 g	3 oz	½ cup
Hot chicken or beef stock (Pages 8 and 10)	120 ml	4 fl oz	½ cup
Freshly chopped parsley and dill	2 tsp	2 tsp	2 tsp

Prepare the stuffing first. Heat oil over medium flame in small frying pan until hot. Add garlic, shallot, celery and onion. Sauté until lightly browned. Place bread in medium-sized bowl. Add sautéed mixture, duxelles, herbs, cayenne and apple. Toss well. Add stock to bread mixture and blend. Using a tablespoon, press the bread against the side of bowl, mashing it slightly. The mixture should be damp enough to hold together. Add more stock, if necessary, to accomplish this.

Trim and discard all fat from chops. Make a pocket in each chop as follows: Lay chop flat. With sharp knife cut horizontally from outer edge through centre to bone. Open pocket. Fill each pocket with 2 tablespoons stuffing. Sew up pocket. (If you don't have a poultry needle, use a large-eyed needle.)

Mix flour with dried herbs and cayenne. Dredge chops with mixture, shaking off excess. Heat oil in large heavy frying pan. (An iron frying pan with heat-proof handle is a must because it will later go into the oven.) Add chops, and brown well on both sides. Add finely chopped onion, garlic and shallot just a minute or two before the browning on the second side is done.

Combine stock, wine and tomato paste in a sauce-pan and heat. Pour 80 ml/3 fl oz/⅓ cup over browned chops. Cover with foil and bake in preheated 180°C/350°F/Gas mark 4 oven for 45 minutes, turning once halfway through cooking.

Add rest of hot stock-wine mixture, together with mushrooms and orange rind. Reheat on top of stove until bubbling, turning meat once. Re-cover and return to oven for 20 minutes.

Transfer to individual heated plates, spooning sauce over chops. Sprinkle with fresly chopped parsley and dill, and serve with any of my green vegetables.

Yield: Serves 4

CAL	F	P:S	SOD	CAR	CHO
363	18	2.1:1	95	6	81
With beef stock					
363	18	2.1:1	116	6	81
Stuffing					
134	4	4.6:1	18	12	0
With beef stock					
134	4	4.6:1	26	12	0

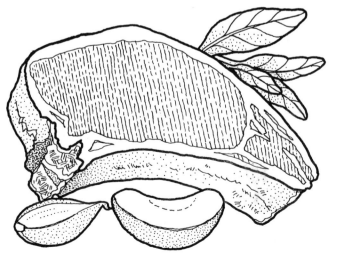

FRIED PORK CHOPS WITH MUSHROOMS

Here's a pork chop dish that you can prepare rapidly in a frying pan, and everybody will think you slaved over it for hours.

	Metric	Imperial	American
Loin pork chops, 1.5 cm/½ inch thick, well trimmed (680 g/1½ lb)	4	4	4
Dried thyme leaves, crushed	½ tsp	½ tsp	½ tsp
Dried basil leaves, crushed	½ tsp	½ tsp	½ tsp
Corn oil	1 tbsp	1 tbsp	1 tbsp
Large cloves garlic, finely chopped	2	2	2
Shallots, finely chopped	2	2	2
Green pepper, cut into 5 mm/¼ inch strips	½	½	½
Wine vinegar	1 tbsp	1 tbsp	1 tbsp
Tomato paste, no salt added	1 tsp	1 tsp	1 tsp
Tomato juice, no salt added	150 ml	¼ pt	⅔ cup
Brown beef stock (Page 11)	3 tbsp	3 tbsp	3 tbsp
Freshly chopped parsley	1 tbsp	1 tbsp	1 tbsp
Fresh mushrooms, washed, trimmed and sliced	225 g	8 oz	½ lb

At least 2 hours before cooking time, wipe chops dry with paper towels, and rub with dried herbs. Cover and refrigerate until ready to cook.

Heat oil until hot in large heavy frying pan. Brown chops well on both sides (about 12-15 minutes). Lower heat to medium. Add garlic and vegetables, except mushrooms, and brown together with chops. Add vinegar and cook for 2 minutes.

Combine tomato paste with tomato juice and brown beef stock. Pour over chops. Sprinkle with chopped parsley. Bring to simmering point. Cover and simmer for 30 minutes, turning chops once. Uncover and add mushrooms. Bring to simmering point. Re-cover and simmer for another 20 minutes, turning once, or until chops are tender.

Yield: Serves 4

CAL	F	P:S	SOD	CAR	CHO
378	22	2.1:1	106	2	112

BAKED LAMB STEAKS

Here's a lamb dish that tastes as if it takes a full day to prepare. Actually, it's made in a very short time. The tangy marinade with its adventurously delicious blending of flavours not ordinarily associated with lamb lifts this dish far out of the commonplace.

	Metric	Imperial	American
Corn oil	2 tbsp	2 tbsp	2 tbsp
Large clove garlic, finely chopped	1	1	1
Shallot, finely chopped	1	1	1
Carrot, peeled and grated	1 tsp	1 tsp	1 tsp
Cider vinegar	1 tbsp	1 tbsp	1 tbsp
Unsweetened orange juice	60 ml	2 fl oz	¼ cup
Pineapple juice, no sugar added, taken from canned pineapple chunks	60 ml	2 fl oz	¼ cup
Ground ginger	1 tsp	1 tsp	1 tsp
Honey	1 tbsp	1 tbsp	1 tbsp
Sodium-free soya sauce	4 dashes	4 dashes	4 dashes
Lamb steaks, cut from leg, 1.5 cm/½ inch thick (570 g/1¼ lb)	4	4	4
Navel orange, peeled and cut into chunks	1	1	1

	Metric	Imperial	American
Pineapple chunks, packed in own juices, no sugar added	80 ml	3 fl oz	1/3 cup
Arrowroot, dissolved in 2 tsp water	2 tsp	2 tsp	2 tsp

Place all ingredients, with the exception of meat, fruit chunks and arrowroot, in blender. Purée for 1 minute to make marinade.

Wipe meat slices dry with paper towels. Place in shallow baking dish in one layer. Pour puréed marinade over meat. Cover and let stand for 2-3 hours.

Place in preheated 180°C/350°F/Gas mark 4 oven and bake for 45 minutes. Add orange and pineapple chunks. Cover and bake until tender (about 20 minutes).

Transfer meat to serving platter and keep warm. Sprinkle arrowroot mixture into gravy, a little at a time, stirring well, using only enough to thicken gravy lightly. Pour over meat and serve.

Yield: Serves 4

Note: Lean lamb chops may be substituted for lamb steaks.

CAL	F	P:S	SOD	CAR	CHO
299	36	1.3:1	112	16	80
Chops					
325	40	1.2:1	112	16	80

HERB-GRILLED SPRING LAMB CUTLETS

Here's a simple way to add the right herbs to lamb and transform just another grilled cutlet into a treat.

	Metric	Imperial	American
Spring lamb cutlets, (680 g/1½ lb), well trimmed, ends of bone removed	8	8	8
Corn oil	1 tbsp	1 tbsp	1 tbsp
Large clove garlic, finely chopped	1	1	1
Shallot, finely chopped	1	1	1
Dried rosemary leaves, crushed	1 tsp	1 tsp	1 tsp
Dried sage leaves, crushed	½ tsp	½ tsp	½ tsp
Dried mint leaves, crushed	½ tsp	½ tsp	½ tsp
Freshly chopped parsley			

Wipe chops dry with paper towels. In a small non-stick frying pan, heat oil until warm. Sauté garlic and shallot for 2 minutes. Avoid browning. Remove from heat. Transfer to small bowl. Add dried herbs and blend with fork. Spoon half the mixture over one side of chops.

Place chops on rack in shallow roasting tin, and grill 4 cm/1½ inches from flame, coated side up, for 8 minutes. Turn. Spread with rest of herbed mixture. Grill for another 5-8 minutes, or until just lightly browned. Meat should remain pink on the inside. Do not overcook.

Serve immediately, sprinkled with freshly chopped parsley.

Yield: Serves 4

Note: If you're using best end of neck, these chops are not as tender and, because of the bones between the meat, will require a longer cooking time. Follow the recipe, but turn twice instead of once, so that the meat will have a chance to cook through. Allow one chop per person, total weight 680 g/1½ lb.

CAL	F	P:S	SOD	CAR	CHO
292	12	1.7:1	79	1	100
Best end of neck					
277	11	1.8:1	79	1	100

FRENCH STYLE ROAST LEG OF LAMB

A French dish, consisting of lean pink lamb cooked to perfection with slivers of garlic and sprinklings of herbs.

	Metric	Imperial	American
½ leg of lamb	1.75 kg	4 lb	4 lb
Large cloves garlic, cut into thin slivers	3	3	3
Dried rosemary leaves, crushed	¼ tsp	¼ tsp	¼ tsp
Dried sage leaves, crushed	¼ tsp	¼ tsp	¼ tsp
Dried thyme leaves, crushed	¼ tsp	¼ tsp	¼ tsp
Cayenne pepper	3 pinches	3 pinches	3 pinches
Corn oil	1 tbsp	1 tbsp	1 tbsp
Veal or chicken stock (Pages 10 and 8)	240 ml	8 fl oz	1 cup
Dry red wine	120 ml	4 fl oz	½ cup
Fresh tomatoes, cored and chopped	2	2	2
Brown beef stock (Page 11)	1 tbsp	1 tbsp	1 tbsp
Tomato paste, no salt added	1 tbsp	1 tbsp	1 tbsp
Dried mint leaves, crushed	1 tsp	1 tsp	1 tsp

Have meat at room temperature before preparing. Trim away all fat. Wipe dry with paper towels. Cut several 5 mm/¼ inch slits into surface of meat. Insert garlic slivers. Rub meat with crushed herbs and cayenne. Preheat over to 220°C/425°F/Gas mark 7. Place lamb on rack in shallow roasting tin, and roast, uncovered, for 20 minutes. Reduce oven temperature to 200°C/400°F/Gas mark 6. Brush meat with oil. Return to oven and roast for 15 minutes.

Heat stock and wine to simmering point and pour over meat. Roast for an additional 40 minutes, basting frequently. Remove from roasting tin to heated platter and keep warm. Remove rack from roasting tin, and

place tin on top of stove over medium high flame. Scrape any brown particles into pan juices. Add tomatoes, brown beef stock, tomato paste and mint, and cook until liquid is reduced by a third. Pour into a sieve, pressing out juices into saucepan. Return to heat and reheat. Pour lamb juices into saucepan. Taste. Add more cayenne pepper, if liked. Serve hot in sauceboat, and spoon over thinly sliced meat.

Yield: Serves 8

CAL	F	P:S	SOD	CAR	CHO
343	1	1.3:1	160	4	133
With chicken stock					
343	1	1.3:1	154	4	133

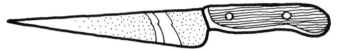

IRISH STEW

Don't let the long list of ingredients deter you. You probably have most, if not all, of them in your kitchen right now. My version of this popular dish is light, delicate and subtly flavoured.

	Metric	Imperial	American
Lean lamb, from shoulder or leg, cut into 5-cm/2-inch chunks	450 g	1 lb	1 lb
Lean beef, cut into 5-cm/2-inch chunks	450 g	1 lb	1 lb
Unbleached flour	40-50 g	1½-2 oz	⅓-½ cup
Corn oil	2 tbsp	2 tbsp	2 tbsp
Large cloves garlic, finely chopped	2	2	2
Large shallot, finely chopped	1	1	1
Large leek, white part only, well washed and coarsely chopped	1	1	1
Dry Vermouth or white wine	120 ml	4 fl oz	½ cup
Beef stock (Page 10)	240 ml	8 fl oz	1 cup
Veal stock (Page 10)	240 ml	8 fl oz	1 cup

Water	450 ml	¾ pt	2 cups
Small bouquet garni	1	1	1
Dried rosemary leaves, crushed	1½ tsp	1½ tsp	1½ tsp
Dried sage leaves, crushed	1 tsp	1 tsp	1 tsp
Onions, cut into eighths	2	2	2
Fresh tomatoes, cored and skinned, or 225 g/8 oz canned tomatoes, no salt added, drained	2	2	2
Carrots, peeled and sliced into 2.5-cm/1-inch pieces	2	2	2
Sticks celery, diced	2	2	2
Large potatoes, peeled and cut into 2.5-cm/1-inch cubes	2	2	2
Swede, peeled, cut into 1.5-cm/½-inch cubes	75 g	3 oz	⅓ cup
Cayenne pepper	6 pinches	6 pinches	6 pinches
Small white onions, peeled	12	12	12
Shelled fresh peas	100 g	4 oz	½ cup
Chopped fresh parsley			

Wipe meat dry with paper towels. Dredge lightly with flour, shaking off excess. Heat half the oil in large flameproof casserole. Brown meat, half at a time, on all sides. Transfer to bowl. Heat remaining oil until hot. Sauté garlic, shallot and leek with rest of meat, and brown lightly. Add wine and cook for 2 minutes. Add stocks, water, bouquet garni and dried herbs. Return first batch of browned meat to casserole and stir to blend. Bring to simmering point. Cover and cook for 1 hour, stirring frequently to prevent sticking.

Add rest of ingredients with exception of peas, white onions and parsley. Bring to simmering point on top of stove. Cover and place in preheated 160°C/325°F/Gas mark 3 oven for 30 minutes. Add white onions and peas. Re-cover and return to oven for 40 minutes.

Pour into heated tureen. Sprinkle with freshly chopped parsley and serve.

CAL	F	P:S	SOD	CAR	CHO
381	12	2.3:1	183	26	89

SIMPLE SAUTÉED STEAKBURGER

Once in a while it's nice to make a meal of a simple prepared meat dish, vegetable and salad. For your meat dish, try this gourmet version of a hamburger. Buy your beef minced only if you can rely on its leanness.

	Metric	Imperial	American
Corn oil	1 tbsp	1 tbsp	1 tbsp
Large shallots, finely chopped	2	2	2
Large cloves garlic, finely chopped	2	2	2
Spring onion, finely chopped	1	1	1
Lean sirloin of beef, minced	450 g	1 lb	1 lb
Carrot, peeled and grated	½	½	½
Cayenne pepper	3 pinches	3 pinches	3 pinches
Dried basil leaves, crushed	¼ tsp	¼ tsp	¼ tsp
Dried thyme leaves, crushed	¼ tsp	¼ tsp	¼ tsp
Sodium-free soya sauce	¼ tsp	¼ tsp	¼ tsp
Fine bread crumbs (Page 00)	2 tbsp	2 tbsp	2 tbsp
Red wine	4 tbsp	4 tbsp	4 tbsp

In large non-stick frying pan, heat ½ teaspoon oil until hot. Sauté for 1 minute with shallots, garlic and spring onion.

In small bowl, combine meat, carrot, cayenne, herbs, sodium-free soya sauce, crumbs and wine. Add sautéed mixture and blend. Shape into 4 steakburgers.

Heat frying pan until hot, adding remaining oil. Add steakburgers and cook until brown on both sides. Meat should be crisp on outside, and pink on inside. Do not overcook. Serve immediately. Delicious with Rocket and Chicory Salad (Page 95).

Yield: Serves 4

CAL	F	P:S	SOD	CAR	CHO
207	8	2.5:1	85	5	80

SAUTÉED STEAKBURGER WITH MUSHROOM SAUCE

This is another gourmet version of a hamburger. It's less strongly spiced than the simple sautéed steakburger (Page 89) because it's accompanied by a creamy mushroom sauce.

	Metric	Imperial	American
For the steakburger:			
Corn oil	1 tbsp	1 tbsp	1 tbsp
Small onion, finely chopped	1	1	1
Large clove garlic, finely chopped	1	1	1
Shallot, finely chopped	1	1	1
Sirloin of beef, minced	450 g	1 lb	1 lb
Fine bread crumbs (Page 145)	15 g	½ oz	¼ cup
Dried thyme leaves, crushed	¼ tsp	¼ tsp	¼ tsp
Low-fat milk	2 tbsp	2 tbsp	⅛ cup
Cayenne pepper	3 pinches	3 pinches	3 pinches
Freshly chopped parsley			
For the sauce:			
Corn oil	1½ tbsp	1½ tbsp	1½ tbsp
Shallot, finely chopped	1	1	1
Clove garlic, finely chopped	1	1	1
Fresh mushrooms, washed, trimmed and sliced	100 g	4 oz	¼ lb
Unbleached flour	1½ tbsp	1½ tbsp	1½ tbsp
Beef stock, heated (Page 10)	240 ml	8 fl oz	1 cup
Dry Vermouth or white wine	2 tbsp	2 tbsp	2 tbsp
Dried thyme leaves, crushed	¼ tsp	¼ tsp	¼ tsp
Cayenne pepper	2 pinches	2 pinches	2 pinches
Curry powder, no salt or pepper added	½ tsp	½ tsp	½ tsp

Note: Co-ordinate the cooking of the sauce with the steakburgers so that they're both finished at the same time.

In non-stick frying pan, heat ½ tablespoon oil until hot. Add onion, garlic and shallot, and sauté until lightly browned.

Meanwhile, combine meat, bread crumbs, thyme, milk and cayenne in small bowl. Blend well. Add sautéed mixture. Shape into 4 burgers about 2 cm/ ¾ inch thick.

Using the same pan, heat remaining oil until hot. Add meat. Brown on one side, turn and brown on second side. Meat should be crisp on outside and pink inside. Avoid overcooking.

Begin preparation of sauce about 10 minutes before burger is ready. In a large non-stick frying pan, heat oil until hot. Add shallot and garlic. Sauté for 1 minute. Add mushrooms. Sauté for 3 minutes until lightly browned. Then sprinkle flour over mixture and cook for 2 minutes, stirring well so that flour cooks through. Combine stock and wine. Add to pan, stirring continually. Add thyme, cayenne and curry powder. Let simmer, uncovered, for 2 minutes.

Pour over steakburgers. Sprinkle with parsley and serve.

Yield: Serves 4

CAL	F	P:S	SOD	CAR	CHO
198	8	2.5:1	80	9	80
Sauce					
69	5	4.5:1	24	3	0

LIGHT MEAT LOAF

Typical meat loaves, filled with egg yolks, salt, pepper and fats were never as delectable as my lighter-than-air version. Make the whole recipe, even if you're not serving four, and have it the next day, hot or cold, served between slices of freshly made bread.

	Metric	Imperial	American
Large potatoes, peeled, each cut into 6 pieces	2	2	2
Corn oil	1 tbsp	1 tbsp	1 tbsp
Onion, finely chopped	1	1	1
Cloves garlic, finely chopped	2	2	2
Large shallot, finely chopped	1	1	1
Beef sirloin, minced	450 g	1 lb	1 lb
Bread crumbs, no salt added (Page 145)	25 g	1 oz	½ cup
Cayenne pepper	4 pinches	4 pinches	4 pinches
Low-fat milk	3 tbsp	3 tbsp	3 tbsp
Egg white, lightly beaten with fork	1	1	1
Freshly chopped dill and parsley	2 tbsp	2 tbsp	2 tbsp
Dried oregano leaves, crushed	¼ tsp	¼ tsp	¼ tsp
Dried marjoram leaves, crushed	¼ tsp	¼ tsp	¼ tsp
Dried thyme leaves, crushed	¼ tsp	¼ tsp	¼ tsp
Tomato paste, no salt added	1 tbsp	1 tbsp	1 tbsp
Tomato juice, no salt added	240 ml	8 fl oz	1 cup

Parboil potatoes for 10 minutes. Drain and set aside. Heat ¾ tablespoon corn oil in non-stick frying pan until hot. Sauté onion, garlic and shallot until lightly browned.

Place meat in medium-sized bowl together with bread crumbs, cayenne, milk, egg white and herbs. Combine tomato paste with tomato juice and add to meat. Stir in sautéed mixture, blending well.

Lightly oil a rectangular baking dish. Do not use a loaf tin. Shape meat with hands into a 20×10-cm/ 8×4-inch loaf. Placed in preheated 180°C/350°F/Gas mark 4 oven, uncovered, and bake for 20 minutes. Remove from oven and pour off any fat that may have dripped from meat. Pour 120 ml/4 fl oz/½ cup tomato juice over loaf. Add boiled potatoes to baking dish and coat with tomato juice. Bake for 15 minutes. Turn potatoes and add rest of tomato juice to baking dish. Return to oven and bake for another 15 minutes, or a total of 50 minutes. Do not overcook.

Serve on heated platter, spooning gravy over meat. Arrange potatoes around loaf, and garnish as liked.

Yield: Serves 4

Note: The reason for not using loaf tin: If meat is placed in loaf tin, there is no way that fat can drip away. It would just go back into meat. Also you would not be able to heat and flavour the potatoes as recommended.

CAL	F	P:S	SOD	CAR	CHO
227	8	2.5:1	104	8	80
Potatoes					
44	0	—	2	6	0

VEAL AND SPINACH LOAF WITH POTATOES

The test of a good cook is the ability to elevate a meat loaf into a gourmet delight. Follow this veal loaf recipe with care, and you'll pass the test.

	Metric	Imperial	American
Fresh spinach, well washed, tough stems removed	450 g	1 lb	1 lb
Small potatoes	8	8	8
Corn oil	1 tbsp	1 tbsp	1 tbsp
Onion, finely chopped	1	1	1
Large cloves garlic, finely chopped	2	2	2
Lean veal, minced	450 g	1 lb	1 lb

Bread crumbs, no salt added (Page 145)	20 g	¾ oz	⅓ cup
Egg white, lightly beaten with fork	1	1	1
Dried marjoram leaves, crushed	¼ tsp	¼ tsp	¼ tsp
Dried basil leaves, crushed	¼ tsp	¼ tsp	¼ tsp
Dried oregano leaves, crushed	¼ tsp	¼ tsp	¼ tsp
Cayenne pepper	2 pinches	2 pinches	2 pinches
Veal stock (Page 10)	120 ml	4 fl oz	½ cup
Tomato paste, no salt added	2 tbsp	2 tbsp	2 tbsp
Large fresh tomatoes, cored, skinned and drained	2	2	2
Low-fat milk	60 ml	2 fl oz	¼ cup
Fresh parsley and dill, stems removed	20 g	¾ oz	⅓ cup

Place spinach in large heavy-bottomed saucepan. Cover and cook over medium-high heat for 4-5 minutes, or until tender. Pour into colander and drain well. Chop.

Boil potatoes in their jackets for 10 minutes. Plunge into cold water and peel. Set aside.

Heat ¾ tablespoon oil in non-stick frying pan until hot. Sauté onion and garlic until softened. Transfer to mixing bowl with veal, spinach, crumbs, egg white, dried herbs and cayenne. Blend well.

In a blender, combine stock, tomato paste, tomatoes, milk, parsley and dill, and blend until smooth. Pour half of mixture over veal, blending well. Reserve rest for sauce.

Shape into 20 × 10-cm/8 × 4-inch loaf, and place in lightly oiled rectangular baking dish. Bake in pre-heated 180°C/350°F/Gas mark 4 oven for 45 minutes. Remove from oven and pour off any fat that may have dripped from meat. Add potatoes, coating well with juices from pan, and bake for 30 minutes. Remove from oven, cover loosely with greaseproof paper, and let stand for 5 minutes before slicing.

Place on platter surrounded by potatoes. Heat remaining blended mixture to simmering point, and pour over loaf.

Yield: Serves 4

Note: See note for Light Meat loaf (Page 91)

CAL	F	P:S	SOD	CAR	CHO
257	9	2.4:1	228	17	105
Potatoes					
46	0	—	2	11	0

SWEDISH MEAT BALLS

Three kinds of tender lean meat, finely minced, mixed with herbs and spices, and gently simmered in a rich stock, produce a meat ball that's as light as it is tasty.

	Metric	Imperial	American
Lean veal, minced	100 g	4 oz	¼ lb
Lean pork, minced	100 g	4 oz	¼ lb
Sirloin beef, minced	225 g	8 oz	½ lb
Freshly chopped parsley and dill	1 tbsp	1 tbsp	1 tbsp
Fine bread crumbs (Page 145)	25 g	1 oz	½ cup
Low-fat milk	80 ml	3 fl oz	⅓ cup
Egg white, lightly beaten with fork	1	1	1
Carrot, peeled and grated	½	½	½
Ground ginger	⅛ tsp	⅛ tsp	⅛ tsp
Ground allspice	½ tsp	½ tsp	½ tsp
Corn oil	2 tbsp	2 tbsp	2 tbsp
Onion, finely chopped	1	1	1
Stick celery, finely chopped	1	1	1
Cloves garlic, finely chopped	2	2	2
Large shallot, finely chopped	1	1	1
Unbleached flour	1½ tsp	1½ tsp	1½ tsp
Beef stock, warmed (Page 10)	300-360 ml	½ pt-12 fl oz	1¼-1½ cups
Large sprig fresh dill	1	1	1

Combine meats with herbs and bread crumbs. Mix well with fingers (the only way to get a smooth blend). Add milk, egg white, carrot and spices. Blend well.

Heat 1 tablespoon oil in large non-stick frying pan until hot. Sauté onion, celery, garlic and shallot until lightly browned. Pour into meat mixture and blend. Shape into 24-26 smooth balls. (At this point, you can cover and refrigerate meat until ready to cook.)

Heat ½ tablespoon oil in same large pan until hot. Brown half the meatballs on all sides, turning carefully with spatula. Transfer to bowl. Add rest of oil, and brown remaining meat balls and return first batch to pan. Sprinkle with flour and cook for 1 minute. Add 300 ml/½ pt/1¼ cups stock and dill sprig. Bring to simmering point, stirring well. Cover and simmer for 15 minutes.

Uncover, and turn meat balls. If sauce is too thick, add remaining 60 ml/2 fl oz/¼ cup stock. Re-cover, and cook for another 15 minutes. Serve immediately with plain Parsleyed Potatoes (Page 20).

Yield: Serves 4

Note: When you're planning a buffet dinner, why not include hot Swedish meat balls. Shaped into small balls, and served with cocktail sticks, they're also delicious as hot hors d'oeuvres.

CAL	F	P:S	SOD	CAR	CHO
285	10	2.3:1	226	12	64

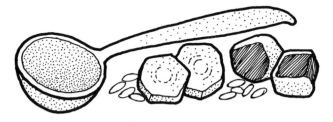

SPAGHETTI AND MEAT BALLS

Here are meat balls, spicy and satisfying and yet as light as air. They make a perfect match for my spaghetti with tomato and mushroom sauce.

	Metric	Imperial	American
Corn oil	2 tbsp	2 tbsp	2 tbsp
Onion, finely chopped	1	1	1
Large cloves garlic, finely chopped	2	2	2
Shallots, finely chopped	2	2	2
Minced lean beef	100 g	4 oz	¼ lb
Minced lean pork	100 g	4 oz	¼ lb
Egg white, lightly beaten with fork	1	1	1
Cayenne pepper	3 pinches	3 pinches	3 pinches
Fine bread crumbs (Page 145)	15 g	½ oz	¼ cup
Dried thyme leaves, crushed	½ tsp	½ tsp	½ tsp
Recipe Spaghetti with Tomato and Mushroom Sauce (Page 27)	1	1	1
Freshly chopped parsley	2 tbsp	2 tbsp	2 tbsp

To prepare meat balls, heat 1 tablespoon oil in non-stick frying pan until hot. Sauté onion, garlic and shallots until softened. Let cool.

Combine meats, egg white, cayenne, crumbs and thyme in bowl, mixing well. Add sautéed ingredients and blend. Mixture should hold together when rolled into small balls. If not, add a little more bread crumbs. Shape into 12 balls.

Heat remaining oil in pan until hot. Add meat balls and brown well on all sides. Set aside.

Prepare recipe for Tomato and Mushroom Sauce up to the point where mushrooms are about to be added. Add mushrooms and browned meat balls. Bring to simmering point. Cover and simmer for 45 minutes stirring and turning twice. Spoon sauce and meat balls over cooked spaghetti. Sprinkle with parsley, and serve.

Yield: Serves 6

CAL	F	P:S	SOD	CAR	CHO
Meat balls					
121	6	3.0:1	55	1	27
Spaghetti and sauce					
267	3	4.5:1	29	59	0

SALADS

GREEN SALAD WITH FLAVOURFUL SALAD DRESSING

There's no end to the variety of greens that can be combined into a salad. But it's not the greens or the dressing that make a successful salad—it's the freshness of the greens. Avoid brown-edged leaves and leaves that don't feel crunchy to the touch. Serve the crispiest of green salads by following these simple instructions:

Remove each leaf and wash under cold running water. Drain, and refrigerate in an uncovered bowl for 1 hour before serving. Pat each leaf dry with paper towels (or use a salad shaker). Tear leaves—do not cut—into bite-size pieces.

Here is a delicious combination of greens with a herbed dressing.

	Metric	Imperial	American
For the salad:			
Small head cos lettuce	350 g	12 oz	¾ lb
Endive	100 g	4 oz	¼ lb
Escarole leaves	100 g	4 oz	¼ lb
Bunch watercress, leaves only	½	½	½
Onion, thinly sliced	1	1	1
Spring onions, sliced	2	2	2
Crisp radishes, sliced	8	8	8
Chicory (optional)	75 g	3 oz	3 oz
Freshly chopped basil, or freshly chopped parsley and dill	2 tbsp	2 tbsp	2 tbsp
For the flavourful salad dressing:			
Cider vinegar	80 ml	3 fl oz	⅓ cup
Corn oil	150 ml	¼ pt	⅔ cup
Dried onion flakes	2 tsp	2 tsp	2 tsp
Cloves garlic, finely chopped	2	2	2
Shallots, finely chopped	2	2	2
Combined dried marjoram and tarragon leaves, crushed, and dill and fennel seeds, crushed	¾ tsp	¾ tsp	¾ tsp
Cayenne pepper	4 pinches	4 pinches	4 pinches
Freshly chopped chives	1 tsp	1 tsp	1 tsp

Prepare vegetables and greens according to preceding directions. Combine all ingredients except freshly chopped herbs and refrigerate for 1 hour.

Prepare salad dressing by combining all ingredients in a jar and shaking well. Let stand 1 hour before serving. Shake again before serving.

Allow 1½ tablespoons dressing per serving. Pour over salad to which freshly chopped herbs have been added. Toss well. Serve immediately.

Yield: Salad serves 4; salad dressing, about 240 ml/8 fl oz/1 cup

Variation: Add 3 tablespoons tomato juice, no salt added, to salad dressing and shake well.

Note: This salad dressing and its variation will keep well in refrigerator for a week. Remove 1 hour before serving.

CAL	F	P:S	SOD	CAR	CHO
37	0	—	25	14	0
With chicory					
38	0	—	26	15	0
With dressing					
129	14	4.5:1	28	16	0
With tomato juice					
130	14	4.5:1	28	16	0

FRESH GREEN BEANS WITH TOASTED CORIANDER

Here's a tantalizing aromatic salad built around just one green vegetable, tossed in a sweet-and-pungent marinade, and raised far beyond the ordinary by that favoured seed of Indian cuisine, the coriander.

	Metric	Imperial	American
Fresh green beans	450 g	1 lb	1 lb
Corn oil	1 tbsp	1 tbsp	1 tbsp
Shallots, finely chopped	2	2	2
Large clove garlic, finely chopped	1	1	1
Coriander seeds, toasted (see method)	2 tsp	2 tsp	2 tsp
Cayenne pepper	4 pinches	4 pinches	4 pinches
Cider vinegar	1 tsp	1 tsp	1 tsp
Wine vinegar	1 tsp	1 tsp	1 tsp
Honey	2 tsp	2 tsp	2 tsp
Freshly chopped parsley	1 tbsp	1 tbsp	1 tbsp

Fill a large pan with water and bring to boil. Add beans to water and boil, partially covered, for 7 minutes. Colour should remain bright green. Do not overcook!

Drain in colander and rinse immediately under cold water to prevent further cooking.

Heat oil in heavy-bottomed saucepan until hot. Sauté shallots and garlic until softened. Add beans and toss well to coat. Remove from heat.

To toast coriander seeds, heat small frying pan until hot. Add seeds, shaking around in pan for 2 minutes. Crush seeds finely in pestle and mortar. Add to green beans together with cayenne and vinegars. Shake saucepan to mix. Add honey and shake to blend.

Pour into small jar or bowl. Chill. Serve cold, sprinkled with freshly chopped parsley.

Yield: Serves 4

Variation: Do not refrigerate. Reheat, and serve hot, sprinkled with freshly chopped parsley.

CAL	F	P:S	SOD	CAR	CHO
77	4	4.5:1	10	8	0

ROCKET AND CHICORY SALAD

In good Italian restaurants, this is often the simplest dish on the menu—and the most sophisticated. Incredibly easy to assemble, it's a study in contrasting textures, colours and shades of mellowed bitterness.

	Metric	Imperial	American
Bunch crisp rocket	1	1	1
Large chicory (about 225 g/8 oz)	2	2	2
Flavourful Salad Dressing (Page 94)			

Wash rocket well under cold running water. Gently pat dry with paper towels. Never wring dry, as the leaves are very delicate. Snip off and discard any long stems.

Gently remove each leaf from chicory. Wash and pat dry.

Arrange individual servings by placing equal amounts of chicory, hollow sides up, on each plate then arrange a layer of rocket on the plates. Spoon enough dressing over each salad to moisten (about 1½ tablespoons per serving). Do not toss. Serve immediately.

Yield: Serves 4

CAL	F	P:S	SOD	CAR	CHO
49	13	4.5:1	12	4	0

TOMATO AND WATERCRESS SALAD WITH YOGURT DRESSING

The sharpness of yogurt is mellowed by the sweetness of tomato paste and juice and a suggestion of honey to produce a rich, smooth, herb-accented dressing for this crispy salad.

	Metric	Imperial	American
For the salad:			
Fresh tomatoes, skinned and cored	4	4	4
Bunch watercress	1	1	1
Cucumbers, peeled and cut into 4 lengthwise sections	2	2	2
For the yogurt dressing:			
Tomato juice, no salt added	4 tbsp	4 tbsp	4 tbsp
Tomato paste, no salt added	1 tbsp	1 tbsp	1 tbsp
Wine vinegar	2 tb	2 tbsp	2 tbsp
Freshly chopped onion	4 tb.	4 tbsp	4 tbsp
Freshly chopped parsley	4 tbsp	4 tbsp	4 tbsp
Freshly chopped basil or chives	2 tsp	2 tsp	2 tsp
Honey	1 tbsp	1 tbsp	1 tbsp
Low-fat plain yogurt	240 ml	8 fl oz	1 cup

Prepare dressing first. In small bowl, blend tomato juice with tomato paste. Add vinegar, onion, parsley, herbs and honey. Stir well. Add yogurt. Blend. Let stand while preparing the salad.

Skin and core tomatoes.

Wash watercress very well under cold running water. Pat dry with paper towels. Remove stalks and refrigerate. Refrigerate cucumbers until ready to use. Do not peel until ready to cut.

Slice tomatoes and arrange on serving platter. Garnish with watercress. Pour Yogurt Dressing over salad, and serve.

Yield: Serves 4

Note: Use all of the dressing for this salad.

CAL	F	P:S	SOD	CAR	CHO
40	0	—	7	9	0
Dressing					
70	1	0.6:1	36	14	2

CONTINENTAL CUCUMBER SALAD

The inspriation for this piquant salad—built around crisp cucumber slices marinated in a clear sweet-and-pungent sauce—comes from Hungary and Germany.

	Metric	Imperial	American
Cider vinegar	60 ml	2 fl oz	¼ cup
Honey	1 tbsp	1 tbsp	1 tbsp
Freshly chopped dill	1 tbsp	1 tbsp	1 tbsp
Cayenne pepper	3 pinches	3 pinches	3 pinches
Ground cloves	3 pinches	3 pinches	3 pinches
Cucumbers, scrubbed and thinly sliced	4	4	4

Combine all ingredients except cucumbers in a jar. Cover and shake well. Drop sliced cucumbers into jar, one by one, shaking gently to coat. Cover jar tightly. Turn gently upside down and back several times to distribute liquid evenly. Refrigerate for one day, turning jar upside down from time to time. Serve cold.

Yield: Serves 4

CAL	F	P:S	SOD	CAR	CHO
29	0	—	5	8	0

CUCUMBER AND ONION SALAD

Sweet and tart, this easy-to-make salad is just the thing to enliven a meal of simply prepared chicken or chops. Or enjoy it by itself as an appetizing starter.

	Metric	Imperial	American
Spanish onion, peeled and thinly sliced	1	1	1
Small cucumbers, peeled and thinly sliced	6	6	6
Freshly chopped chives	2 tbsp	2 tbsp	2 tbsp
Yogurt Dressing (Page 96)	80 ml	3 fl oz	⅓ cup

Place onion and cucumber in bowl. Toss with chives. Add dressing to moisten. Cover and refrigerate for at least 3 hours before serving.

Yield: Serves 4

CAL	F	P:S	SOD	CAR	CHO
41	0	—	17	9	0

GERMAN-STYLE POTATO SALAD

This vinegary yet herb-sweetened delicacy from north of the Rhine is the lightest possible potato salad.

	Metric	Imperial	American
Large potatoes, peeled and halved	3	3	3
Wine vinegar	2 tbsp	2 tbsp	2 tbsp
Cider vinegar	1 tbsp	1 tbsp	1 tbsp
Corn oil	1 tbsp	1 tbsp	1 tbsp
Dried thyme leaves, crushed	¼ tsp	¼ tsp	¼ tsp
Dried basil leaves, crushed	¼ tsp	¼ tsp	¼ tsp
Cayenne pepper	4 pinches	4 pinches	4 pinches
Small onion, grated	1	1	1
Large cloves garlic, finely chopped	2	2	2
Shallots, finely chopped	2	2	2
Freshly chopped parsley and dill	2 tsp	2 tsp	2 tsp

Place potatoes in saucepan, adding enough water to cover. Bring to boil and cook, partially covered, until tender but still firm. Drain. Let cool.

Cut into 1.5-cm/½-inch slices and place in bowl. Combine vinegars and oil, and pour over potatoes. Add dried herbs, cayenne, onion, garlic and shallots, and toss gently. Cover and refrigerate for 4-5 hours before serving, stirring from time to time. Sprinkle with parsley and dill.

Yield: Serves 4

Variations: Half green pepper, parboiled for 1 minute and thinly sliced, or one well drained sliced pimento may be added before salad is refrigerated.

CAL	F	P:S	SOD	CAR	CHO
124	4	4.5:1	9	21	0

Variations
No appreciable difference

COLE SLAW

Textured with cabbagy crunchiness, this familiar salad is elevated to new taste heights by a mixture of sweet and pungent vegetables sharpened by the slight bite of my eggless mayonnaise.

	Metric	Imperial	American
¾ head loose-leafed green cabbage	450 g	1 lb	1 lb
Carrot, peeled and shredded	1	1	1
Large radishes, trimmed and thinly sliced	6	6	6
Onion, peeled and grated	1	1	1
Green pepper, finely chopped	1	1	1
Cayenne pepper	4 pinches	4 pinches	4 pinches
Juice of ½ lemon			
Honey	1 tbsp	1 tbsp	1 tbsp
Eggless Mayonnaise (Page 103)	80 ml	3 fl oz	⅓ cup

Cut cabbage in quarters and remove core. Slice each quarter into 5-mm/¼-inch slivers. Add carrot, radishes, onion, green pepper, cayenne and lemon juice which has been blended with honey. Add Eggless Mayonnaise to coat. Stir well. Cover and refrigerate several hours before serving, stirring often.

Yield: Serves 4

Variation: Substitute Flavourful Salad Dressing (Page 94) for Eggless Mayonnaise using just enough to moisten (about 80 ml/3 fl oz/⅓ cup).

CAL	F	P:S	SOD	CAR	CHO
With mayonnaise					
186	15	4.5:1	47	14	0
With salad dressing					
160	11	4.5:1	44	15	0

RUSSIAN SALAD

This is a colourful potpourri of raw and cooked vegetables, hard-boiled egg whites, and my mustardy Eggless Mayonnaise. No reason why, with slices of one of my breads, you can't relish it as a complete luncheon meal.

	Metric	Imperial	American
Fresh peas, cooked, drained and cooled	225 g	8 oz	½ lb
Sweet red onion or shallot, thinly sliced	1	1	1
Shallot, finely chopped	1	1	1
Stick celery, diced	1	1	1
Spring onions, diced	2	2	2
Carrot, peeled and thinly sliced	½	½	½
Cucumbers, scrubbed and diced	2	2	2
Small potatoes, cooked in jackets, peeled and cooled	8	8	8
Firm tomato, cored, skinned and cubed	1	1	1
Hard-boiled egg whites, cooled, cut in half, then quarters	3	3	3
Ground thyme	¼ tsp	¼ tsp	¼ tsp
Freshly chopped dill	1 tbsp	1 tbsp	1 tbsp
Cayenne pepper	4 pinches	4 pinches	4 pinches
Eggless Mayonnaise (Page 103)	3 tbsp	3 tbsp	3 tbsp
Low-fat plain yogurt	2 tbsp	2 tbsp	2 tbsp
Watercress sprigs	4	4	4

Combine all vegetables and egg whites. Sprinkle with herbs and cayenne and toss. Add mayonnaise and gently toss again. Add yogurt and stir well to coat. Refrigerate, covered, until well chilled. Garnish with watercress sprigs, and serve.

Yield: Serves 4, one portion left over

CAL	F	P:S	SOD	CAR	CHO
151	7	3.9:1	66	19	0

COLD BEAN SALAD

For the gourmet with one eye on the budget, here's a main-course salad that's as nutritious and tasty as it's economical.

	Metric	Imperial	American
Red kidney beans	175 g	6 oz	1 cup
Spanish onion, thinly sliced	1	1	1
Cucumbers, peeled and diced	2	2	2
Combined dried thyme, oregano, marjoram and basil leaves, crushed	¾ tsp	¾ tsp	¾ tsp
Freshly chopped dill and parsley	50 g	2 oz	¼ cup
Cayenne papper	4 pinches	4 pinches	4 pinches
Flavourful Salad Dressing (Page 94)	4 tbsp	4 tbsp	4 tbsp
Cos lettuce leaves	8	8	8
Tomato, skinned, cored and sliced	1	1	1
Watercress sprigs	8	8	8

Soak beans overnight in water to cover. Drain well. Place beans in heavy-bottomed saucepan. Add enough water to cover and bring to boil. Turn heat down to simmering point, partially cover, and simmer gently for about 45 minutes, or until tender. Drain and let cool.

Transfer beans to bowl. Add onion, cucumber, herbs and cayenne. Toss. Pour Flavourful Salad Dressing over beans to moisten. Cover and refrigerate for 5-6 hours before serving.

Serve on a bed of Cos lettuce leaves and garnish with tomato and watercress.

Yield: Serves 4

CAL	F	P:S	SOD	CAR	CHO
181	9	4.5:1	19	16	0

VEAL SALAD

With your Braised Veal leftovers, prepare this elegant and colourful main-course salad. It's mildly spiced with curry, sharpened by a touch of lime juice, and textured with crunchy nuts and vegetables.

	Metric	Imperial	American
Cooked veal, diced (Page 77)	450 g	1 lb	2 cups
Fresh lime juice	2 tsp	2 tsp	2 tsp
Stick celery, coarsely diced	1	1	1
Carrot, peeled and grated	½	½	½
Shallots, finely chopped	2	2	2
Onion, finely chopped	1	1	1
Ground thyme	½ tsp	½ tsp	½ tsp
Curry powder, no salt or pepper added	2 tsp	2 tsp	2 tsp
Eggless Mayonnaise (Page 103)	3 tbsp	3 tbsp	3 tbsp
Whole pimento, no salt added, drained, cut into thin slivers	1	1	1
Cos lettuce leaves, washed and dried	8	8	8
Walnuts, coarsely chopped	50 g	2 oz	¼ cup

Place meat in large bowl. Sprinkle with lime juice. Add celery, carrot, shallots and onion, and toss well. Sprinkle with thyme and curry. Add mayonnaise, stirring well to coat. Stir in pimento. Cover and refrigerate for at least 2 hours before serving.

Serve on lettuce leaves. Sprinkle with walnuts.

Yield: Serves 4

CAL	F	P:S	SOD	CAR	CHO
255	16	5.9:1	71	11	39

LENTIL SALAD

Like Cold Bean Salad, this is an inflation beating one-course meal. The carnivores among us love its meaty taste, and the vegetarians like its all-round nutritional goodness. The garnish of fresh raw vegetables gives it an attractive visual appeal.

	Metric	Imperial	American
Dried lentils, washed and drained	175 g	6 oz	1 cup
Bay leaf	1	1	1
Vegetable concentrate (optional)	½ tsp	½ tsp	½ tsp
Whole cloves	3	3	3
Shallots, finely chopped	2	2	2
Cayenne pepper	3 pinches	3 pinches	3 pinches
Freshly chopped basil or freshly chopped parsley and dill	2 tbsp	2 tbsp	2 tbsp
Dry mustard, dissolved in 1 tsp water	¾ tsp	¾ tsp	¾ tsp
Onion, cut into quarters and sliced	1	1	1
Spring onions, finely chopped	2	2	2
Flavourful Salad Dressing (Page 94)			
Cos lettuce leaves, washed and dried	8	8	8
Tomato, cored, skinned and sliced	1	1	1
Crisp radishes, washed, trimmed and cut into roses	8	8	8
Cucumber, peeled and sliced	1	1	1

Soak lentils overnight in water to cover. Drain. Transfer to heavy-bottomed saucepan. Add bay leaf, vegetable concentrate, cloves and enough water to cover. Bring to boil. Turn heat down, partially cover, and simmer for about 30 minutes, or until lentils are tender. Drain well.

Transfer lentils to bowl. Add shallots, cayenne, freshly chopped herbs, mustard, onions and spring onions, and toss well. Add just enough dressing to moisten (about 3-4 tablespoons) and toss. Serve on a bed of Cos lettuce leaves, garnished with tomato, radishes and cucumber.

Yield: Serves 4

CAL	F	P:S	SOD	CAR	CHO
226	7	4.5:1	24	32	0

TURKEY SALAD DE LUXE

Here's a perfect summer meal made with leftover roast turkey accented with herbs and enriched with a subtly spiced dressing.

	Metric	Imperial	American
Cooked turkey, white and dark meat, cut into 1.5-cm/½-inch cubes	680 g	1½ lb	3 cups
Dry Vermouth or white wine	60 ml	2 fl oz	¼ cup
Chicken stock (Page 8)	120 ml	4 fl oz	½ cup
Mushrooms, washed, trimmed and quartered	100 g	4 oz	¼ lb
Coriander seeds, toasted (see method)	2 tbsp	2 tbsp	2 tbsp
Celery, diced	75 g	3 oz	⅓ cup
Small red onion, thinly sliced	1	1	1
Small potatoes, cooked in jackets, cut into 1.5-cm/½-inch cubes, cooled	2	2	2

Fresh peas, cooked and cooled	225 g	8 oz	½ lb
Walnuts, coarsely chopped	3 tbsp	3 tbsp	3 tbsp
Navel oranges, peeled, sliced crosswise, then cut into quarters	2	2	2
Carrot, peeled and grated	½	½	½
Dried tarragon leaves, crushed	½ tsp	½ tsp	½ tsp
Freshly chopped parlsey and dill	2 tbsp	2 tbsp	2 tbsp
Cayenne pepper	4 pinches	4 pinches	4 pinches
Fruit Dressing (Page 102)			
Cos lettuce leaves, washed and dried	8	8	8
Watercress sprigs	8	8	8

Place turkey in large bowl. Add wine, toss well and marinate, covered, for 1 hour.

Pour stock into small saucepan and bring to simmering point. Add mushrooms. Partially cover, and simmer for 2 minutes. Drain, reserving stock to be used again in a soup or gravy. Set aside.

Heat small frying pan until hot. Add coriander seeds and shake around in pan for 2 minutes. Crush seeds finely in pestle and mortar.

To the marinated turkey, add celery, onion, potatoes, peas, walnuts, oranges, mushrooms and carrot. Sprinkle with herbs, cayenne and coriander seeds, and toss gently. Pour only enough dressing over salad to moisten (about 4-6 tablespoons). Toss well to coat. Chill before serving.

Serve on a bed of lettuce and garnish with watercress.

Yield: Serves 4, one portion left over

Note: Poached Chicken Breasts may be substituted for turkey (Page 56).

CAL	F	P:S	SOD	CAR	CHO
297	8	5.0:1	139	21	36
Chicken					
290	4	4.3:1	127	23	40

CHEF SALAD

My version of this classic one-course meal for weight watchers is built around crisp cos and spinach leaves enhanced with an array of hot, mild, sweet and pungent vegetables, and topped with fragrant toasted sesame seeds. Not least of its virtues is a flavour-imparting cupful of my toasted French Herb Bread cubes.

	Metric	Imperial	American
For the salad:			
Spinach leaves, washed, dried and torn into 2.5-cm/1-inch pieces	450 g	1 lb	5 cups
Cos lettuce leaves, washed, dried and torn into 2.5-cm/1-inch pieces	225 g	8 oz	3 cups
Small red onion, very thinly sliced	1	1	1
Spring onions, finely chopped	1	1	1
Freshly toasted bread cubes (Page 145)	50 g	2 oz	1 cup
Sesame seeds, toasted	2 tbsp	2 tbsp	2 tbsp
Tomatoes, skinned, cored and cut into wedges	2	2	2
For the salad dressing:			
Cider vinegar	1 tbsp	1 tbsp	1 tbsp
Juice of ½ lemon			
Sodium-free soya sauce	1 tsp	1 tsp	1 tsp
Flavoured honey, such as thyme	2 tsp	2 tsp	2 tsp
Corn oil	3 tbsp	3 tbsp	3 tbsp
Unsweetened pineapple juice	80 ml	3 fl oz	⅓ cup
Shallot, finely chopped	1	1	1
Clove garlic, finely chopped	1	1	1

Prepare salad dressing first by combining all ingredients in jar, shaking well. Let stand for 30 minutes before serving, shaking again before pouring over salad.

Combine spinach and Cos with onion, spring onion and bread cubes, tossing well. Add only enough salad dressing to moisten vegetables (about 2 tablespoons per serving).

To toast sesame seeds, heat a small frying pan until hot. Pour seeds into pan and spread in one layer. Continue cooking while shaking pan at intervals until seeds brown lightly. Sprinkle on top of prepared salad. Garnish with tomatoes, and serve.

Yield: Salad serves 4; dressing, about 180 ml/ 6 fl oz/¾ cup

Variations:
1. Pile low-fat cottage cheese into the centre of the salad before adding dressing.
2. Add 225 g/8 oz/1 cup slivered cooked turkey, veal or chicken to salad and toss.
3. Add 50 g/2 oz/¼ cup low-fat cheese, cut into thin slivers, and toss.

CAL	F	P:S	SOD	CAR	CHO
93	1	4.8:1	48	22	0
Dressing					
56	5	4.5:1	6	2	0
With cottage cheese					
96	1	4.8:1	50	22	0
With turkey					
135	3	3.3:1	78	22	16
With veal					
129	3	3.1:1	66	23	18
With chicken					
129	4	3.0:1	67	25	17
With low-fat cheese					
143	6	1.3:1	49	32	10

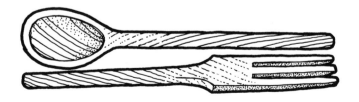

VEGETABLE-FRUIT SALAD

Here's an original vegetarian salad.

	Metric	Imperial	American
For the salad:			
Large cos lettuce leaves, washed and dried	8	8	8
Carrot, peeled and shredded	1	1	1
Stick celery, diced	1	1	1
Seedless raisins	75 g	3 oz	½ cup
Crisp sweet apples	3	3	3
Banana, sliced	1	1	1
Fresh lemon juice	1 tbsp	1 tbsp	1 tbsp
For the fruit dressing:			
Banana, sliced	½	½	½
Unsweetened apple juice	120 ml	4 fl oz	½ cup
Unsweetened pineapple or orange juice	60 ml	2 fl oz	¼ cup
Carrot, peeled and grated	¼	¼	¼
Corn oil	2 tbsp	2 tbsp	2 tbsp
Ground ginger	¼ tsp	¼ tsp	¼ tsp
Ground allspice	¼ tsp	¼ tsp	¼ tsp
Cottage cheese, no salt	1 tbsp	1 tbsp	1 tbsp

Combine vegetables and fruit with lemon juice and toss. Arrange Cos on individual serving plates. Top leaves with vegetable-fruit mixture.

Prepare salad dressing by combining all ingredients in blender and puréeing until smooth. Pour over salad.

Yield: Salad serves 4; Fruit Dressing, about 300 ml/ ½ pt/1¼ cups

CAL	F	P:S	SOD	CAR	CHO
134	0	—	39	44	0
Dressing					
44	2	4.5:1	2	6	0

HORS D'OEUVRES, BREAKFAST AND LUNCHEON DISHES, AND RELISHES

Dinner for most of us is the gastronomic highlight of the day, and too often the little dishes that sustain us for the rest of the day are rarely bothered with. What a pity! Light, but fulfillingly nutritious, breakfasts and lunches should be as varied as your evening meal. Here is an interesting selection of recipes to transform the little meals, and the evening's precursor to the grand meal, into small gems, often by using humble leftovers.

Of the few condiments in this section, I'm particularly proud of my mayonnaise. It has all of the right flavours and none of the wrong ingredients. And you'll be surprised by my non-saline pickles.

MELBA TOAST

Use any of my firm textured breads such as Pumpernickel, Ryes, Four Flour Bread, Whole Wheat, Cracked Wheat, etc. (see bread section). Slice bread very thin, and lay on baking tray in one layer. Bake in preheated 220°C/425°F/Gas mark 7 oven for 10 minutes, or until completely dry. Cool. Store in airtight tin.

To prepare melba toast for dips, cut each slice into quarters before baking.

Yield: As much as you'd like to make

CAL	F	P:S	SOD	CAR	CHO
Per piece (about)					
13	0	—	0	3	0
For dips (about)					
3+	0	—	0	1	0

EGGLESS MAYONNAISE

	Metric	Imperial	American
Cider vinegar	1 tbsp	1 tbsp	1 tbsp
Wine vinegar	1 tsp	1 tsp	1 tsp
Water	80 ml	3 fl oz	⅓ cup
Powdered gelatine	1½ tsp	1½ tsp	1½ tsp
Dry mustard	½ tsp	½ tsp	½ tsp
Fresh lemon juice	1 tbsp	1 tbsp	1 tbsp
Garlic powder, no salt added	¼ tsp	¼ tsp	¼ tsp
Low-fat dry milk	1 tbsp	1 tbsp	1 tbsp
Low-fat milk	60 ml	2 fl oz	¼ cup
Honey	1 tsp	1 tsp	1 tsp
Freshly chopped dill or ¼ tsp dried dill, crushed	½ tsp	½ tsp	½ tsp
Dried tarragon leaves, crushed	¼ tsp	¼ tsp	¼ tsp
Cayenne pepper	3 pinches	3 pinches	3 pinches
Corn oil	180 ml	6 fl oz	¾ cup

Combine vinegars and water in saucepan. Bring to boil. Turn off heat. Add gelatine and stir to dissolve. Let cool to lukewarm.

In small bowl combine mustard, lemon juice and garlic powder. Beat well with small wire whisk. Add gelatine mixture and blend again with whisk.

In another bowl, whisk together dry and liquid milks, honey, herbs and cayenne pepper. Slowly add to blended gelatine milk mixture, beating constantly with whisk. Add oil, a little at a time, beating vigorously after each addition, until all oil is absorbed.

Refrigerate until partially set (about 20 minutes). Whisk again until smooth and creamy.

Pile into ½-litre/1-pint jar and refrigerate until set (about 2 hours).

CAL	F	P:S	SOD	CAR	CHO
Per tablespoon					
71	8	4.5:1	4	1	0

MAKE-YOUR-OWN PICKLES

	Metric	Imperial	American
Large firm cucumbers, scrubbed and thinly sliced	2	2	2
Pickling spices, no salt added	2 tsp	2 tsp	2 tsp
Honey	2 tsp	2 tsp	2 tsp
Freshly chopped dill	1 tsp	1 tsp	1 tsp
White vinegar	3 tbsp	3 tbsp	3 tbsp
Wine vinegar	1 tbsp	1 tbsp	1 tbsp
Cayenne pepper	4 pinches	4 pinches	4 pinches

Place cucumber slices in small bowl. Combine rest of ingredients in saucepan. Bring to simmering point, and cook for 1 minute. Pour over cucumber slices. Let stand uncovered until cucumbers have given up some of their juices (about 1 hour). Transfer to covered jar and refrigerate for 24 hours before serving, turning jar upside down 3-4 times.

Yield: Serves 4

CAL	F	P:S	SOD	CAR	CHO
24	0	—	10	5	0

APPLE RELISH

	Metric	Imperial	American
Crisp eating apples, peeled, cored and diced	6	6	6
Honey	60 ml	2 fl oz	¼ cup
Cider vinegar	180 ml	6 fl oz	¾ cup
Freshly chopped parsley	1 tsp	1 tsp	1 tsp
Whole cloves	6	6	6
Ground ginger	1 tsp	1 tsp	1 tsp
Garlic powder, no salt added	¼ tsp	¼ tsp	¼ tsp
Medium-sized green pepper, finely chopped	1	1	1
Medium-sized onion, finely chopped	1	1	1
Large shallot, finely chopped	1	1	1
Lime, sliced and cubed	½	½	½
Seedless raisins	100 g	4 oz	¾ cup

Combine all ingredients in saucepan. Stir well to blend. Bring to boil. Turn heat down to simmering point. Cover and simmer for 1½-2 hours, until very thick, stirring from time to time. Finished relish should be the consistency of thick soured cream. Partially remove cover and let cool in pan. Transfer to jars and refrigerate. Storage life: about 2 weeks.

Yield: About 1 litre/1¾ pints/1 quart

Note: Delicious served with grilled or roasted meats.

CAL	F	P:S	SOD	CAR	CHO
Per tablespoon					
34	0	—	2	9	0

THREE-FLOUR PANCAKES

Serve these for breakfast.

	Metric	Imperial	American
Buckwheat flour	50 g	2 oz	½ cup
Whole wheat flour	25 g	1 oz	¼ cup
Unbleached white flour	25 g	1 oz	¼ cup
Low sodium baking powder	2½ tsp	2½ tsp	2½ tsp
Ground ginger	¼ tsp	¼ tsp	¼ tsp
Unsweetened apple juice	60 ml	2 fl oz	¼ cup
Corn oil	1 tbsp	1 tbsp	1 tbsp
Buttermilk, no salt added	300–360 ml	10–12 fl oz	1¼–1½ cups
Corn oil to brush pan	¼ tsp	¼ tsp	¼ tsp

Combine flours, baking powder and ginger in bowl. Stir to blend. Add apple juice and stir. Then add oil and most of the buttermilk and stir again. Mixture should be the consistency of thick soured cream—yet pourable.

Heat non-stick frying pan until hot. Brush lightly with oil. For each pancake, pour 2 tablespoons batter into pan, making 3 or 4 pancakes at a time. Cook until top is lightly bubbled and edges are brown. Turn and brown on second side. Serve immediately with honey, jam (no sugar added), or sprinkled with cinnamon.

Yield: 12 pancakes, 7.5 cm/3 inches in diameter

CAL	F	P:S	SOD	CAR	CHO
Per pancake					
58	1	4.5:1	39	9	0

BILBERRY GRIDDLE CAKES

Delicious for breakfast.

	Metric	Imperial	American
Buckwheat flour	40 g	1½ oz	⅓ cup
Unbleached flour	60 g	2½ oz	⅔ cup
Low sodium baking powder	2½ tsp	2½ tsp	2½ tsp
Low-fat plain yogurt	120 ml	4 fl oz	½ cup
Low-fat milk	120 ml	4 fl oz	½ cup
Fresh bilberries	50 g	2 oz	¼ cup
Corn oil to coat pan	½ tsp	½ tsp	½ tsp

Combine flours and baking powder in bowl. Blend yogurt with most of the milk and add to flour mixture. Stir. The consistency should be thick yet pourable. If too thick, add a little more milk.

Pick over bilberries. Pour into sieve and rinse under cold running water. Drain well. Gently stir into batter.

Heat large non-stick frying pan until hot enough for a drop of water to bounce off. Coat very lightly with oil for the first batch of griddle cakes. Sauté 3 or 4 griddle cakes at a time. Turn when edges brown and top bubbles (about 3 minutes). Sauté on second side until lightly brown and griddle cakes puff up slightly. Serve with honey or your favourite jam, no sugar added.

Yield: 12 griddle cakes, serves 4

CAL	F	P:S	SOD	CAR	CHO
Per pancake					
47	0	—	9	10	0

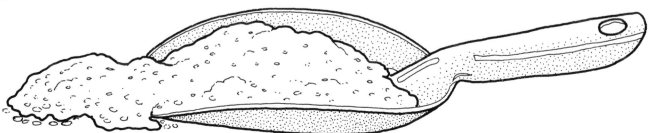

FRENCH TOAST

For breakfast.

	Metric	Imperial	American
Egg whites	4	4	4
Low-fat milk	120 ml	4 fl oz	½ cup
Cayenne pepper	2 pinches	2 pinches	2 pinches
Ground cinnamon	2 pinches	2 pinches	2 pinches
Bread slices, 1.5 cm/½ inch thick, 7.5 cm/3 inches square, including crusts (see Note)	4	4	4
Corn oil	1 tbsp	1 tbsp	1 tbsp

In small bowl, combine egg whites, milk, cayenne and cinnamon. Beat until frothy with fork. Soak bread in mixture, one slice at a time, until moistened through uniformly. Transfer each slice to plate. Pour any left-over mixture over bread slices.

Heat oil in large heavy frying pan until hot but not smoking. Add bread, pouring any unabsorbed liquid over bread. Sauté over medium high heat until brown on both sides. Serve immediately, topped with honey, jam (no sugar added), or sprinkled with cinnamon.

Yield: Serves 4

Note: My breads which are suitable for French Toast are: Featherbread, Cracked Wheat Bread, Cardamom Bread, My French Bread, and My French Herb Bread. If using My French Breads, allow two 1.5-cm/½-inch slices per portion.

CAL	F	P:S	SOD	CAR	CHO
118	4	4.5:1	74	15	0

WHOLE WHEAT CREPES WITH CHEESE FILLING

For lunch or breakfast. Filling 1 is sweet. Filling 2 is spicy.

	Metric	Imperial	American
For the crepe batter:			
Egg whites	3	3	3
Egg yolk	½	½	½
Low-fat milk	180 ml	6 fl oz	¾ cup
Whole wheat flour	90 g	3½ oz	¾ cup
Unbleached flour	25 g	1 oz	¼ cup
Toasted wheat germ, no sugar added	2 tsp	2 tsp	2 tsp
Corn oil	1½ tbsp	1½ tbsp	1½ tbsp
Corn oil for oiling pan	½ tsp	½ tsp	½ tsp
Ground cinnamon	½ tsp	½ tsp	½ tsp
Vanilla essence	½ tsp	½ tsp	½ tsp
Cheese filling 1:			
Cottage cheese, no salt added	350 g	12 oz	1½ cups
Fresh lemon juice	1 tbsp	1 tbsp	1 tbsp
Ground nutmeg	2 pinches	2 pinches	2 pinches
Small egg (use ½ yolk and all of white)	1	1	1
Vanilla essence	½ tsp	½ tsp	½ tsp
Ground cinnamon	2 pinches	2 pinches	2 pinches
Honey	1 tsp	1 tsp	1 tsp
Cheese filling 2:			
Cottage cheese, no salt added	350 g	12 oz	1½ cups
Chopped chives or spring onions	1 tbsp	1 tbsp	1 tbsp
Mild paprika	3 pinches	3 pinches	3 pinches
Cayenne pepper	2 pinches	2 pinches	2 pinches
Small egg (use ½ yolk and all of white)	1	1	1

Prepare batter first. Combine all ingredients in blender and blend for 1 minute. Cover and let stand at room temperature for 1 hour.

To prepare fillings: Combine all ingredients in small bowl. Blend well with small wire whisk. Refrigerate until ready to fill crepes.

To cook and assemble crepes: Brush non-stick crepe pan lightly with oil for first crepe only. Heat pan until hot. Add 60 ml/4 tbsp/¼ cup batter to centre of pan. Tilt so that batter flows to sides and makes complete circle. Cook until lightly brown and edges start to come away from pan. Turn. Cook on second side for just 10 seconds. Stack crepes between alternating layers of greaseproof paper, first-cooked side down. Continue to cook crepes until all batter is used.

To fill, remove crepes from stack one by one, adding 1 tablespoon filling to second-cooked side of each crepe. Fold over ends and tuck in sides.

Brush crepe pan lightly with oil. Heat until hot. Place filled crepes in pan, 4 at a time, seam side down, and brown lightly. Turn and brown on other side. Remove to serving platter and keep warm. Repeat cooking procedure for balance of crepes. Serve immediately.

Yield: 8 crepes

CAL	F	P:S	SOD	CAR	CHO
Each crepe					
82	1	2.7:1	32	12	16
Cheese filling 1					
39	0	—	28	4	16
Cheese filling 2					
36	0	—	30	3	16

CORN MUFFINS

	Metric	Imperial	American
Fresh lemon juice	2 tsp	2 tsp	2 tsp
Unsweetened orange or apple juice	60 ml	2 fl oz	¼ cup
Large egg (use ½ yolk and all of the white)	1	1	1
Low-fat milk	180 ml	6 fl oz	¾ cup
Honey	1 tbsp	1 tbsp	1 tbsp
Corn oil	2½ tbsp	2½ tbsp	2½ tbsp
Yellow cornmeal	175 g	6 oz	1 cup
Unbleached flour	75 g +1 tbsp	3 oz +1 tbsp	¾ cup +1 tbsp
Low sodium baking powder	2½ tsp	2½ tsp	2½ tsp
Ground cinnamon	½ tsp	½ tsp	½ tsp
Corn oil to oil tin	½ tbsp	½ tbsp	½ tbsp

In mixing bowl, combine lemon juice with orange or apple juice. Blend. Add egg, milk and honey and blend again. Add oil and stir.

Combine cornmeal, flour, baking powder and cinnamon in one bowl. Stir to blend. Add to liquid mixture, 120 ml/4 fl oz/½ cup at a time, blending with wooden spoon after each addition. Mixture should be thick yet pourable. If too thin, add an additional tablespoon flour.

For a crisp crust, lightly oil tartlet tin. Place in preheated 220°C/425°F/Gas mark 7 oven for 10 minutes. Remove from oven and fill with batter, filling each cup almost to top. Return to oven and bake for 20 minutes. Remove from oven and let muffins cool for 5 minutes in tin. Remove muffins from tin and serve warm.

Yield: 9 large muffins

Variation: If you prefer smaller muffins, fill each cup ⅔ full. Yield will be 12 muffins.

CAL	F	P:S	SOD	CAR	CHO
Each large muffin					
143	4	4.5:1	17	5	14
Each small muffin					
106	2	4.5:1	12	3	10

MAKE-YOUR-OWN GRANOLA

For breakfast.

	Metric	Imperial	American
Rolled oats, toasted	350 g	12 oz	3 cups
Unprocessed bran flakes	50 g	2 oz	½ cup
Sesame seeds	40 g	1½ oz	¼ cup
Toasted wheat germ, no sugar added	75 g	3 oz	½ cup
Chopped walnuts	50 g	2 oz	¼ cup
Ground cinnamon	1 tsp	1 tsp	1 tsp
Dried dates, chopped	50 g	2 oz	¼ cup
Dried apricots, chopped	50 g	2 oz	¼ cup
Seedless raisins	75 g	3 oz	½ cup

Toss toasted oats with remaining ingredients and store in glass jar in refrigerator.

Yield: About 750 g/1½ lb/5½ cups granola

Note: Allow 3 tablespoons per portion.

CAL	F	P:S	SOD	CAR	CHO
Per portion					
104	2	7.9:1	4	17	0

LUNCHEON OMELETTES

For each omelette:	Metric	Imperial	American
Egg whites	2	2	2
Freshly chopped parsley and dill	1½ tsp	1½ tsp	1½ tsp
Corn oil	½ tsp	½ tsp	½ tsp
Onion, finely chopped	1 tsp	1 tsp	1 tsp
Small shallot, chopped	1	1	1
Freshly chopped chives	¼ tsp	¼ tsp	¼ tsp
Dried tarragon leaves, crushed	⅛ tsp	⅛ tsp	⅛ tsp
Cayenne pepper	2 pinches	2 pinches	2 pinches

Place egg whites in small bowl and beat with fork until frothy. Add 1 teaspoon parsley and dill and remaining ingredients and beat again with fork.

Brush non-stick frying pan with oil. Heat until hot but not smoking. Pour egg mixture into pan, tilting pan from side to side so that mixture forms a complete circle. Turn heat down and cook only until lightly browned on one side. The centre should remain moist. Slide onto dish, fold half over. Serve with herbs.

Variations:

1. Add 2 tablespoons chopped cooked, drained spinach to uncooked mixture. Blend well with fork.

2. Add 2 tablespoons finely diced warm cooked chicken or veal to centre of cooked omelette.

3. Make basic omelette and pour Creamy Mushroom Sauce over it (Page 81).

Yield: Serves 1

CAL	F	P:S	SOD	CAR	CHO
62	2	4.5:1	120	2	0
Spinach					
74	2	4.5:1	139	5	0
Chicken					
103	4	3.6:1	139	6	12
Veal					
100	4	3.0:1	135	0	13
Mushroom sauce					
184	9	4.5:1	156	10	0

CREAMY MUSHROOMS ON TOAST

For lunch.

	Metric	Imperial	American
Corn oil	2 tbsp	2 tbsp	2 tbsp
Shallots, finely chopped	2	2	2
Cloves garlic, finely chopped	2	2	2
Fresh mushrooms, washed, trimmed and sliced	350 g	12 oz	¾ lb
Unbleached flour	2 tbsp	2 tbsp	2 tbsp
Cayenne pepper	3 pinches	3 pinches	3 pinches
Dry Vermouth or white wine	3 tbsp	3 tbsp	3 tbsp
Chicken stock	150 ml	¼ pt	⅔ cup
Dried tarragon leaves, crushed	¾ tsp	¾ tsp	¾ tsp
Low-fat milk	180 ml	6 fl oz	¾ cup
Thin slices any of my breads (Pages 134 to 145)	4	4	4
Freshly chopped parsley	1 tbsp	1 tbsp	1 tbsp

Heat oil in large non-stick or heavy frying pan until hot. Add shallots and garlic. Sauté for 1 minute. Add mushrooms and sauté for 3 minutes, turning constantly. Sprinkle with flour and cook for 1 minute, stirring well. Add cayenne, wine and stock, and blend. Add tarragon and milk. Simmer until thickened. If too thick to your taste, add a little milk and blend well. Do not over-cook.

Pour over just-toasted slices of bread. Sprinkle with parsley, and serve.

Yield: Serves 4

CAL	F	P:S	SOD	CAR	CHO
147	7	4.5:1	36	13	0

LUNCHEON TREAT WITH FRUIT JUICE DRESSING

	Metric	Imperial	American
For the salad:			
Large cos lettuce leaves	8	8	8
Cottage cheese	225 g	8 oz	1 cup
Large navel orange, peeled and sliced	1	1	1
Large banana, sliced	1	1	1
Seedless raisins	50 g	2 oz	¼ cup
For the fruit juice dressing:			
Unsweetened orange juice	120 ml	4 fl oz	½ cup
Unsweetened apple juice	60 ml	2 fl oz	¼ cup
Unsweetened pineapple juice	120 ml	4 fl oz	½ cup
Lemon juice	3 tbsp	3 tbsp	3 tbsp
Corn oil	3 tbsp	3 tbsp	3 tbsp
Honey	1 tbsp	1 tbsp	1 tbsp

Prepare the salad dressing an hour before serving. Place all ingredients in 0.5-litre/1-pint jar. Cover and shake well. Chill.

Set out 4 salad plates. Wash and pat lettuce leaves dry. Place 2 lettuce leaves on each plate. Spoon 50 g/2 oz/¼ cup cottage cheese per serving on top of lettuce. Distribute orange and banana slices equally around cottage cheese. Sprinkle with raisins. Serve with fruit dressing on the side in sauceboat.

Yield: Salad: Serves 4; Fruit Dressing, about 360 ml/12½ fl oz/1½ cups—allow 2 tablespoons per serving

CAL	F	P:S	SOD	CAR	CHO
Salad					
141	0	—	30	29	0
Dressing					
48	4	4.5:1	0	4	0

VEAL STUFFED EGGS

For luncheon.

	Metric	Imperial	American
Cooked veal, finely diced, leftovers are fine (Page 77)	75 g	3 oz	1/3 cup
Crisp eating apple, peeled, cored and finely diced	1/2	1/2	1/2
Chopped pickles (Page 104)	1 tbsp	1 tbsp	1 tbsp
Cayenne pepper	2 pinches	2 pinches	2 pinches
Eggless Mayonnaise (Page 103)	2-3 tbsp	2-3 tbsp	2-3 tbsp
Hard-boiled egg whites (see method)	6	6	6
Crisp cos lettuce leaves	8	8	8
Radishes, cut into roses	8	8	8

In small bowl, combine veal, apple and pickles. Add cayenne and enough mayonnaise to bind mixture.

Bring eggs to room temperature. Fill saucepan with warm water. Place eggs in pan and slowly bring water to boil. Turn heat down. Simmer slowly, uncovered, for 15 minutes. Cool eggs under cold running water, and remove shells as soon as eggs are cool enough to handle. Cut eggs in half and discard yolk.

Lightly stuff egg halves with veal mixture. Arrange on lettuce leaves, surrounded by remaining veal mixture. Garnish with radish roses.

Yield: Serves 4

CAL	F	P:S	SOD	CAR	CHO
106	6	4.5:1	82	1	6

SALMON STUFFED EGGS

For hors d'oeuvres or luncheon.

	Metric	Imperial	American
Hard-boiled egg whites	7	7	7
Canned salmon, no salt added, well drained	100 g	3 1/2 oz	3 1/2 oz
Eggless Mayonnaise (Page 103)	1 tbsp	1 tbsp	1 tbsp
Finely chopped onion	2 tsp	2 tsp	2 tsp
Cayenne pepper	2 pinches	2 pinches	2 pinches
Dry mustard, dissolved in 1/2 tsp water	1/2 tsp	1/2 tsp	1/2 tsp
Fresh lemon juice	1 tsp	1 tsp	1 tsp
Freshly chopped dill and parsley	1 tsp	1 tsp	1 tsp

Remove shells from eggs while still warm. Cut eggs in half and discard yolks. Chop 2 halves well, leaving rest of halves intact.

Mash salmon together with mayonnaise and chopped egg white. Add onion, cayenne, mustard, lemon juice and herbs, blending well. Stuff egg halves with mixture. Cover and chill before serving.

Yield: 12 stuffed halves; serves 4

CAL	F	P:S	SOD	CAR	CHO
32	2	3.3:1	98	0	7

CRUDITÉS

Colourful cold vegetable platter.

	Metric	Imperial	American
Cottage cheese	3 tbsp	3 tbsp	3 tbsp
Cayenne pepper	2 pinches	2 pinches	2 pinches
Tomato juice, no salt added (see method)	1 tbsp	1 tbsp	1 tbsp
Freshly chopped parsley			
Chicory leaves	10	10	10
Broccoli florets	12	12	12
Cauliflower florets	8	8	8
Fresh lemon juice	1 tsp	1 tsp	1 tsp
Carrots, peeled and cut lengthwise into thin sticks	2	2	2
Cherry tomatoes	15-20	15-20	15-20
Watercress sprigs	8	8	8
Radishes, cut into roses	8	8	8

Combine cottage cheese in blender with cayenne pepper and enough tomato juice to make a spreadable mixture. Sprinkle with parsley and lightly fill chicory leaves with mixture.

Parboil broccoli for 1 minute, drain in colander and place under cold running water until cooled. Parboil cauliflower for 2 minutes, drain in colander and place under cold running water until cooled. Sprinkle with lemon juice. Arrange all the vegetables on platter in attractive pattern and serve with or without dip (Page 116).

Yield: Serves 8 for hors d'oeuvres; serves 4 for light lunch

CAL	F	P:S	SOD	CAR	CHO
For hors d'oeuvres					
39	0	—	38	7	0
For luncheon					
78	0	—	76	14	0

SARDINE CANAPÉS

	Metric	Imperial	American
Canned Norwegian dietetic brisling sardines, packed in water, no salt or oil added	105 g	3¾ oz	3¾ oz
Fresh lemon juice	2 tsp	2 tsp	2 tsp
Cayenne pepper	pinch	pinch	pinch
Hard-boiled egg whites, cooled and mashed	3	3	3
Drained pickles, finely chopped (Page 104)	80 ml	5 tbsp	⅓ cup
Eggless Mayonnaise (Page 103)	2 tbsp	2 tbsp	2 tbsp

Drain sardines. Transfer to small bowl. Add lemon juice and cayenne. Mash well with fork. Add egg whites, pickles and mayonnaise, and blend. Cover and refrigerate until well chilled.

Spread on 5 slices of any of my breads, thinly sliced, each slice cut into quarters (Pages 134 to 145).

Yield: 20 canapés

Variation: For luncheon. Wash and pat dry 4 large Cos lettuce leaves. Arrange on luncheon plates. Spoon equal amounts of sardine mixture over lettuce. Garnish with strips of pimento (no salt added), and slices of pickles.

Yield: Serves 4

CAL	F	P:S	SOD	CAR	CHO
Each canapé					
26	1	3.0:1	9	1	3
Luncheon serving					
114	7	3.0:1	48	3	13

TUNA FISH FOR CANAPÉS

	Metric	Imperial	American
Canned tuna, packed in water, no salt added	*185 g*	*6½ oz*	*6½ oz*
Juice of 1 lemon			
Onion, finely chopped	*1*	*1*	*1*
Spring onion, finely chopped	*1*	*1*	*1*
Stick celery, finely chopped	*½*	*½*	*½*
Small pepper, finely chopped	*1*	*1*	*1*
Cayenne pepper	*2 pinches*	*2 pinches*	*2 pinches*
Eggless Mayonnaise (Page 103)	*2 tbsp*	*2 tbsp*	*2 tbsp*
Freshly chopped parsley	*2 tsp*	*2 tsp*	*2 tsp*

Drain tuna well and transfer to bowl. Add lemon juice and mash well with fork. Add remaining ingredients and blend. Spread on 5 slices of any of my breads, thinly sliced, each slice cut into quarters.

Yield: 20 canapés

Variations: For luncheon:
1. Sandwiches. Set out 6 slices of any of my breads, thinly sliced (Pages 134 to 145). Spread the tuna fish on 3 slices of bread. Add a half leaf crisp Cos lettuce to each sandwich. Spread balance of bread with ½ teaspoon Eggless Mayonnaise per slice and cover sandwich. Cut each sandwich into 4 triangles. Serve 3 triangles per person.

Yield: Serves 4

2. Salad. Spoon all of mixture onto crisp Cos lettuce leaves. Garnish Cos with watercress, tomato wedges and radish roses.

Yield: Serves 4

CAL	F	P:S	SOD	CAR	CHO
Each canapé					
26	0	—	7	2	6
Sandwich serving					
171	9	4.5:1	30	15	21
Salad serving					
110	4	4.5:1	35	9	29

MY HOT CANAPÉS

Four kinds of canapés: meat, fish, chicken and gratineed.

	Metric	Imperial	American
Cooked meat, finely diced (e.g. leftovers)	*225 g*	*8 oz*	*1 cup*
Duxelles (Page 12)	*3 tbsp*	*3 tbsp*	*3 tbsp*
Finely chopped walnuts	*1 tsp*	*1 tsp*	*1 tsp*
Freshly chopped parsley	*2 tsp*	*2 tsp*	*2 tsp*
Chicken stock (Page 8)	*3 tbsp*	*3 tbsp*	*3 tbsp*
Cayenne pepper	*3 pinches*	*3 pinches*	*3 pinches*
Combined dried thyme and rosemary leaves, crushed	*¼ tsp*	*¼ tsp*	*¼ tsp*
Thin slices of any of my breads (Pages 134 to 145)	*6*	*6*	*6*

In food processor or blender combine all ingredients except bread, and blend until smooth. (If using blender, blend small amounts at a time.) Spread over sliced bread. Place in shallow baking tin and bake in pre-heated 220°C/425°F/Gas mark 7 oven for about 7 minutes, or until heated through. Cut each slice into 4 triangles, and serve.

Yield: 24 canapés

Variations:
1. Substitute fish for meat, fish stock for chicken stock, and crushed fennel seeds for rosemary leaves.
2. Substitute chicken for meat, and sage leaves for thyme leaves.

3. Sprinkle any of heated canapés with 2 tablespoons grated low-fat cheese (the sharper the better), and place under grill for 2-3 minutes, or until cheese is melted.

CAL	F	P:S	SOD	CAR	CHO
Per canapé, meat					
16	0	—	3	1	2
Per canapé, fish					
14	0	—	2	1	2
Per canapé, chicken					
17	0	—	4	0	2
Cheese, add					
3	0	—	0	0	0

CHOPPED EGG HORS D'OEUVRES

	Metric	Imperial	American
Hard-boiled egg whites (see method)	4	4	4
Small onion, finely chopped	1	1	1
Spring onion, finely chopped	1	1	1
Freshly chopped dill	1 tsp	1 tsp	1 tsp
Cayenne pepper	2 pinches	2 pinches	2 pinches
Eggless Mayonnaise (Page 103)	1 tbsp	1 tbsp	1 tbsp
Pimento, no salt added, well drained, cut into thin strips	1	1	1

Bring eggs to room temperature. Fill saucepan with warm water. Place eggs in pan and slowly bring water to boil. Turn heat down. Simmer slowly, uncovered, for 15 minutes. Cool eggs under cold running water, and remove shells as soon as eggs are cool enough to handle.

Cut eggs in half, discarding yolks, and mash well with fork. Add rest of ingredients with exception of pimento, and blend well.

Serve spread on 4 thin slices of any of my breads (Pages 134 to 145). Cut each slice into quarters. Garnish with pimento strips.

Yield: 16 canapés

Variation: For luncheon—open sandwiches. Spread on 4 slices of any of my breads, thinly sliced, and garnish with pimento strips.

Yield: Serves 4

CAL	F	P:S	SOD	CAR	CHO
Each canapé					
16	0	—	14	2	0
Each sandwich					
37	0	—	14	7	0

COLD FISH SPREAD

	Metric	Imperial	American
Cooked fish removed from bone (leftovers are fine)	100 g	4 oz	¼ lb
Juice of ½ lemon			
Dry mustard, dissolved in ¼ tsp water	⅛ tsp	⅛ tsp	⅛ tsp
Cayenne pepper	3 pinches	3 pinches	3 pinches
Finely chopped shallots	½ tsp	½ tsp	½ tsp
Eggless Mayonnaise (Page 103), enough to moisten and make spreadable	1 tbsp	1 tbsp	1 tbsp
Thin slices any of my breads (Pages 134 to 145)	3	3	3
Pimento slivers, no salt added, for garnish	12	12	12

Sprinkle fish with lemon juice and mash well. Add remaining ingredients, except pimento, and blend. Spread on sliced bread. Cut each slice into quarters. Garnish with pimento and serve.

Yield: 12 canapés

CAL	F	P:S	SOD	CAR	CHO
Per canapé					
21	1	2.5:1	4	2	4

PINEAPPLE-WALNUT CHEESE SPREAD

For hors d'oeuvres.

	Metric	Imperial	American
Cottage cheese, no salt added	100 g	4 oz	½ cup
Crushed pineapple in its own juices, drained, no sugar added	75 g	3 oz	¼ cup
Fresh lemon juice	1 tsp	1 tsp	1 tsp
Ground ginger	¼ tsp	¼ tsp	¼ tsp
Cayenne pepper	2 pinches	2 pinches	2 pinches
Garlic powder, no salt added	2 pinches	2 pinches	2 pinches
Chopped walnuts	1 tbsp	1 tbsp	1 tbsp
Sodium-free soya sauce	2 dashes	2 dashes	2 dashes

Combine all ingredients in blender or food processor. Blend until smooth. Spread on 4 slices of any of my breads, thinly sliced (Pages 134 to 145). Cut each slice into quarters, and serve.

Yield: Enough for 16 canapés

Variation: For luncheon dish. Make thin sandwiches using Date-nut Cake (Page 129). Cut into quarters and serve on a bed of Cos lettuce. Garnish with radish roses.

CAL	F	P:S	SOD	CAR	CHO
Per canapé					
17	0	0	4	3	0
Per sandwich					
149	2	4.1:1	7	35	10

APPLE-WALNUT SPREAD

For hors d'oeuvres.

	Metric	Imperial	American
Shelled walnuts, finely chopped	75 g	3 oz	½ cup
Crisp eating apple, peeled and chopped	½	½	½
Cloves garlic, finely chopped	2	2	2
Bread crumbs (Page 145)	3 tbsp	3 tbsp	3 tbsp
Fresh lemon or lime juice	1½ tsp	1½ tsp	1½ tsp
Corn oil	1 tsp	1 tsp	1 tsp
Ground cinnamon	¼ tsp	¼ tsp	¼ tsp
Unsweetened apple juice (optional)	2 tsp	2 tsp	2 tsp

Using a food processor: Place walnuts, apple, garlic and bread crumbs in food processor bowl. Blend into paste. Add lemon or lime juice, oil and cinnamon. Blend until smooth. If too thick to your taste, add apple juice, if liked, and blend again. Pour into jar and chill.

Using a blender: Place chopped walnuts in pestle and mortar and pulverize to a paste. Transfer to blender together with apple, oil and cinnamon. Blend until smooth. Add crumbs, lemon or lime juice and garlic, and blend. If mixture is too thick to your taste, add apple juice and blend again. Pour into jar and chill.

Cut 6 thin slices of any of my breads (Pages 134 to 145). Spread 1 tablespoon mixture over each slice. Cut each slice into 4 triangles. Serve.

Yield: 24 hors d'oeuvres

Variation: Curry powder, no salt or pepper added, or ground ginger can be substituted for cinnamon.

CAL	F	P:S	SOD	CAR	CHO
Each hors d'oeuvre					
36	3	12:1	1	6	0

Variations and option make no appreciable difference.

MUSHROOM-EGG SPREAD

For hors d'oeuvres.

	Metric	Imperial	American
Corn oil	1 tbsp	1 tbsp	1 tbsp
Onion, finely chopped	1	1	1
Cloves garlic, finely chopped	2	2	2
Spring onion, finely chopped	1	1	1
Duxelles (Page 12)	3 tbsp	3 tbsp	3 tbsp
Cider vinegar	1 tsp	1 tsp	1 tsp
Hard-boiled egg whites	4	4	4
Fresh chopped parley and dill	2 tsp	2 tsp	2 tsp
Dry mustard, dissolved in ½ tsp water	¼ tsp	¼ tsp	¼ tsp
Eggless Mayonnaise (Page 103)	2 tsp	2 tsp	2 tsp

Heat oil in small heavy frying pan until hot. Sauté onion, garlic and spring onion until lightly browned. Add duxelles and stir to blend. Add vinegar and cook for 1 minute.

In small bowl, mash egg whites to fine consistency. Combine with sautéed mixture, herbs and mustard, blending well. Add mayonnaise and blend again. Serve immediately, spread on 4 slices of any of my breads, thinly sliced, each slice cut into quarters.

Yield: 16 canapés

CAL	F	P:S	SOD	CAR	CHO
Each canapé					
29	2	4.5:1	15	2	0

CURRIED SPREAD

For hors d'oeuvres.

	Metric	Imperial	American
Stick celery, diced	½	½	½
Carrot, peeled and sliced	½	½	½
Large spring onion, sliced	1	1	1
Hard-boiled egg whites	3	3	3
Cayenne pepper	4 pinches	4 pinches	4 pinches
Curry powder, no salt or pepper added	½ tsp	½ tsp	½ tsp
Dried thyme leaves, crushed	⅛ tsp	⅛ tsp	⅛ tsp
Freshly chopped parsley and dill	1 tsp	1 tsp	1 tsp
Shelled walnuts	25 g	1 oz	¼ cup
Fresh lemon juice	1 tsp	1 tsp	1 tsp
Eggless Mayonnaise (Page 103)	1 tbsp	1 tbsp	1 tbsp

If you're using a mincer, mince all vegetables and egg whites. Then add spices, herbs, walnuts, lemon juice and mayonnaise, blending well.

If you're using a food processor, combine all ingredients in processing bowl and blend, using sharp metal knife attachment.

Spread on 4 slices of any of my breads, thinly sliced (Pages 134 to 145). Cut each slice into quarters, and serve.

Yield: Enough for 16 canapés

CAL	F	P:S	SOD	CAR	CHO
Each canapé					
17	8	—	16	2	0

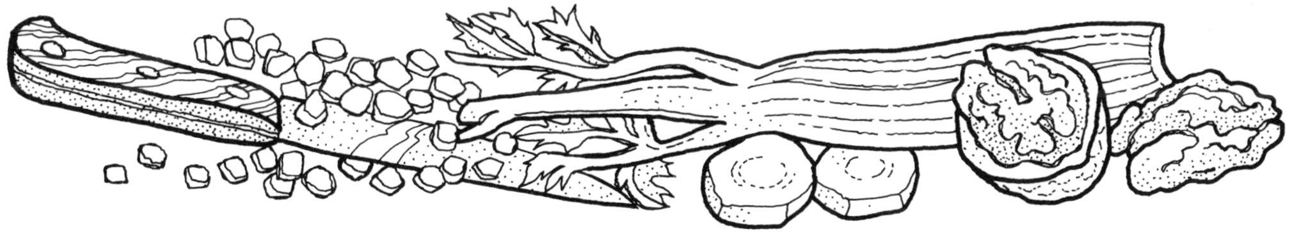

BOMBAY CHICKEN BALLS

For hors d'oeuvres.

	Metric	Imperial	American
Cooked chicken breast, finely chopped, or cooked turkey, white meat only	175 g	6 oz	¾ cup
Diced shallots	1 tbsp	1 tbsp	1 tbsp
Diced onions	1 tbsp	1 tbsp	1 tbsp
Diced celery	1 tbsp	1 tbsp	1 tbsp
Diced carrot	1 tbsp	1 tbsp	1 tbsp
Freshly chopped parsley and dill	1 tbsp	1 tbsp	1 tbsp
Curry powder, no salt or pepper added	1 tsp	1 tsp	1 tsp
Corn oil	1 tbsp	1 tbsp	1 tbsp
Tomato juice, no salt added	1 tbsp	1 tbsp	1 tbsp
Cayenne pepper	2 pinches	2 pinches	2 pinches
Bread crumbs (Page 145)	15 g +1 tbsp	½ oz +1 tbsp	¼ cup +1 tbsp
Paprika			

This hors d'oeuvre is best made using a food processor, but it can be made successfully with a blender.

If using a food processor, combine all ingredients, except crumbs and paprika, in processing bowl. Purée until smooth. If using blender, combine all ingredients except crumbs and paprika in blender. Blend for 10 seconds. Stop machine and stir with spoon. Repeat process until mixture is smooth. Turn mixture into bowl.

Scoop up ½ teaspoon puréed chicken mixture, and shape into smooth balls by rolling between palms. Roll in crumbs. Then sprinkle with paprika. Arrange in flat dish in one layer. Cover and refrigerate for 2 hours before serving.

Pierce with cocktail sticks and serve.

Yield: About 18 balls

Variation: Substitute pineapple juice for tomato juice; add one pineapple chunk from can of pineapple in its own juices, no sugar added, and blend with remaining ingredients.

CAL	F	P:S	SOD	CAR	CHO
Each ball					
26	1	2.5:1	3	4	2
With pineapple					
27	1	2.5:1	2	5	2
Turkey					
32	1	2.5:1	1	5	2

SAVOURY CHEESE DIP

	Metric	Imperial	American
Cottage cheese, no salt added	225 g	8 oz	1 cup
Low-fat plain yogurt	80 ml	3 fl oz	⅓ cup
Shallot, finely chopped	1	1	1
Small onion, finely chopped	1	1	1
Dried tarragon leaves, crushed	½ tsp	½ tsp	½ tsp
Cayenne pepper	3 pinches	3 pinches	3 pinches
Freshly chopped parsley and dill	1 tsp	1 tsp	1 tsp
Fresh lemon juice	1 tsp	1 tsp	1 tsp
Garlic powder, no salt added	⅛ tsp	⅛ tsp	⅛ tsp
Dry mustard, dissolved in ½ tsp water	¼ tsp	¼ tsp	¼ tsp
Tomato juice, no salt added	1 tbsp	1 tbsp	1 tbsp

Combine all ingredients in blender or food processor and purée until smooth. Serve with melba toast (Page 103), allowing one teaspoon per dip.

Yield: About 350 ml/12 fl oz/1½ cups

CAL	F	P:S	SOD	CAR	CHO
Per dip					
6	0	—	2	1	0

HOT STUFFED MUSHROOMS

For hors d'oeuvres.

	Metric	Imperial	American
Large fresh mushrooms, washed and trimmed	225 g	8 oz	½ lb
Corn oil	1 tbsp	1 tbsp	1 tbsp
Clove garlic, finely chopped	1	1	1
Shallot, finely chopped	1	1	1
Dried tarragon leaves, crushed	½ tsp	½ tsp	½ tsp
Cayenne pepper	2 pinches	2 pinches	2 pinches
Dry Vermouth or white wine	1 tbsp	1 tbsp	1 tbsp
Bread crumbs (Page 145)	15 g	½ oz	¼ cup
Freshly chopped parsley and dill	2 tsp	2 tsp	2 tsp
Sodium-free soya sauce (optional)	2 dashes	2 dashes	2 dashes

Gently separate stalks from mushroom caps. Finely chop stalks.

Heat ½ tablespoon oil in non-stick frying pan until hot. Add chopped mushrooms, garlic and shallot, and sauté until softened. Add tarragon and cayenne. Stir. Pour in wine and cook for 1 minute. Pour into small bowl. Add bread crumbs and 1 teaspoon chopped fresh herbs, and optional sodium-free soya sauce. Blend well with spoon. Set aside.

In same pan, heat rest of oil until hot. Sauté mushroom caps for 30 seconds on each side. Transfer to shallow baking dish. Fill each mushroom with prepared stuffing. Sprinkle with remaining freshly chopped parsley and dill. Bake in preheated 200°C/400°F/Gas mark 6 oven for 10 minutes or until heated through. Do not overbake.

Yield: About 12 stuffed mushrooms

CAL	F	P:S	SOD	CAR	CHO
Each mushroom					
32	0	—	4	4	0

SPICY HOT COCKTAIL SAUSAGES

	Metric	Imperial	American
Minced lean beef, rump or boneless sirloin	100 g	4 oz	¼ lb
Carrot, peeled and grated	½	½	½
Freshly chopped parsley	1 tsp	1 tsp	1 tsp
Spring onion, finely chopped	1	1	1
Clove garlic, finely chopped	1	1	1
Finely chopped celery	1 tsp	1 tsp	1 tsp
Bread crumbs (Page 145)	1 tsp	1 tsp	1 tsp
Dried thyme leaves, crushed	⅛ tsp	⅛ tsp	⅛ tsp
Ground cloves	⅛ tsp	⅛ tsp	⅛ tsp
Allspice	⅛ tsp	⅛ tsp	⅛ tsp
Cayenne pepper	3 pinches	3 pinches	3 pinches
Corn oil to oil baking tray	½ tsp	½ tsp	½ tsp
Moderately hot paprika			

Combine all ingredients except paprika in small bowl and blend well. Shape into small sausages by taking 1 teaspoon mixture and rolling it between moist palms. Place on lightly oiled baking tray. Sprinkle liberally with paprika. Cover with foil and refrigerate for 2 hours before grilling.

Grill under medium high heat, until browned.

Yield: 20 small sausages

Variation: Use a combination of half pork and half beef, minced.

CAL	F	P:S	SOD	CAR	CHO
Each beef sausage					
12	0	—	55	0	6
Each beef-pork sausage					
12	0	—	59	1	6

DESSERTS

STRAWBERRY CREPES

Light airy crepes with a delicious strawberry filling make the kind of dessert that stirs memories of champagne and candlelight.

	Metric	Imperial	American
For the crepe batter:			
Egg whites	3	3	3
Egg yolk	½	½	½
Low-fat milk	180 ml	6 fl oz	¾ cup
Whole wheat flour	90 g	3½ oz	¾ cup
Unbleached flour	25 g	1 oz	¼ cup
Toasted wheat germ, no sugar added	2 tsp	2 tsp	2 tsp
Corn oil	1½ tbsp	1½ tbsp	1½ tbsp
Corn oil for oiling pan	½ tsp	½ tsp	½ tsp
Ground cinnamon	½ tsp	½ tsp	½ tsp
Vanilla essence	½ tsp	½ tsp	½ tsp
For the strawberry filling:			
Fresh strawberries, washed, hulled and sliced	450 g	1 lb	2 cups
Fresh lemon juice	1 tsp	1 tsp	1 tsp
Unsweetened apple juice	80 ml	3 fl oz	⅓ cup
Arrowroot	1½ tbsp	1½ tbsp	1½ tbsp
Unsweetened apple juice, to dissolve arrowroot	30 ml	1 fl oz	⅛ cup
Honey	2 tbsp	2 tbsp	2 tbsp
Corn oil to oil baking dish	½ tsp	½ tsp	½ tsp
Finely chopped walnuts	2 tbsp	2 tbsp	2 tbsp

Combine all ingredients for batter in blender and blend for 1 minute. Cover and let stand at room temperature for 1 hour.

Brush non-stick crepe pan lightly with oil for first crepe only. Heat pan until hot. Add 60 ml/4 tbsp/¼ cup batter to centre of pan. Tilt so that batter flows to sides and makes complete circle. Cook until lightly brown and edges start to come away from pan. Turn, cook on second side for just 10 seconds. Stack crepes between alternating layers of greaseproof paper, first-cooked side down. Continue to cook crepes until all batter is used.

Combine strawberries with lemon and apple juices in small heavy-bottomed saucepan. Bring to boil. Turn heat down and simmer, uncovered, for 3 minutes. Add dissolved arrowroot mixture and honey and continue cooking for 2 minutes, stirring constantly, until thickened. Cool until just warm.

Spoon 1 tablespoon warm mixture into centre of second cooked side of each crepe. Fold ends over. Arrange in lightly oiled baking dish. Bake in preheated 220°C/425°F/Gas mark 7 oven for 5 minutes. Sprinkle with nuts and serve.

Yield: 8 crepes

Variation: Prepare 8 crepes. Fill each crepe with 1 tablespoon of your favourite jam (no sugar added). Fold ends over and proceed as above recipe, adding ½ teaspoon cinnamon to chopped nuts.

CAL	F	P:S	SOD	CAR	CHO
Each crepe					
82	1	2.7:1	32	12	16
Filling					
29	0	—	0	8	0

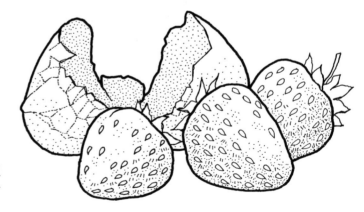

118

BAKED PEARS IN RED WINE

In my version of this masterpiece of haute cuisine, baked pears are bathed in a rich sauce fragrant with the heady essence of Burgundy.

	Metric	Imperial	American
Firm-skinned pears	4	4	4
Whole cloves	4	4	4
Burgundy wine	240 ml	8 fl oz	1 cup
Honey	3 tbsp	3 tbsp	3 tbsp
Unsweetened apple juice	4 tbsp	4 tbsp	4 tbsp
Ground cinnamon	1 tsp	1 tsp	1 tsp
Seeds from 4 pods of cardamom, crushed			
Ground nutmeg	4 pinches	4 pinches	4 pinches

Select pears that are not quite ripe, but not rock hard. If necessary, keep them at room temperature until they reach this degree of ripeness. Leaving stalks on, gently peel from top to bottom in strips, removing as little skin as possible. Stick a clove on to bottom of each pear, and place, standing up and touching each other, in casserole.

Combine wine, honey, apple juice and remaining spices in saucepan. Heat to simmering point. Pour over fruit. Cover and bake in preheated 150°C/ 300°F/Gas mark 2 oven for 30 minutes, basting twice.

Baste again and return, uncovered, to oven. Bake for another 10-15 minutes. Pears should retain shape and not be oversoft. Remove cloves.

Transfer to dish and spoon over wine juices. Cover loosely with greaseproof paper until cooled. Serve at room temperature or cover tightly and refrigerate. Serve chilled.

Yield: Serves 4

Variation: Serve with 1 tablespoon Vanilla Sauce spooned over each pear (Page 122).

CAL	F	P:S	SOD	CAR	CHO
113	0	—	7	27	0

POACHED PEARS

This dessert, light in taste and low in calories, is perfect to follow one of your heavier main courses.

	Metric	Imperial	American
Juice of ½ lemon			
Pears, not quite ripe	4	4	4
Unsweetened apple juice	120 ml	4 fl oz	½ cup
Ground cinnamon	¼ tsp	¼ tsp	¼ tsp
Ground nutmeg	3 pinches	3 pinches	3 pinches
Whole cloves or ¼ tsp cardamom seeds, crushed	3	3	3

Strain lemon juice into wide saucepan. Peel, core and quarter pears. (If they're rock hard when you buy them, keep them unwrapped at room temperature for a day or two until they show just some resistance when you press with thumb.) As each pear is cut, drop into lemon juice in saucepan, turning to coat. Lemon juice keeps the fruit from turning brown.

Add rest of ingredients. Bring to simmering point. Partially cover and simmer for 7-10 minutes, depending upon the ripeness of fruit. Pears when cooked should remain firm yet tender.

Remove cover. Let cool in liquid. Remove cloves. Store in glass jar in refrigerator. Serve, chilled, with cooking liquid poured over pears.

Yield: Serves 4

Variation: Add 1 tablespoon honey during last 5 minutes of cooking time.

CAL	F	P:S	SOD	CAR	CHO
76	0	—	2	18	0
With honey					
92	0	—	2	22	0

APRICOT-PINEAPPLE MÉLANGE

The old favourite fruit compote, with sweet spices, apple juice and honey, becomes a new dessert. For devotees of the sweet and the tart.

	Metric	Imperial	American
Dried apricots	300 g	11 oz	11 oz
Unsweetened apple juice	450 ml	¾ pt	2 cups
Slice lemon	1	1	1
Honey	2 tbsp	2 tbsp	2 tbsp
Ground cinnamon	1 tsp	1 tsp	1 tsp
Seeds from 4 pods of cardamom, crushed			
Crushed pineapple in its own juice, no sugar added, drained	225 g	8 oz	1 cup
Arrowroot, dissolved in 2 tbsp water	2 tbsp	2 tbsp	2 tbsp
Powdered gelatine, dissolved in 1 tbsp boiling water	1½ tsp	1½ tsp	1½ tsp

Soak apricots overnight in enough water to cover, Next day pour apricots into sieve and drain, pressing fruit with spoon. Transfer apricots to saucepan. Add apple juice, lemon slice, honey, cinnamon and cardamom. Bring to boil. Turn heat down, cover and simmer for about 20 minutes or until tender but firm. Add pineapple and dissolved arrowroot. Cook until thickened (about 5 minutes). Add dissolved gelatine and stir to blend. Pour mixture into 8 dessert dishes and let cool to room temperature. Then refrigerate until set.

Yield: Serves 8

Variation: Serve topped with 1 tablespoon Vanilla Sauce per serving (Page 122).

CAL	F	P:S	SOD	CAR	CHO
224	0	—	0	52	0

SPICED BAKED BANANAS

There's a sunny touch of the tropics in this easy-to-make sweet.

	Metric	Imperial	American
Unsweetened apple juice	80 ml	3 fl oz	⅓ cup
Fresh lemon juice	1 tsp	1 tsp	1 tsp
Ground cinnamon	¼ tsp	¼ tsp	¼ tsp
Seedless raisins	1 tbsp	1 tbsp	1 tbsp
Corn oil for brushing	¼ tsp	¼ tsp	¼ tsp
Ripe bananas, peeled, sliced lengthwise, then in half	3	3	3
Ground mace	4 pinches	4 pinches	4 pinches

In small saucepan, heat apple juice to simmering point. Add lemon juice, cinnamon and raisins. Bring to simmering point again and cook, partially covered, for 5 minutes.

Brush shallow baking dish lightly with oil. Place sliced bananas on dish and pour hot apple juice mixture over them. Sprinkle with mace, and bake, uncovered, in preheated 200°C/400°F/Gas mark 6 oven for 15 minutes. Serve warm.

Yield: Serves 4

CAL	F	P:S	SOD	CAR	CHO
97	0	—	2	23	0

STRAWBERRY PARFAIT

Pastel pinks and the ripe redness of fresh strawberries make this amazingly low-calorie sweet as colourful as it is delicious. Two textures, one coarse and one smooth, are arranged in alternate layers to provide contrast.

	Metric	Imperial	American
Unsweetened apple juice	360 ml	12½ fl oz	1½ cups
Powdered gelatine	2 tsp	2 tsp	2 tsp
Fresh strawberries, washed, hulled and sliced	275 g	10 oz	1¼ cups
Honey	3 tsp	3 tsp	3 tsp
Low-fat plain yogurt	120 ml	4 fl oz	½ cup
Almond essence	4 drops	4 drops	4 drops
Whole strawberries	4	4	4
Mint leaves for garnish	8	8	8

Heat apple juice to boiling point. Add gelatine and stir to dissolve. Measure out 120 ml/4 fl oz/½ cup of this mixture and set aside, leaving remainder for the next step.

For the smooth-textured mixture: In a blender, purée 100 g/4 oz/½ cup strawberries with 2 teaspoons honey. Pour into small bowl. Add remainder of apple juice mixture and stir well. Whisk in yogurt. Pour into 20.5 × 23-cm/8¼ × 9-inch loaf tin. Refrigerate until set (about 2 hours).

For the coarse-textured mixture: Coarsely mash rest of sliced strawberries. Add remaining honey and cook over very low heat for 2 minutes. Cool. Add almond essence and 120 ml/4 fl oz/½ cup apple juice mixture which had been set aside. Stir well. Refrigerate until slightly thickened.

When mixture in loaf tin has set, cut into 2.5 cm/1-inch cubes, and remove from pan with spatula carefully to avoid breaking. In 4 parfait glasses, arrange cubes and slightly thickened strawberry mixture in alternate layers. Refrigerate again until set.

Serve, garnished with 1 whole strawberry and 2 mint leaves on top of each dessert.

Yield: Serves 4

Note: If strawberries are particularly sweet, you can eliminate the honey. If honey is eliminated, cook the strawberries with 1 tablespoon unsweetened apple juice.

CAL	F	P:S	SOD	CAR	CHO
114	0	—	18	27	1
Without honey					
72	0	—	16	16	1

SPICED BAKED APPLES

Where prepared with a generous lacing of spiced apple juice, this traditional dish is transformed.

	Metric	Imperial	American
Medium-sized cooking apples	4	4	4
Unsweetened apple juice	180 ml	6 fl oz	¾ cup
Honey	2 tbsp	2 tbsp	2 tbsp
Ground mace	4 pinches	4 pinches	4 pinches
Ground cinnamon	1 tsp	1 tsp	1 tsp
Ground ginger	½ tsp	½ tsp	½ tsp
Fresh lemon juice	½ tsp	½ tsp	½ tsp

Wash and core apples. Make several slits in skin to depth of one third of apple starting from top centre. Arrange in shallow baking dish.

Combine apple juice, honey, spices and lemon juice in saucepan. Heat to simmering point. Pour over apples. Bake in preheated 180°C/350°F/Gas mark 4 oven for 45 minutes, basting 3 times. Remove from oven. Let cool in baking dish, lightly covered with greaseproof paper. Serve warm or chilled.

Yield: Serves 4

CAL	F	P:S	SOD	CAR	CHO
129	0	—	3	35	0

CINDERELLA APPLESAUCE

Here is a recipe for apple sauce that lifts this ordinary sweet to a spicy treat.

	Metric	Imperial	American
Crisp, sweet apples cored and sliced	4	4	4
Unsweetened apple juice	80 ml	3 fl oz	1/3 cup
Ground ginger	1/4 tsp	1/4 tsp	1/4 tsp
Whole cloves	3	3	3
Ground nutmeg	2 pinches	2 pinches	2 pinches
Flavoured honey, such as thyme	3 tbsp	3 tbsp	3 tbsp

Combine all ingredients except honey in saucepan. Bring to boil. Lower heat. Cover and simmer for 10-15 minutes, or until apples are tender yet firm when pierced with sharp knife. Uncover, and let cool in pan for 10 minutes. Pour into food mill or blender and purée. Add honey to taste, not to exceed 3 tablespoons.

Serve warm or chilled.

Yield: Serves 4 with one left over portion

CAL	F	P:S	SOD	CAR	CHO
107	0	—	4	26	0

BILBERRY MOUSSE WITH VANILLA SAUCE

This sweet captures the essence of bilberry in a blend of sweet creaminess and contrasting tartness.

	Metric	Imperial	American
For the bilberry mousse:			
Fresh bilberries, washed and picked over	225 g	8 oz	1 cup
Cottage cheese, no salt added	2 tbsp	2 tbsp	2 tbsp
Low-fat plain yogurt	4 tbsp	4 tbsp	4 tbsp
Honey	2 tbsp	2 tbsp	2 tbsp
Juice of 1/2 lemon			
Grated rind of 1/2 lemon			
Unsweetened apple juice	60 ml	2 fl oz	1/4 cup
Agar-agar flakes	1 tsp	1 tsp	1 tsp
Grand Marnier Liqueur or 1/2 tsp Cognac essence	1 tsp	1 tsp	1 tsp
Egg whites	2	2	2

Combine bilberries, cottage cheese, yogurt, honey, lemon juice and lemon rind in blender. Purée for 30 seconds. Pour into bowl.

Heat apple juice to boiling point in small saucepan. Sprinkle with agar-agar. Turn heat down to simmering point and cook, uncovered, for 4 minutes, stirring to blend, skimming foam that rises to top. Let cool. Pour into blended mixture. Add liqueur or essence and blend with whisk.

Beat egg whites, starting machine on medium speed. When egg whites start to whisk up increase speed gradually to top speed until firm but before dry peaks form. Whisk one-third of mixture into berries, and fold in balance. Folding is done by making a down motion with the spoon, and then a scooping up and folding over motion. Spoon into dessert dishes and chill until thickened (about 2 hours). Serve with 1 tablespoon vanilla sauce spooned over each dessert or to taste.

	Metric	Imperial	American
For the vanilla sauce:			
Low-fat dry milk	4 tbsp	4 tbsp	4 tbsp
Water	120 ml	4 fl oz	1/2 cup
Honey	1 tbsp	1 tbsp	1 tbsp
Vanilla essence	2 tsp	2 tsp	2 tsp
Arrowroot, dissolved in 1 tbsp water	1 tbsp	1 tbsp	1 tbsp
Ground nutmeg	3 pinches	3 pinches	3 pinches

Combine milk, water and honey in blender. Blend for 1 minute on high speed. Pour into small heavy-bottomed saucepan. Stir in vanilla. Add dissolved arrowroot mixture and cook over very low heat, stirring constantly, until thickened. Sprinkle with nutmeg and stir. Pour through fine-meshed sieve, pressing with spoon. Serve warm or chilled.

Yield: About 180 ml/6 fl oz/¾ cup

Variations:

1. *Almond Sauce:* Substitute ¼ teaspoon almond essence for vanilla essence. Yield: About 180 ml/ 6 fl oz/¾ cup.

2. *Mocha Sauce:* Dissolve 1 teaspoon coffee substitute in 1 teaspoon hot water. Add to blender with milk mixture before blending. Yield: About 180 ml/ 6 fl oz/¾ cup.

3. *Fruit Sauce:* Add 50 g/2 oz/¼ cup fresh fruit to blender with milk mixture. Try berries, sliced ripe peeled peaches, or bananas. Substitute a few drops of almond essence for vanilla essence. Yield: About 240 ml/8 fl oz/1 cup.

4. *Carob Sauce:* Cook 1 tablespoon carob powder in 60 ml/2 oz/¼ cup water for 5 minutes. Cool. Add to blender with milk mixture and blend. Yield: About 240 ml/8 fl oz/1 cup.

CAL	F	P:S	SOD	CAR	CHO
97	0	—	35	23	0
With Grand Marnier					
100	0	—	35	23	0
Vanilla sauce					
28	0	—	8	6	0
Almond sauce					
28	0	—	8	6	0
Mocha sauce					
30	0	—	8	6	0
Raspberry sauce					
33	0	—	8	7	0
Peach sauce					
33	0	—	8	7	0
Banana sauce					
34	0	—	8	8	0
Carob sauce					
31	0	—	8	7	0

BANANA WHIP

Light, frothy, fruity, with just a touch of tartness, this banana whip is as original as it is delicious.

	Metric	Imperial	American
Combination of raisins and unsweetened chopped dates	60 g	2½ oz	⅓ cup
Unsweetened apple juice	240 ml	8 fl oz	1 cup
Agar-agar flakes	1½ tsp	1½ tsp	1½ tsp
Large ripe banana	1	1	1
Almond essence	⅛ tsp	⅛ tsp	⅛ tsp
Vanilla essence	¼ tsp	¼ tsp	¼ tsp
Ground cinnamon	4 pinches	4 pinches	4 pinches
Low-fat plain yogurt	4 tbsp	4 tbsp	4 tbsp
Egg whites	2	2	2
Small banana for garnish	½	½	½

In small saucepan, combine date-raisin mixture and apple juice. Bring to boil. Turn heat down and simmer for 5 minutes. Add agar-agar and simmer for 5 minutes, skimming foam that rises to top. Let cool. Pour into blender and purée for 30 seconds. Pour into bowl.

Mash banana with fork. Combine with apple juice mixture. Add essences and cinnamon, stirring to blend. Whisk in yogurt.

To beat egg whites, start mixing machine on medium speed. As egg whites begin to whisk up, turn speed up gradually to top speed and beat until firm but before dry peaks form. Drop third of egg whites into banana mixture blending well with whisk. Fold in balance of egg whites gently using wooden spoon. Folding is done by making a down motion with the spoon, and then a scooping up and folding over motion. In this way, all the egg white is incorporated into the mixture while air bubbles remain intact.

Pour into 4 dessert dishes. Top each serving with 2 slices of banana.

Yield: Serves 4

CAL	F	P:S	SOD	CAR	CHO
138	0	—	59	30	0

PRUNE MOUSSE

You'll never know this recipe is from prunes. A prune whip must be prepared before making the mousse, and the whip stands on its own as a dessert or as a breakfast treat.

For the whip:	Metric	Imperial	American
Prunes, unsweetened	350 g	12 oz	12 oz
Unsweetened apple juice	300 ml	½ pt	1¼ cups
Large slice of orange	1	1	1

Place prunes in a saucepan and barely cover with apple juice. Add orange slice. Bring to simmering point, cover and cook for 10 minutes. Turn off heat and let stand in covered saucepan until completely cold.

Purée in food mill. (Do not use blender.) Store in jar in refrigerator.

For the prune mousse:	Metric	Imperial	American
Unsweetened apple juice	80 ml	3 fl oz	⅓ cup
Agar-agar flakes	1 tsp	1 tsp	1 tsp
Prune whip, room temperature	180 ml	6 fl oz	¾ cup
Ground cinnamon	½ tsp	½ tsp	½ tsp
Low-fat plain yogurt	2 tbsp	2 tbsp	2 tbsp
Egg whites	2	2	2

Heat apple juice in small saucepan. Sprinkle agar-agar into juice and simmer for 5 minutes, uncovered, stirring often. Skim off foam. Let cool.

Prune whip should have the consistency of thick, pourable soured cream for this recipe. If too thick, thin down with small amount of apple juice before proceeding with recipe. Pour prune whip into large mixing bowl. Add cooled agar-agar mixture, together with cinnamon and yogurt, and blend with whisk.

To beat egg whites, start mixing machine on medium speed. As egg whites begin to whisk up, turn speed up gradually to top speed and beat until firm but before dry peaks form. Add egg whites to prunes as follows:

Blend third of egg whites into prune mixture with whisk. Then with wooden spoon, fold balance of whites into prunes, using a down motion with the spoon followed by a scooping up and folding over motion. Spoon into dessert dishes. Refrigerate for 2 hours before serving.

Yield: Prune Whip: about 240 ml/8 fl oz/1 cup, serves 4. Prune Mousse: serves 4

CAL	F	P:S	SOD	CAR	CHO
Whip					
229	0	—	11	55	0
Mousse					
250	0	—	39	58	0

HONEYDEW SHERBET

The pure fruit essence of honeydew melon is captured in a frozen dessert almost as light as a meringue.

	Metric	Imperial	American
Puréed ripe honeydew melon (see method) (about ¾ of average size melon)	600 ml	1 pt	2½ cups
Juice of 1 lemon			
Grated rind of ½ lemon			
Honey	2 tbsp	2 tbsp	2 tbsp
Egg whites	3	3	3
Honeydew melon balls for garnish			

Cut and dice honeydew melon flesh. Purée in blender. Pour into mixing bowl. Add lemon juice and rind and blend with whisk. Add honey and blend again.

To beat egg whites, start mixing machine on medium speed. As egg whites begin to whisk up, turn speed up gradually to top speed and beat until firm but before dry peaks form. Whisk third of egg whites into the puréed melon then fold in remainder gently using wooden spoon. Folding is done by making a down motion with the spoon, and then a scooping up and folding over motion. In this way, all the egg white is incorporated into the mixture while air bubbles remain intact.

Pour into 23 × 13-cm/9 × 5-inch loaf tin that has been rinsed in cold water and dried. Cover with foil and place in freezing compartment of refrigerator.

Remove from freezer after 45 minutes. At this point, top has started to solidify and the bottom has become watery. Fold bottom over top with wooden spoon until most of liquid is absorbed. Return, covered, to freezer.

Repeat the freezing, stirring, and folding process twice more. After 3 hours, remove from freezer, and using wire whisk or portable mixing machine, beat until smooth. At this point, the dessert will look and taste like sherbert. Return, covered, to freezer.

Sherbet will be fully ripened in flavour in about 5 hours from starting time. Remove from freezer 20 minutes before serving if you prefer a softer consistency. Serve in parfait or dessert dishes, garnished with 2 honeydew balls on top of each dessert.

Yield: Serves 4, one portion left over

Note: If melon is very sweet, honey may be eliminated.

CAL	F	P:S	SOD	CAR	CHO
72	0	—	47	15	0
Without honey					
47	0	—	47	9	0

PINEAPPLE SHERBET

A light, crisp dessert with the refreshing taste of pineapple.

	Metric	Imperial	American
Canned pineapple chunks, in their own juices, no sugar added	550 g	1¼ lb	20 oz
Juice of ½ lemon			
Honey	2 tbsp	2 tbsp	2 tbsp
Egg whites	3	3	3

Pour pineapple into blender, together with lemon juice and honey. Blend at high speed for 1 minute. Pour into large mixing bowl.

Beat egg whites, folding them into fruit, following directions for Honeydew Sherbet (Page 124).

Yield: Serves 6

Note: If you're fortunate enough to find a very ripe fresh pineapple (outer skin brown, and fruit soft to touch), by all means use it. Replace canned pineapple with 350-450 g/12 oz-1 lb/2½ cups cubed fresh pineapple, plus juices. Very ripe pineapple is as sweet as sugar, so eliminate the honey.

CAL	F	P:S	SOD	CAR	CHO
88	0	—	29	20	0
Fresh pineapple					
40	0	—	29	7	0

DATE-CHEESE DELIGHT

An interesting—and easy to prepare—sweet.

	Metric	Imperial	American
Very thin slices of Munster, Swiss, or other low-fat sliceable cheese	8	8	8
Stoned fresh dates	16	16	16
Ground cinnamon			

Set out 4 individual ovenproof ramekins. Place a slice of cheese in bottom of each dish, add 4 dates and top with a slice of cheese. Sprinkle with cinnamon.

Bake in preheated 180°C/350°F/Gas mark 4 oven for 10-15 minutes or until cheese is melted and dates are well heated. Let cool for 2 minutes before serving.

Yield: Serves 4

CAL	F	P:S	SOD	CAR	CHO
75	6	6:1	0	35	14

PINEAPPLE CHIFFON PIE

This rich extravagant dessert should satisfy your most compulsive craving for sweets.

	Metric	Imperial	American
For the pastry case:			
Rye flour	65 g	2¼ oz	½ cup
Whole wheat flour	130 g	4½ oz	1 cup
Buckwheat flour	65 g	2¼ oz	½ cup
Finely chopped walnuts	50 g	2 oz	¼ cup
Ground cinnamon	½ tsp	½ tsp	½ tsp
Corn oil	120 ml	4 fl oz	½ cup
Iced water	3 tbsp	3 tbsp	3 tbsp

In medium-sized bowl, combine flours, walnuts and cinnamon. Add oil, a little at a time, and blend with fork. Finally, sprinkle iced water, 1 tablespoon at a time, into mixture, blending with fork, using enough water to hold the mixture together.

Turn into a 20-cm/8-inch or 25-cm/10-inch pie plate (not glass), and press even amounts against bottom and sides. Bake in preheated 190°C/375°F/Gas mark 5 oven for 35-40 minutes until lightly browned. Cool tin on wire rack.

Note: If there are some dried beans on hand, sprinkle handful over unbaked case so that dough won't rise while baking. When fully baked, remove beans and save for next baking.

	Metric	Imperial	American
For the filling:			
Unsweetened orange juice	240 ml	8 fl oz	1 cup
Canned crushed pineapple in its own juices, no sugar added	350 g	12 oz	12 oz
Honey (optional)	2 tbsp	2 tbsp	2 tbsp
Powdered gelatine	2 tbsp	2 tbsp	2 tbsp
Cottage cheese, no salt added	175 g	6 oz	6 oz
Low-fat plain yogurt	120 ml	4 fl oz	½ cup
Vanilla essence	1½ tsp	1½ tsp	1½ tsp
Almond essence	4 drops	4 drops	4 drops
Grated rind of ½ lemon			
Large egg whites	2	2	2
Walnuts, coarsely chopped	2 tbsp	2 tbsp	2 tbsp

Add enough orange juice to juice from can of pineapple to equal 360 ml/12 fl oz/1½ cups liquid. Pour into saucepan together with honey. Bring to simmering point. Add gelatine, stirring to dissolve. Let cool to room temperature.

Combine cottage cheese, yogurt and pineapple in blender. Add essences and lemon rind, and purée on low speed for 1 minute. Pour into cooled gelatine mixture, and refrigerate until mixture begins to thicken.

To beat egg whites, start mixing machine on medium speed. As egg whites begin to whisk up, turn speed up gradually to top speed and beat until firm but no dry peaks forming.

Drop one third beaten egg whites into cheese mixture. Blend well with whisk. Pour balance of egg whites into mixture and fold gently using wooden spoon. Folding is done by making a down motion with the spoon, and then a scooping up and folding over motion. In this way, all the egg white is incorporated into the mixture while air bubbles remain intact. Don't overfold. Cool in refrigerator until almost set. This will take about 45 minutes.

Turn cooled filling into baked pastry case. Sprinkle with coarsely chopped nuts and refrigerate. Allow 2 hours to set.

Yield: Serves 10

Variations:
1. *Alternative pie crust:*

	Metric	Imperial	American
Crunchy rolled oats pastry case:			
Rolled oats	175 g	6 oz	1 cup
Finely chopped walnuts	75 g	3 oz	½ cup
Corn oil	60 ml	2 fl oz	¼ cup
Honey	4 tbsp	4 tbsp	4 tbsp

Toast oats by spreading them on baking tray and baking for 10 minutes. Transfer to polythene bag.

Press all air out of bag. Then tie securely. Roll oats with rolling pin until they are broken up but not pulverized.

In a bowl, combine oats with nuts. Add oil, a little at a time, mixing with spoon. Lift mixture into centre of 20-cm/8-inch ungreased pie plate and press to bottom and sides. Dribble honey on to pastry and gently spread along sides and bottom. Refrigerate for at least 1 hour before filling.

2. The filling alone makes a superb dessert. Just pour into 8 dessert dishes and chill until firm. Sprinkle with chopped nuts and serve.

CAL	F	P:S	SOD	CAR	CHO
Pastry case					
123	4	5.4:1	0	42	0
Filling					
71	0	—	25	13	0
Filling with honey					
86	0	—	25	16	0
Rolled oats pastry case					
117	7	4.5:1	0	14	0

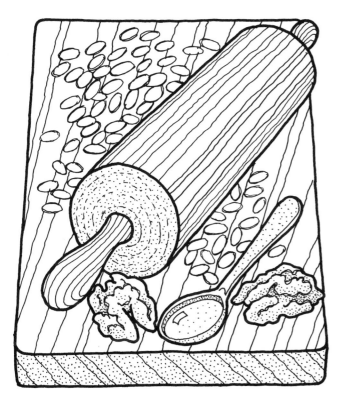

5-MINUTE SPICE CAKE

This spicy cake makes a wonderful finale to your meal. And with no beating, just stirring, it's almost effortless to make.

	Metric	Imperial	American
Unbleached flour	130 g	4½ oz	1 cup
Low sodium baking powder	1½ tsp	1½ tsp	1½ tsp
Ground cinnamon	1 tsp	1 tsp	1 tsp
Ground ginger	1 tsp	1 tsp	1 tsp
Ground nutmeg	¼ tsp	¼ tsp	¼ tsp
Large egg (use ½ of the yolk)	1	1	1
Honey	1 tbsp	1 tbsp	1 tbsp
Grated orange rind	1 tsp	1 tsp	1 tsp
Buttermilk, no salt added	120 ml	4 fl oz	¾ cup
Corn oil	3 tbsp	3 tbsp	3 tbsp
Corn oil to oil tin	¼ tsp	¼ tsp	¼ tsp

Sift flour, baking powder and spices into a bowl.

In another bowl, combine egg beaten lightly with fork, honey, rind, buttermilk and oil. Stir to blend. Pour liquid ingredients into bowl with flour mixture. Stir well with wooden spoon to blend.

Turn into lightly oiled small loaf tin (18 × 9 × 5.5 cm/7⅜ × 3⅝ × 2¼ inches), and bake in preheated 180°C/350°F/Gas mark 4 oven for 45-50 minutes, or until fine skewer inserted through centre of cake comes out dry.

Place tin on wire rack to cool for 15 minutes. Using blunt knife, loosen around sides and invert. Serve slightly warm.

Yield: 1 loaf, serves 6

CAL	F	P:S	SOD	CAR	CHO
131	7	4.1:0	47	19	16

APPLE COFFEE CAKE

This cake, and the one that follows, are delicious. Quality cold-pressed corn oil (lighter by far than commercial corn oils) is a must, and so is strongly flavoured honey. Wild thyme honey is my choice.

	Metric	Imperial	American
For the cake:			
Unbleached flour, sifted	250 g	9 oz	2¼ cups
Low sodium baking powder	3 tsp	3 tsp	3 tsp
Corn oil	60 ml	2 fl oz	¼ cup
Honey	4 tbsp	4 tbsp	4 tbsp
Egg whites	3	3	3
Egg yolk	½	½	½
Low-fat plain yogurt, room temperature	200 ml	7 fl oz	scant 1 cup
Vanilla essence	1 tsp	1 tsp	1 tsp
Corn oil for oiling baking tin	½ tsp	½ tsp	½ tsp
For the topping:			
Crisp apples, quartered, peeled and cored	4	4	4
Small lemon, including grated rind of ½ lemon	1	1	1
Corn oil	1 tsp	1 tsp	1 tsp
Honey	2 tbsp	2 tbsp	2 tbsp
Ground cinnamon, plus several sprinklings	½ tsp	½ tsp	½ tsp
Ground cloves	4 pinches	4 pinches	4 pinches
Seedless raisins	25 g	1 oz	¼ cup
Coarsely chopped walnuts	2 tbsp	2 tbsp	2 tbsp

Slice apple quarters lengthwise 5 mm/¼ inch thick. Place in bowl, together with lemon juice and rind, turning to coat. Add combined oil and honey, tossing gently. Add cinnamon and cloves, and toss again. Set aside.

Sift flour and baking powder into mixing bowl. Combine oil, honey and eggs. Beat lightly with fork. Add to dry ingredients. Blend on medium speed of mixing machine for 1 minute. Add yogurt and vanilla, and blend again. Pour into lightly oiled 23-cm/9-inch square baking tin, spreading mixture evenly.

Arrange coated apples close together in a neat pattern on top of cake mixture. Sprinkle with raisins and nuts, pouring any leftover juices over cake as well. Press entire mixture slightly into cake mixture, using spatula. Sprinkle with cinnamon.

Bake in preheated 180°C/350°F/Gas mark 4 oven for 50 minutes. When cake is baked, it should shrink slightly from sides of pan, and be lightly browned. Remove from oven and place on wire rack to cool. Cut into 8 serving pieces. Remove carefully with spatula, and serve slightly warm.

Yield: Serves 12

Note: If all cake isn't used on baking day, wrap each piece in foil and freeze. When you want a slice, reheat in foil in preheated 180°C/350°/Gas mark 4 oven for 15 minutes. Serve warm.

Variation: Fresh peaches or blueberries can be substituted for apples. If either are used, add ⅛ teaspoon almond essence to topping mixture.

CAL	F	P:S	SOD	CAR	CHO
215	8	4.7:1	26	37	11
Peaches					
208	8	4.7:1	26	35	11
Blueberries					
218	8	4.7:1	26	38	11

BANANA CRAZY CAKE

It looks like a cake, tastes like a pudding.

	Metric	Imperial	American
Chopped dates, no sugar added	50 g	2 oz	¼ cup
Unsweetened apple juice, brought to boiling point	120 ml	4 fl oz	½ cup

BREAD FOR STUFFING

Bread for stuffing and bread crumbs (the recipe follows) should be kept in your refrigerator at all times. Mine add herby flavours to many of my dishes, and are amazingly low in calories.

Cut one loaf of My French Bread into 1.5-cm/½-inch slices (Page 134), and then into cubes. Spread cubes on baking tray in one layer. Bake in preheated 220°C/425°F/Gas mark 7 oven for 10 minutes, turning cubes with spatula after 5 minutes. Cool. Store in glass jar in refrigerator until ready to use.

Yield: About 225 g/8 oz/4 cups

Note: Any yeast bread can be made similarly into bread for stuffing.

CAL	F	P:S	SOD	CAR	CHO
Per 50 g/2 oz/1 cup					
190	2	4.6:1	6	47	0

FINE BREAD CRUMBS

1 loaf My French Bread, cut into cubes and toasted (Page 134)

Place cubes in blender, half at a time, and blend until smooth. Store in glass jar in refrigerator.

Yield: 50 g/2 oz/1 cup

Variation: Combine 40 g/1½ oz/¾ cup bread crumbs with 50 g/2 oz/¼ cup wheat germ, no sugar added, and blend.

Yield: 50 g/2 oz/1 cup

CAL	F	P:S	SOD	CAR	CHO
Per 50 g/2 oz/1 cup					
760	6	4.6:1	25	186	0
Per tablespoon					
48	0	—	2	12	0
Variation:					
Per 50 g/2 oz/1 cup					
680	8	4.8:1	20	153	0
Per tablespoon					
43	0	—	1	10	0

ABOUT WINE

Wine has heightened the enjoyment of food since Biblical times.

I cook with wine because it marries so felicitously with my new gourmet cuisine. About 240 ml/8 fl oz/½ pt red wine or dry white wine contribute about 168 calories. But since most of those calories are derived from alcohol, and since alcohol evaporates in cooking leaving only the flavoursome essence of wine, about 85 per cent of those calories disappear. 120 ml/4 fl oz/½ cup of wine as a recipe ingredient adds only about 13 calories to a dish, plus 3 grams of carbohydrate, 4 milligrams of sodium, and no fats or cholesterol.

White wine—that is wine made from white-skinned grapes (blanc de blanc) or from the pulp of white or red grapes—when it's used for cooking must be dry (not sweet) and assert its flavour authoritatively. I prefer dry Vermouth, a herb-flavoured wine, either from Italy or from France. Not quite as flavoursome, and a little more expensive, is a French Macon.

Red wine for cooking has to be exuberantly vigorous, so use a full-bodied younger wine. A French Beaujolais, Burgundy or St. Emilion of recent vintage produces exquisite results, as do the following one-to-three-year-olds: Italian Barolos, Caremas and Spannas.

For drinking, the varieties of wine seem almost limitless. There's no problem about making your choice if you can afford a vintage Lafite, Latour, Margaux, a Charmes Chambertin or a Musigny. But there are many superb wines within a sane price range. (Even if you're on a budget, do avoid really cheap wines except when you're making stock.) Traditionally, we're supposed to have white wine with fish, and drier white wine with shellfish; light red wine with poultry and white meats; robust red wines with red meats. But there is no need to follow this rigidly.

Here's a list of good wines, and the kind of dishes with which they blend perfectly.

Barbara D'Asti, 1971 (Italian), red. Hamburgers, meat loaves, salads (fish, poultry and meat), my simpler chicken dishes, baked tuna with broccoli, cod fish cakes.

Borgogno Barolo, 1971 (Italian), red. For the more extravagant meat dishes.

Spanna, 1964 (Italian), red. Use it as you would a Barolo. It's a bit subtler, a little bit more aristocratic.

The wines of Bourg, Blaye and Fronsac, 1973 and 1975 (French), red. Lamb dishes and all my stews, and fish chowder.

Ruffino Chianti Classico, Riserva, Gold Label, 1969 (Italian), red. Pasta, chicken cacciatore, prawn Italian style, and so on.

Muscadet Sur Lie of recent vintage (French), white. Incomparable with any of my prawn or heavier fish dishes.

Vouvray of recent vintage (French), white. A light-hearted wine for fish or poultry.

Pouilly Fumé, 1976, (French), white. For fish, poultry, sautéed escalopes of veal and veal birds.

MEAL PLANNING

It saves money and time to set up a general plan for your weekly menus, then, at least 24 hours in advance, decide on each day's specific menus. Here's a general plan.

For dinner main courses: Meat twice a week, fish twice a week, chicken or turkey twice a week, pasta or vegetables on the remaining day. Rounding out the dinner are hors d'oeuvres, green salads, soups (occasionally), vegetables, desserts, and beverages which include wine.

For lunch: Salads and luncheon dishes, and even sandwiches filled with leftovers. (That's why some of my recipes yield four portions and one leftover, or serve six.) For a sweet, small portions of low-fat dessert cheeses and/or fresh and dried fruits. Beverages include herb teas, coffee substitute, fruit juices, no-salt-added tomato juice, low-fat milk, and, of course, my Chocolate Milk Shake.

For breakfast: My breakfast dishes are supplemented by a variety of hot and cold breakfast cereals, no sugar, salt or coconut added. They range from shredded wheat to sophisticated granolas. Jams made with honey as the sweetening agent are bright morning accompaniments to my oven-fresh bread and rolls along with herb teas and fruit juices.

I like a general plan because I can buy in larger quantities, and that always costs less in the long run, and I don't have to make as many treks to the shops. I like planning my specific menus a day ahead because then I can make whatever preliminary preparations are necessary, like thawing out or marinating, and I'm well organized when I get down to the actual cooking. It adds up to extra hours of free time, and the right amount of time to prepare meals with the care they deserve.

MONEY-SAVING HINTS

In practising my new cuisine, the big savings come from using the more healthful and less expensive cuts of meat; limiting meat as a dinner main course to twice a week; making generous use of leftovers for luncheon dishes and hors d'oeuvres; relying in part on grain-based breakfasts and on salads for lunch; and setting up a general weekly menu pattern so you can plan ahead and buy in bulk. Here are some additional ways you can save money while eating better.

Since you're planning well ahead, stock up in large quantities on special offers of ingredients you're going to need anyway. These can be shared with neighbours or friends on a bulk-buy basis, with substantial savings.

Whole fish are less expensive by far than fish steaks or fillets.

Remember that some of my more interesting recipes are for the less expensive fish.

When you're shopping for chickens, keep in mind that young chickens are consistently lower-priced than roasters, and are 10 per cent less fatty. Chicken portions cost more, so joint them yourself with sharp utensils. Refer to my utensil list on Page 148.

Overripe tomatoes and slightly bruised apples make excellent tomato soups and apple sauce respectively, and the price is low.

Herbs are an integral and important ingredient in many of my recipes. It is so easy—and very satisfying—to grow your own. A few pots of greenery will brighten any window ledge or balcony, and fresh herbs are then available year-round. Many shops stock fresh-frozen herbs, or small quantities in packets. Most herb varieties can be dried or frozen at home.

When travelling abroad, be on the lookout for fresh or dried spices. They are always less expensive—and fresher—in their country of origin.

Many of the recipes of my new cuisine call for parsley, dill and watercress. If they're not stored properly they'll rot, and you'll lose part or all of your investment. Here are the secrets of extending their storage life to 10 days:

Wash crisp green parsley well under cold running water. Store in covered jar, stems down, with just enough water to cover the stems. Refrigerate. Change water after 4 days. Treat watercress the same way. Green dill (don't buy it if there's even a suggestion of brown) should never be washed before storing. Place it in a covered jar and refrigerate.

Refrigerate your flours and grains in tightly closed containers and they'll retain freshness for at least 6 months.

A surprisingly large portion of most households' food budgets slips away in wasted food. Here are some ways to save food that you would otherwise discard:

Let's suppose you need a small quantity of stock. You remove a jar from the freezer, thaw and extract what you need. It's too dangerous to refreeze the remaining stock, so you refrigerate, and if you don't use it in a few days, it's gone rancid. Instead, store some of your stock in miniature ice-cube trays and freeze. Each miniature ice cub equals about 1 tablespoon of stock. Use one or more as required—without waste.

Overripe berries can be redeemed by cooking them in a small amount of unsweetened apple juice for 2 minutes, and serving as a cold dessert, a topping, or as a flavouring for my Chocolate Milk Shake. Thicken with arrowroot, and you have an instant jelly.

Instead of discarding cooking liquids, add them to stocks, or use them to boost the flavour of soups and sauces.

A number of my recipes call for unsweetened pineapple juice, so save the juice from cans of unsweetened pineapples when my recipes call for the pineapples but not the juice.

After you've squeezed a lemon, grate the rind and freeze it. When one of my recipes demands grated lemon rind, you're ready.

And, finally, there's no such thing as stale bread. My

stale breads can always be used—converted into Melba toast (Page 103), cut into cubes for stuffing (Page 145), or blended into fine bread crumbs (Page 145).

TERMS USED IN THIS BOOK

Al dente. Firm-textured. Said of pasta.

Baste. To spoon liquid over food while roasting or braising.

Bouquet garni. A combination of aromatic herbs which are used in the preparation of soups, stews, sauces and braised dishes to add flavour. In my new cuisine, it's usually made with 3-4 sprigs of parsley wrapped around one bay leaf and tied into a small bundle with thread.

Braise. To cook with a small amount of liquid over low heat, after food has been browned.

Brush. To cover a surface of the food lightly with liquid, usually using a pastry brush.

Coat. To roll food in flour, bread crumbs or other ingredients until coated.

Court bouillon. An aromatic broth of water, herbs, seasonings and sometimes wine.

Diced. Cut into 3-mm/⅛-inch cubes.

Flake. Refers to the flesh of cooked fish which comes loose in flakes when touched with a fork.

Fold in. A method to obtain an even combination of ingredients. Usually applied to egg whites.

Garnish. To decorate savoury food.

Grate. Extremely small pieces of food obtained by rubbing on a grater.

Marinate. To soak food in a flavourful liquid prior to cooking.

Parboil. To cook partially in water.

Peel, core and drain. Refers to fresh tomatoes. Skin pulls off easily after tomato has been immersed in boiling water for 30 seconds. Core is then cut away, and liquid is drained and reserved.

Poach. To cook in a broth just below the boiling point.

Preheat. To turn oven on at a specified temperature 15 minutes before using.

Purée. To put through a blender, food mill or food processor to obtain a smooth pulpy consistency.

Reduce. To continue cooking to concentrate liquid and, consequently, heighten flavour.

Rolling boil. Boiling at high heat so stream of bubbles circulate in a rolling motion.

Sauté. To cook in a small amount of oil over low or medium heat.

Score. To make shallow gashes, usually through the skin of fish.

Sift. To put through sieve or flour sifter.

Simmer. To cook just below boiling point over low heat.

Skewer. To fasten with skewers.

Skim. To clear floating substances such as scum and fat from a liquid. For rapid fat-skimming leave liquid until all fat has come to top, remove with large spoon, and finally blot gently with paper towels. If liquid is to be used after day of cooking, refrigerate overnight, then remove solid layer of fat from surface.

Sliver. A long thin slice.

Steam. To cook with steam rather than with liquid.

Toss. To mix with fork and spoon, as for salads.

Trimmed. Unwanted parts removed.

Truss. To fasten body of fowl before cooking so that it holds its shape.

Whisk. To beat rapidly in a circular motion using a wire whisk.

THE UTENSILS I USE

1. Large non-stick frying pan (30 cm/12 inches in diameter).
2. Large heavy frying pan (30 cm/12 inches in diameter).
3. Medium-sized frying pan (25 cm/10 inches in diameter), either cast-iron or non-stick lining.
4. Small non-stick frying pan or electric non-stick frying pan for making crepes or for reheating leftovers.
5. Large saucepan with lid for making soups and stocks.
6. Covered cast-iron casserole (or enamelware to go

from stove to table) for making stews, with removable rack.

7. Rectangular aluminium, non-stick, or enamelware shallow roasting tin with removable rack, for roasting foods uncovered, permitting fats to drip.
8. Heavy-bottomed saucepan, for general heating and cooking and saucemaking.
9. Saucepans of varied sizes in which to cook rice, pasta and vegetables.
10. Stainless steel pan for making soups and stews; necessary to retain cooking juices.
11. Sharp straight-edged knives—5-7 cm/2-3 inches for paring and mincing, and 25-30 cm/10-12 inches for cutting and chopping.
12. Butcher's steel for sharpening knives.
13. Serrated knife for cutting bread, slicing tomatoes, and so on.
14. Heavy shears for cutting chicken bones through and cutting fins from fish.
15. Mallet for flattening meat and chicken breasts.
16. Long-pronged fork for lifting meats and testing to see if they are cooked.
17. Slotted spoons for removing meats, chicken, vegetables or fish from liquid. Also large spoons for basting and stirring.
18. Various spatulas for turning meats and fish.
19. Wooden spoons for stirring foods while cooking, and beating batters of breads, cakes and biscuits.
20. Four-sided grater to grate vegetables, orange, lemon and lime peels, cheese, and so on.
21. Casseroles of varying sizes for baking rice, casseroles, and so on.
22. Various sized whisks for blending sauces, mayonnaise and egg whites.
23. Measuring spoons and cups.
24. Loaf tins for breads and cakes 18 × 9 × 5.5 cm (7⅜ × 3⅝ × 2¼ inches) and 20 × 23 × 5.5 cm (8¼ × 9 × 2¼ inches). Also Swiss roll tin (28 × 40 × 2.5 cm/11½ × 15½ × 1 inch), square (23-cm/9-inch) baking tin, and aluminium pie plate, 20 cm/8 inches or 25 cm/10 inches in diameter.
25. French bread baking tins (35.5 cm/14 inches long). I prefer double tins.
26. Stainless steel straight-sided bowl for bread risings.
27. Freezerproof containers for freezing stocks and leftovers.
28. Colander for draining vegetables, rice, pasta and so on.
29. Sieve with bowl for draining and pressing out juices in making stocks, stews and so on.
30. Pestle and mortar for crushing dried herbs and seeds.
31. Poultry needle to sew up stuffed cavities of chicken, turkey, chops and so on.
32. Blender. Indispensable for many recipes throughout this book.
33. Mixing machine for beating egg whites, cakes and breads. Dough hook attachment is helpful once you've learned how to make bread by hand.
34. Food mill for puréeing soups, apple sauce, prune whip and so on.
35. Mincer or food processor for mincing cooked and uncooked meats, fish and vegetables, and for making dips and spreads.
36. Chopping board for all types of chopping, and for kneading bread.
37. Pastry brush for brushing meats, poultry and breads.
38. Fine sieve for preparation of smooth sauces.
39. Small wire whisk.
40. Swivel bladed peeler.

MENU PLANNERS

Calorie content

Fat content in grams

Ratio of P:S

0 Apple Juice Rye Bread **138**
Apple Relish **104**
Apple-rice Pudding **133**
Apple-rice Pudding with Dates or Raisins **133**
Apricot-pineapple Mélange **120**
Baked Pears in Red Wine **119**
Banana Whip **140**
Beef Stock **10**
Bilberry Mousse with Sauces **122**
Bilberry Griddle Cakes **105**
Brown Beef Stock **11**
Buckwheat Rye Bread **140**
Carob Milk Shake **132**
Carob Milk Shake with Berries **132**
Carob Milk Shake with Coffee Substitute **152**
Cheese Filling for Whole Wheat Crepes (1 and 2) **106**
Chicken Stock **8**
Chopped Egg Hors d'Oeuvres **113**
Cinderella Apple Sauce **122**
Clear Vegetable Consommé **31**
Cod in Court Bouillon **46**
Cracked Wheat Bread **142**
Creamy Mushroom Sauce for Veal Loaf **80**
Continental Cucumber Salad **96**
Crudités for Hors d'Oeuvres and Luncheon **111**
Cucumber and Onion Salad **97**
Curried Spread for Hors d'Oeuvres **115**
Extraordinary Kasha with Beef, Chicken or Veal Stock **24**
Kasha, Variation **24**
Feather Bread **141**
Fine Bread Crumbs (per tablespoon) **145**
Fish Stock **9**
French Green Beans *au naturel* **13**
Green Salad with Chicory **94**
Green Salad with Flavourful Salad Dressing **94**
Herb-flavoured Roast Chicken Stuffing **61**
Honeydew Sherbet **124**
Honeydew Sherbet without Honey **124**
Hot Stuffed Mushrooms **117**
Luncheon Treat with Fruit Juice Dressing (salad only) **109**
Make-your-own Pickles **104**
Melba Toast **103**
My French Bread **134**
My Hot Canapés—Meat, Fish, Chicken or Cheese **112**
Near-east Chicken Sauce **63**
Norwegian Rye Bread **139**
Orange-pineapple Chicken Sauce or Stuffing **64**
Pineapple Chiffon Pie Filling **126**
Pineapple Chiffon Pie Filling with Honey **126**
Pineapple Sherbet **125**
Pineapple Sherbet with Fresh Pineapple **125**
Pineapple-walnut Cheese Spread **114**
Poached Sole or Flounder with Savoury Sauce **41**
Poached Pears **119**
Poached Pears with Honey **119**
Potatoes for Light Meat Loaf **91**

0 Potatoes for Veal and Spinach Loaf **91**
Prune Mousse **124**
Prune Mousse Whip **124**
Pumpernickel **144**
Rich Carob Pudding **133**
Sautéed Prawns **53**
Sautéed Prawns Italian Style **55**
Savoury Cheese Dip **116**
Spiced Baked Apples **121**
Spiced Baked Bananas **120**
Spicy Hot Cocktail Sausages **117**
Strawberry Crepes Filling **118**
Strawberry Parfait **121**
Strawberry Parfait without Honey **121**
Stuffed Roast Turkey Stuffing **71**
Tomato-watercress Salad with Yogurt Dressing (Dressing: 0.6:1) **96**
Veal Stew with Tomatoes and Mushrooms **82**
Veal Stock **10**
Vegetable Fruit Salad **102**
Whole Wheat Bread **140**
0.6:1 Tomato-watercress Salad **96**
1:1 Twelve-vegetable Beef Soup **32**
Twelve-vegetable Beef Soup with Fresh Broad Beans or Split Peas **32**
Veal Loaf with Creamy Mushroom Sauce **80**
1.2:1 Baked Lamb Steaks **86**
Sweet and Sauerbraten with Yogurt **75**
1.3:1 Baked Lamb Steaks **86**
Sweet and Sauerbraten **75**
Chef Salad with Low Fat Cheese **101**
French Style Roast Leg of Lamb **88**
French Style Roast Leg of Lamb with Chicken Stock **88**
1.5:1 Sautéed Escalopes of Veal **76**
Sautéed Escalopes of Veal with Veal Stock **76**
1.6:1 Steak Pizzaiola **74**
1.7:1 Herb-grilled Lamb Cutlets **87**
1.8:1 Apple Chicken **59**
Chicken Breasts in Creamy Sauce **56**
Herb Grilled Lamb Cutlets **87**
Near-east Chicken **63**
Near-east Chicken with Sauce **63**
Poached Chicken Breasts **56**
1.9:1 Poached Sole or Flounder with Savoury Sauce **41**
Savoury Sauce for Poached Sole or Flounder **41**
2.0:1 Baked Herbed Veal Chops **80**
2.1:1 Braised Veal **79**
Fried Pork Chops with Mushrooms **86**
Stuffed Pork Chops in Red Wine **84**
Stuffed Pork Chops in Red Wine with Beef Stock **84**
2.2:1 Swiss Steak **74**
2.3:1 Irish Stew **88**
Swedish Meat Balls **92**
2.4:1 Grilled Salmon with Green Sauce **52**
Veal and Spinach Loaf **91**

2.5:1 Bombay Chicken Balls with Pineapple (each ball) **116**
Bombay Chicken or Turkey Balls (each ball) **116**
Cold Fish Spread (per canapé) **113**
Light Meat Loaf **91**
Paella **54**
Paella with Curry **54**
Paella with Tomato Juice **54**
Roast Stuffed Turkey **71**
Simple Sautéed Steakburger **89**
Veal Birds **83**
2.6:1 Orange-pineapple Chicken **64**
Orange-pineapple Chicken with Stuffing **64**
Orange-pineapple Chicken with Sauce **64**
Orange-pineapple Chicken with Stuffing and Sauce **64**
Potato Pancakes **23**
Simple Grilled Chicken **58**
2.7:1 Herb-flavoured Roast Chicken **61**
Herb-flavoured Roast Chicken with Stuffing **61**
Sautéed Chicken with Apples **66**
Sautéed Prawns **53**
Sautéed Prawns Italian Style **55**
Strawberry Crepes (each) **118**
Veal Stew **82**
Whole Wheat Crepes with Cheese Filling (each Crepe) **106**
2.8:1 Braised Boned and Rolled Leg of Veal **77**
Chicken Marengo **70**
Chicken Tandoori **62**
Grilled Chicken Paprikash **59**
3:1 Baked River Trout **49**
Whiting Baked in Red Wine **45**
Chef Salad with Chicken **101**
Grilled Halibut with Dill Sauce **49**
Luncheon Omelettes with Veal **108**
Sardine Canapés (each) **111**
Sardine Canapés Luncheon Serving **111**
Spaghetti and Meat Balls **93**
3.1:1 Chef Salad with Veal **101**
Four-flour Bread (slice) **143**
Sautéed Chicken Legs with Pimentos **60**
Grilled Chicken Legs with Pimentos **60**
3.2:1 Beef Bourguignon **73**
Brunswick Stew **67**
Brunswick Stew with Peas **67**
Chicken à l'Orange **66**
Miracle Chicken **69**
Cucumber-tomato Soup **33**
Mushroom and Barley Soup **39**
Mogul Chicken with Mushrooms **62**
Simple Sautéed Chicken Rosemary **60**
3.3:1 Chef Salad with Turkey **101**
Salmon Stuffed Eggs **110**
3.4:1 Spiced Potatoes **21**
Stuffed Roll-ups of Sole **42**
3.5:1 Chicken Cacciatore **68**
Hearty Cabbage Soup **38**
3.6:1 Luncheon Omelettes with

Chicken **108**
3.7:1 Baked Pike **43**
Puréed Swede **19**
Turkey Supreme **71**
3.8:1 Creamy Asparagus Soup **30**
3.9:1 Russian Salad **98**
Stuffed Potatoes **21**
Vichyssoise **36**
4:1 Baked Tuna with Broccoli **51**
Baked Tuna with Broccoli and Curry **51**
Carob Swirl Cake (per slice) **130**
Herbed Cauliflower Gratinéed **18**
4.1:1 Chinese-steamed Sea Bass **50**
Broccoli-vegetable Purée with Yogurt **17**
Five-minute Spice Cake **127**
Pineapple-walnut Cheese Spread (per Sandwich) **114**
Quennelles with Mushroom Sauce Starter **46**
Quennelles with Mushroom Sauce Main Course **46**
Sautéed Cod Fishcakes **48**
4.2:1 Banana Crazy Cake **128**
Banana Crazy Cake with Honey **128**
Chicken Divan **57**
Fresh Tomato Soup **33**
Turkey Divan **57**
4.3:1 Chicken Bolognese **58**
Chicken Salad de Luxe **100**
Chinese Sweet and Pungent Soup **36**
Simple Sautéed Lemon Sole (recipe 1 or 2) **44**
4.4:1 Braised Chicory sprinkled with Cheese **12**
Bracing Fish Soup (Cod or Haddock) **40**
Grilled Cod Cakes **48**
Spaghetti with Tomatoes and Mushrooms sprinkled with Cheese **27**
Tomato-watercress Soup with Yogurt **34**
4.5:1 Asparagus with Toasted Coriander **13**
Baked Barley Casserole **24**
Baked Barley Casserole with Chicken Stock and Apple Juice **24**
Baked Barley Casserole with Veal Stock **24**
Baked Barley Casserole with Veal Stock and Apple Juice **24**
Baked Mashed Sweet Potatoes **23**
Braised Chicory **12**
Broccoli-vegetable Purée **17**
Broccoli Magic **17**
Broccoli Magic Variation with Cheese **17**
Broccoli-vegetable Purée with Vegetables **17**
Carob-honey Biscuits (each) **132**
Cold Bean Salad **99**
Cole Slaw with Mayonnaise or Salad Dressing **98**
Corn Muffins (each) **107**
Courgette and Tomato Casserole **15**
Creamed Spinach **19**
Creamy Mushroom Soup **30**

153

4.5:1 Creamy Mushrooms on Toast 109
Dill Sauce for Grilled Halibut 49
Chef Salad Dressing 101
Luncheon Treat Fruit Juice Dressing 109
Duxelles 12, 83
Eggless Mayonnaise (per tablespoon) 103
French Green Beans 13
French Toast 106
Gazpacho 35
Giblet Gravy for Roast Stuffed Turkey 71
Green Salad with Flavourful Salad Dressing or Tomato Juice 94
Fresh Green Beans with Toasted Coriander 95
Grilled Salmon with Green Sauce 52
Herbed Cauliflower with Dill Sauce 18
Herbed Cauliflower 18
Honeyed Carrots 16
Honeyed White Onions 16
Lentil Salad 100
Luncheon Omelettes with Spinach 108
Luncheon Omelette 108
Luncheon Omelette with

Mushroom Sauce 108
Meatless Lentil Soup 37
Mushroom and Barley Soup 39
Mushroom Egg Spread (per canapé) 115
Mustard Sauce for Baked Pike 43
Orange-pineapple Rice 26
Parsleyed Potatoes 20
German-style Potato Salad 97
Quennelles with Mushroom Sauce 46
Mushroom Sauce for Quennelles 46
Rich Sauté Potatoes 22
Risotto 28
Risotto with Beef Stock 28
Risotto with Veal Stock 28
Rocket and Chicory Salad 95
Rolled Oats Pastry Case for Pineapple Chiffon Pie 126
Mushroom Sauce for Sautéed Steakburger 90
Sautéed Swede 19
Spaghetti with Tomato and Mushroom Sauce 27
Spaghetti and Sauce for Meat Balls 93
Spiced Red Cabbage 20
Split Pea Soup 38

4.5:1 Stir-fried Courgettes 14
Stuffing for Stuffed Veal 78
Veal Birds Stuffing 83
Three-flour Pancakes (each) 105
Tomato-watercress Soup 34
Tuna Fish for Canapés (sandwich serving) 112
Tuna Fish for Canapés Salad Serving 112
Veal Stuffed Eggs 110
Vegetable Fruit Salad Dressing 102
4.6:1 Bread for Stuffing (per 50g/2oz/1 cup) 145
Cardamom Bread or Rolls (per slice) 137
Fine Bread Crumbs (per 50g/2oz/1 cup) 145
Sourdough Rye Bread (average slice) 136
Stuffing for Stuffed Pork Chops in Red Wine with Beef Stock 84
Stuffing for Stuffed Pork Chops in Red Wine 84
4.7:1 Apple Coffee Cake 128
Bilberry Coffee Cake 128
Peach Coffee Cake 128
4.8:1 Bread Crumbs, Variation (per 50g/2oz/1 cup) 145

4.8:1 Chef Salad with Cottage Cheese 101
Chef Salad 101
My French Herb Bread (per slice) 135
French Onion Soup 35
5:1 Turkey Salad de Luxe 100
5.4:1 Pastry Case for Pineapple Chiffon Pie 126
5.5:1 Apple-oatmeal Biscuits 131
5.9:1 Veal Salad 99
6:1 Date-cheese Delight 125
6.1:1 Stuffed Veal 78
6.3:1 Date-nut Cake 129
6.5:1 Date Dreams 131
6.9:1 Grilled Salmon with Green Sauce 52
7:1 Sautéed Steakburger with Mushroom Sauce 90
Veal Birds with Stuffing 83
7.5:1 Grilled Halibut with Dill Sauce 49
7.9:1 Make-your-own Granola 108
8:1 Salmon in White Wine with or without Sauce 52
8.2:1 Baked Pike with Mustard Sauce 43
12.1 Apple-walnut Spread (each hors d'oeuvre) 114
12.5:1 Rich Carob Pudding with Nuts 133

Sodium content in grams

0 Apricot-pineapple Mélange 120
Beef Bourguignon, Rice for 73
Carob-honey Biscuits 132
Date-cheese Delight 125
Luncheon Treat with Fruit Juice Dressing 109
Melba Toast 103
My Hot Canapés—Cheese 112
Pineapple Chiffon Pie Pastry Case 126
Pineapple Chiffon Pie Rolled Oats Pastry Case 126
Pumpernickel 144
Sautéed Prawns, Rice for 53
Sautéed Prawns Italian Style, Rice for 55
Strawberry Crepes Filling 118
Veal Stew with Tomatoes and Mushrooms, Rice for 82
1 Apple Juice Rye Bread 138
Apple-walnut Spread (each hors d'oeuvre) 114
Bombay Turkey Balls (each) 116
Bread Crumbs Variation (per tablespoon) 145
Whole Wheat Bread (per slice) 140
2 Apple Relish (per tablespoon) 104
Spiced Baked Bananas 120
Bombay Chicken Balls with Pineapple (each ball) 116
Bread Crumbs (per tablespoon) 145
Buckwheat Rye Bread (slice) 140
Cardamom Bread (slice) 137
Cracked Wheat Bread (slice) 142
Vegetable Fruit Salad Dressing 102
Duxelles (per tablespoon) 12, 83
Four-flour Bread (slice) 143
Extraordinary Kasha 24
My French Bread (slice) 134
My French Herb Bread (slice) 135

0 My Hot Canapés-Fish (per canapé) 112
Poached Pears 119
Poached Pears with Honey 119
Potatoes for Light Meat Loaf 91
Savoury Cheese Dip (per dip) 116
Sourdough Rye Bread (slice) 136
Potatoes with Veal and Spinach Loaf 92
3 Spiced Baked Apples 121
Bombay Chicken Balls (each) 116
Cardamom Bread Rolls (per roll) 137
Date-nut Cake 129
Extraordinary Kasha 24
My Hot Canapés—Meat 112
Sauce for Orange-pineapple Chicken 64
4 Apple-oatmeal Biscuits (per biscuit) 131
Cinderella Apple Sauce 122
Cold Fish Spread (per canapé) 113
Eggless Mayonnaise (per tablespoon) 103
Feather Bread (slice) 141
Make-your-own Granola (per portion) 108
My Hot Canapés—Chicken 112
Hot Stuffed Mushrooms (each mushroom) 117
Pineapple-walnut Cheese Spread (per canapé) 114
5 Continental Cucumber Salad 96
6 Bread for Stuffing (per 50g/2oz/1 cup) 145
Chef Salad Dressing 101
7 Baked Pears in Wine 119
Banana Crazy Cake 128
Banana Crazy Cake with Honey 128
French Green Beans *au naturel* 13

7 Pineapple-walnut Cheese Spread (per sandwich) 14
Tomato-watercress Salad 96
Tuna Fish for Canapés (per canapé) 112
8 Bilberry Mousse with Sauces 122
Parsleyed Potatoes 20
9 Bilberry Griddle Cakes (each) 105
Herbed Cauliflower 18
Herbed Cauliflower Gratinéed 18
Carob Milk Shakes 132
German-style Potato Salad 97
Sardine Canapés (per canapé) 111
10 Asparagus with Toasted Coriander 13
Broccoli Magic 80
Fresh Green Beans with Toasted Coriander 95
Make-your-own Pickles 104
Spiced Red Cabbage 20
11 Prune Mousse Whip 124
12 Corn Muffins (each) 107
Rocket and Chicory Salad 95
13 Pea Purée 14
Stir-fried Courgettes 14
14 Chopped Egg Hors d'Oeuvres (per canapé or sandwich) 113
Kasha with Veal Stock 24
15 Date Dreams 131
Gazpacho 35
Mushroom Egg Spread (per canapé) 115
16 Curried Spread (per canapé) 115
French Green Beans 13
Risotto with Chicken Stock 28
Strawberry Parfait without Honey 121
17 Corn Muffins (each) 107
Courgette and Tomato Casserole 15

17 Cucumber and Onion Salad 97
18 Braised Chicory 12
Strawberry Parfait 121
Stuffing for Pork Chops in Red Wine 84
19 Braised Chicory sprinkled with Cheese 12
Cold Bean Salad 99
Near-east Chicken Sauce 63
Stuffing for Stuffed Veal 78
20 Bread Crumbs Variation (per 50g/2oz/1 cup) 145
22 Baked Barley Casserole 24
Dill Sauce for Grilled Halibut 49
Creamy Mushroom Sauce for Veal Loaf 80
Green Bean Purée 14
Honeyed White Onions 16
Tomato-watercress Soup 34
23 Extraordinary Kasha with Beef Stock 24
24 Broccoli-vegetable Purée 17
Lentil Salad 100
Mustard Sauce for Baked Pike 43
Mushroom Sauce for Sautéed Steakburger 90
25 Baked Barley Casserole with Veal Stock and Apple Juice 24
Fine Bread Crumbs (per 50g/2oz/1 cup) 145
Broccoli-vegetable Purée with Yogurt 17
Green Salad 94
Pineapple Chiffon Pie Filling 126
Pineapple Chiffon Pie Filling with Honey 126
26 Apple, Bilberry or Peach Coffee Cake 128
Green Salad with Chicory 94

154

Carbohydrate content in grams

155

Cholesterol content in milligrams

157

INDEX